3D TV and 3D Cinema

3D TV and 3D Cinema

Tools and Processes for Creative Stereoscopy

Bernard Mendiburu

with Yves Pupulin and Steve Schklair

AMSTERDAM • BOSTON • HEIDELBERG • LONDON • NEW YORK • OXFORD
PARIS • SAN DIEGO • SAN FRANCISCO • SINGAPORE • SYDNEY • TOKYO
Focal Press is an imprint of Elsevier

Focal Press is an imprint of Elsevier
225 Wyman Street, Waltham, MA 02451, USA
The Boulevard, Langford Lane, Kidlington, Oxford, OX5 1GB, UK

Notices
Knowledge and best practice in this field are constantly changing. As new research and experience broaden our understanding, changes in research methods, professional practices, or medical treatment may become necessary.

Practitioners and researchers must always rely on their own experience and knowledge in evaluating and using any information, methods, compounds, or experiments described herein. In using such information or methods they should be mindful of their own safety and the safety of others, including parties for whom they have a professional responsibility.

To the fullest extent of the law, neither the Publisher nor the authors, contributors, or editors, assume any liability for any injury and/or damage to persons or property as a matter of products liability, negligence or otherwise, or from any use or operation of any methods, products, instructions, or ideas contained in the material herein.

Library of Congress Cataloging-in-Publication Data
Application submitted

British Library Cataloguing-in-Publication Data
A catalogue record for this book is available from the British Library

ISBN: 978-0-240-81461-2

For information on all Focal Press publications
visit our website at www.elsevierdirect.com

11 12 13 14   5 4 3 2 1

Printed in the United States of America

To frank verpillat*

"Bernard, within a few years, we'll see the first 3D TV channels. For they won't be able to produce enough content for 24/7 operation, they'll rely on content converted into 3D. I want you to design a 2D/3D conversion workflow and pipeline."

*frank verpillat** **(October 1999)**

Contents

Acknowledgments

Thousands of thanks, Fabienne, for your incredible performance as the best supporting wife over the 15 months writing this book, and the 15 years before.

I want to acknowledge help and support from:

Steve and Yves, for agreeing to contribute to this book together, and for finding some time slots in your insane schedules to write and read; Richard Kroon for your tremendous work on audiovisual lingo, and the glossary you provided for this book.

The 3ality and Binocle teams, and all the industry members who answered my questions or provided images;

The CML-3D members, for your expertise and sense of humor;

The most beautiful Caribbean pearl, the Commonwealth of Dominica, West Indies, also known as the "Nature Island."

Foreword

This book is a continuation of my first one, *3D Movie Making: Stereoscopic Digital Cinema from Script to Screen*, which was published in 2009 by Focal Press. It is a continuation both in time and in subject matter. Back in 2008, 3D was not yet definitively installed in movie theaters, as no major live action 3D movie had proven it was feasible and viable to the extent that *Avatar* did. At the time of my first book, my objective was to convince readers that 3D would be more than a fad. My message was that it was complex to produce but worth the effort; that it was a new art form and needed the involvement of new crew members; and that one of them, the stereographer, deserves a supervisor-level seat at the production roundtable. The year 2011 is another world, with flocks of 3D movies now in development, production, and postproduction.

Before 2010, 3D filmmakers were afraid bad content would hit the screens and drive audiences away; and, indeed, bad 3D conversions almost did. With a surprising and positive twist, bad conversions educated viewers about the difference between 3D conversions and 3D filming. It even taught audiences the difference between the rushed afterthoughts that were market-driven conversions and delicately planned art-driven conversions. We are now witnessing the cinema taming the 3D beast, inventing a new grammar, creating new visual tools, and enjoying more adapted hardware. In 3D cinema, the technicians are polishing the tools, and the game is clearly in the hands of the creatives.

The deployment of the 3D medium has always been a chicken-and-egg problem between display and content. In the movie business, that gridlock seems to be solved for good, thanks to digital projection, first fed with CG animation, and now associated with live action 3D movies. In the TV business, it's another story. There's no previous installment of a massively broadcast 3D media one can rely on, such as with the Fifties golden age of 3D. One can see a vintage 3D movie and learn from it. What 3D broadcast would you turn to in order to learn about the practice? Although 3D cinema has a whole family of ancestors that forged a path, 3D TV is a newborn orphan about whom we have much to learn. Around the world, crews are learning and producing 3D content at the same time, mostly for sports events and concerts.

Until very recently, the 3D battle was about education; we had to both justify it and provide it. This battle will soon be won, judging by the number of 3D workshops hosted by the many cinematographic societies around the world; industry members obviously agree that 3D image-making needs special skills and experience. Now, the battle is about the quality of the equipment used in production. We have to debunk the idea that bolting two cameras together is enough. Not all productions or camera positions require a high-end motion-controlled rig, but one needs to correctly animate the interocular distance and use the full extent of the zooms in order to offer some creative range to the director—all while staying within comfortable stereoscopy, of course. We have often seen the lowest bidder getting the deal, and it shows in the recorded material: low-end equipment may not cause discomfort, but it creates bland and uninteresting stereoscopy.

We've gotten to the point where it's unlikely that cheap 3D production will hurt the audience's eyes, but we are now seeing that cheap gear impedes stereoscopic creativity. There's no trick here: If one wants to be able to invent a new imagery, one needs a new camera and monitoring system that reflects the evolution of the produced media. Would you produce color without a calibrated camera, color monitoring, and a color timing pass? Would you edit on an NLE (nonlinear editing) system that drops frames and drifts in frame rate? Some respected names in the industry discard as useless functions they can't offer yet, but they will suddenly insist that these very same functions are necessary as soon as their engineers catch up with the industry requirements. In the meantime, poor 3D is produced and inaccurate knowledge is spread around. For instance, it's not because one cannot calibrate a zoom lens that zooming is useless in 3D, yet we have heard this incorrect opinion voiced loudly all year.

As Yves Pupulin explains in Chapter 6, 3D is an industrial art; as such, it cannot be separated from its exhibiting support. We would add that in its current infancy, neither can 3D be separated from the tools of its creation. In the early years of sound and of color in the movies, reproduction technology was advertised on movie posters and billboards, sometimes just as much as the starring talent—"in Technicolor" or with "Movietone" or "Vitaphone." Shall we soon see the "in 3D" demarcation replaced by "100% real 3D," "Shot with 3ality Digital rigs," or "3D Quality by Binocle Takker," just as we see the Intel brand "InTru3D" on the DreamWorks Studios animation promotional material?

Dear reader, this is the journey awaiting for you. It's time to get to know your new production tools, and use them to extend the cinematographic language like sound and color did. How far stereoscopy will revolutionize audiovisual arts? I can't wait to see your answers reaching TV and theater screens.

Until recently there was no such thing as stereoscopic television. It was a dream, a concept, but now it is a reality—a nascent medium that is being shaped by aesthetic, business, and technological forces.

The quest for 3D moving images is more than a century old, and the quest for 3D television has been evolving for most of that time. Early attempts at broadcast 3D TV were crude by today's standards, but despite the inelegance of these solutions the dream didn't falter. Part of what makes this story so interesting is the convergence of motion picture and television (or video) technology. Digital motion pictures are nothing more than technologically advanced video, and it's this commonality that makes the transition from film to TV so much easier than it might have been had the film medium remained entirely based on the chemistry of silver halide.

The groundwork for stereoscopic television was laid in the 1980s and 1990s by three companies: StereoGraphics, Tektronix, and VRex. StereoGraphics introduced the flicker-free, field-sequential 3D display, and the first wireless shuttering eyewear, CrystalEyes. StereoGraphics also introduced what are now the most commonly used stereoscopic television multiplexing techniques and created the ZScreen electro-optical modulator, which is the basis for the RealD motion picture projection system. Tektronix was first-to-market with a liquid crystal modulator for a display screen that alternated polarization characteristics at field rates allowing for the viewing of a 3D image with passive eyewear. VRex developed manufacturing techniques for an interdigitated micropolarizer for monitors, which allowed for line-sequential viewing of a stereoscopic image using passive eyewear. The techniques created by these three companies are now employed by the manufacturers of stereoscopic televisions and by the people who manufacture the connective infrastructure necessary for the recording and transmission of 3D TV images.

Why, then, did it take two or three decades for stereoscopic television to happen when so much of the technology was in place? There are several reasons for this, some of which have a technological and some of which have a business basis. For one thing, the obsolete NTSC protocol in the United States, and PAL and SECAM in other countries, precluded viable transmission of stereoscopic information because of their limited bandwidth. Stereoscopic television had to await the more open protocols and higher definition of digital television. Curiously, though, the prior dominant display technology, the cathode ray tube, or CRT, was a better vehicle for the viewing of field-sequential stereoscopic TV than the modern pervasive liquid crystal display screen.

It's obvious that the current interest in stereoscopic television derives from the success of stereoscopic cinema, and this success can be laid at the doorstep of three companies: Texas Instruments, with the development of their DLP (digital light processing) light modulator; the Walt Disney Company, with their lead in the charge for 3D movies; and RealD, with its successful deployment of the ZScreen added to the DLP projector. The basis for modern stereoscopic projection technology, and its reason for success, is that only a single projector needs to be employed for the successful display of both left and right images in a field-sequential mode, as originally demonstrated by StereoGraphics for industrial applications. This makes for superior geometric and illumination coordination of the left and right channels, allowing for routinized operations in the projection booth. Similarly, a virtue of today's 3D TV is that both left and right images can be displayed on the surface of a single monitor.

The success of current 3D TV technology, just like 3D motion picture technology, depends on viewers wearing eyewear. The eyewear that are employed today are either passive, using polarizing lenses, or active, using electro-optical shutters, and are identical in function to the products offered in the past. There are advantages and disadvantages to both techniques, yet as this book is being published, no one can predict the level of acceptance on the part of the public for stereoscopic television that requires the use of glasses. Despite the fact that every major television set manufacturer, as well as the manufacturers of cameras, custom integrated circuits, set-top boxes, Blu-ray players, and the like, not to mention cable companies, satellite broadcasters, Internet protocol providers, and manufacturers of multiplexing and switching apparatus for the backbone of the television infrastructure, despite the fact that all these players are making a tremendous amount of effort and outlaying enormous expenditures, everybody in the field is making a big bet on the public's acceptance of 3D TV with individual selection devices—that is, glasses.

There are applications today that do not necessarily require the use of eyewear. These applications, most probably involving laptops and handheld devices, use interdigitated stereo pairs in a vertical columnar format with an at-the-screen selection device, typically a lenticular screen or a raster barrier. In applications where the user can carefully position himself or herself, or by hand-holding the device to position it, and where there is only a single user, an interdigitated stereogram makes sense. Such selection devices have limited head-box area, so proper positioning or the relationship between the display and the viewer's eyes is critical. But such a stereogram is not a general-purpose solution that must await a large number of views and a proper selection technique.

It is safe to say that if an autostereoscopic (non-eyewear) television system could be developed and offered for sale at a reasonable price, and had image quality equal to that of images viewed with eyewear, it would be successful. The basic technology has been under development for about a century. One of the several problems that must be addressed no matter what selection technique is used for an autostereoscopic display is that a tremendous amount of information needs to be displayed. A multiplicity of views is required—something like a hundred views rather than the two views needed for a plano-stereoscopic (two-view) display—which would require either a humongous bandwidth or the means to reconstruct the required information. The latter is more practical, and a great deal of work has gone into solving the reconstruction problem. But what to do about a display panel that requires at least an order of magnitude more pixels than present devices? It is my belief that the autostereo problem will be solved, but is it 5 years or 15 years away?

There are more immediate problems to be solved for successful implementation of a plano-stereoscopic TV system, not the least of which is the camera requirement. For every kind of TV content—news, sitcom, documentary, sports—a specific camera type is required. Today we have kludges of thrown-together adapted cameras. The industry needs integral cameras designed from the ground up. Numerous other issues need to be addressed, such as how to handle text boxes, how to reconcile the different formats that will be favored by particular content providers, and on and on. One interesting issue is the suitability of content created for the large theater screen when it is displayed on small screens at home or in the hand, and vice versa.

There are aesthetic issues to be addressed as well. Producing comfortable content is the first order of business, and there's always the question of style: the photographic approach has to be related to content. Since the 3D medium is so new, at this time creative people have to wing it. Some people have strong opinions, but many of these opinions aren't based on experience because the industry has very little history producing stereoscopic television content. That means that we're in a period of discovery, which can be a good thing, as long as people are open-minded. But we don't know whether or not some of what we suspect to be hard-and-fast rules are truly gospel, or whether these will change in time as the audience learns to look at stereoscopic images. This is an important subject, and there is no room for its contemplation in an introduction—which is fortunate for me, because I don't have the answers.

And the business issues I'll leave to the business people.

The book that you hold in your hands, by Bernard Mendiburu, is an effort to offer the information that creative professionals in the field of stereoscopic television require. There's a lot of work that needs to be done in order to get a stereoscopic image from the camera to somebody's TV set or computer screen or handheld device. Bernard has tackled an enormous subject, and his book is an important part of what will be an ongoing exploration. It will prove to be an invaluable reference for people in the field or for those who wish to enter the field.

Lenny Lipton
Laurel Canyon, California
November 2010

CHAPTER 1

Professional 3D Production in the 2010s

1

In this first chapter, we will try to describe as accurately as possible the landscape in which the concept of 3D production is currently being redefined. This description represents only a snapshot of our professional universe as of summer 2010, as the landscape itself is an ever-changing picture. Still, we feel it is important to set the background before jumping into the story. Describing how new tools are being invented every day will help the reader manage any new task that may be handed out to 3D crew members.

THE 3D TV AND 3D CINEMA LANDSCAPE IN 2010

It's generally accepted that being paid for what you do defines your position as a professional. Movie making adds a twist to that definition, however, because many film professionals started by working for peanuts, sometimes only for a day, sometimes for most of their career. And 3D accentuates that twist, with 3D budgets more often spent on equipment than on pay slips—at least until the new 3D renaissance.

Before this renaissance, 3D was more like a hobby or a craft than a profession. Although there were a few production companies and a handful of specialized movie professionals working mainly for theme parks, corporate communications, and universal exhibitions, 3D was usually not an everyday job that reliably paid bills. Since 2005, though, the renaissance of 3D cinema and the birth of 3D TV has changed the situation dramatically. Droves of 3D movies are in production, and 3D TV channels around the world are looking for thousands of hours of programs to air. Today, 3D is not a geek toy anymore; it's a serious business that needs serious tools.

The last time the entertainment industry experimented with 3D was in 1953 and 1954, but the movement was short-lived, and panoramic cinematography took over as the medium of choice. Stereoscopic imagery stayed out of the main street movie business for more than 50 years and was relegated to theme parks, research labs, and other special venues. For many years, it remained a hobby or a "special projects" technology, both areas where time is not as critical as it is in blockbuster production and TV. (Indeed, spending time may even be the purpose of a hobby—what's the point in building an Eiffel tower with matches if you are done in two hours?) In movies and TV, time is the most expensive resource. To quote Vince Pace, "In event broadcast, all the money on earth won't buy you that shoot again." On a major movie set, tens or hundreds of people are working together, international talents have a tight schedule, and overtime pay can seriously dent a budget. There's no way one can delay a shoot by a day or two—a problem that didn't exist when 3D was produced in universities and labs.

DEFINING 3D TV AND 3D CINEMA

Stereoscopic 3D is not the only new media technology changing production processes and deliveries. Alternative content in theaters, user-created content at home, day-and-date video on demand, Internet televisions, and legally challenged peer-to-peer distributions are other major changes currently affecting both entertainment production and entertainment experience. Let's discuss and define a few key terms:

- *Live shooting* refers to filming events whose timings are not controlled, like sports or music shows.
- *Live broadcast* refers to transmitting images of an event while it's happening in real time.
- *Cinema* refers to prerecorded, post-produced content for the entertainment industry—products that involve talents, stars, and marketing plans.
- *Television* content refers to prerecorded, post-produced content for playback on television sets. Shows such as prime-time dramas, comedies, or sitcoms fall into this category.
- *Postproduction* refers to the process of editing footage, including applying visual effects, before distributing via broadcast or packaged content.
- *Theater* refers to any large-screen public presentation.
- *TV* refers to any screen sized for a living room, regardless of the image source it is using (terrestrial, multipoint, IP, legal, or illegal). A TV is defined by its audience.
- *3D* refers to stereoscopic images. In this text, we may use *S3D* as opposed to 3D, CG, or CGI to distinguish stereoscopic 3D images from rendered computer images based on 3D models.

Cinema Went 3D in 2009

The first year all major U.S. animation studios released CGI movies in S3D was 2009; four of the ten top grossing movies were 3D. A total of 24 3D movies were released or premiered around the world, and tens of projects were green-lighted. This year of the 3D cinema renaissance ended with *Avatar*, the fourth biggest box office moneymaker (adjusting for inflation) in the history of cinema, which brought the 3D experience to millions of moviegoers and convinced its worldwide audience that 3D is now a new storytelling medium. The year 2010 confirmed this trend, with 3D in six of the top ten movies, and retaining the top three spots.

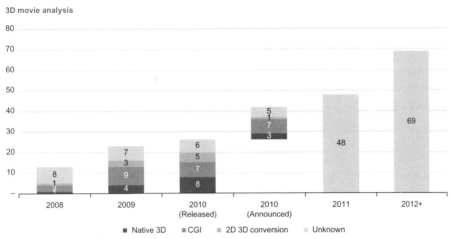

Source: www.3dmovielist.com, PwC analysis. Note: The list includes short movies.

FIGURE 1.1
3D movie releases 2008 to 2012.
Image courtesy of Vincent Teulade, PricewaterhouseCoopers Advisory.

3D TV Is Born in 2010

Now well established in cinema, stereoscopic content will soon invade your living room with 3D TVs showing 3D games, TV channels, and 3D video on demand (VoD). TV is now exactly where cinema was a few years ago in terms of technologies and economic background. For anyone following the 3D revolution, the only thing surprising about the 3D TV deployment is its speed. TV is at the edge of a major shift, and "going HD" is only the tip of the 3D iceberg.

Steve Schklair, one of the forerunners among 3D TV advocates and engineers, recalls the key events leading to 3D at home. Readers willing to learn more about the inception of the entire 3D production system and procedures will find Steve's extensive recapitulations of the early years in Chapter 6.

STEVE SCHKLAIR

In April 2008, 3ality Digital did the first 3D broadcast, with Howie Mandel doing a comedy skit from our offices in Burbank to the Content Theater at NAB as part of my speech. This is the event that kicked off the BSkyB (British Sky Broadcasting Group) launch of the world's first 3D channel by a major broadcaster in 2009.

In September 2008, 3ality broadcast Jeffrey Katzenberg live to the International Broadcasting Convention (IBC) in Amsterdam as part of my keynote speech. This was the first transatlantic broadcast of 3D.

To give you a more general point of view of the 3D industry, we use a classic three-act structure to represent the rapid transition to 3D TV in the few months between 2009 and 2010.

ACT ONE: SEPTEMBER 2009—IBC, AMSTERDAM

In an entertainment industry, the loom of recession generates great caution; communication and marketing budgets are always the first to shrink when cost cuts kick in. Still, at IBC (International Broadcasting Convention) in 2010 we were given many 3D set-top boxes (STB) and chipset projects—even though the STB business is not one of large margins and fast turnovers but of large volumes and long product life. If the STB makers were going 3D, it's because they knew better than we did.

Next came the public release of the Fuji W1, that little marvel of a 3D still camera. It was the first consumer 3D camera since the film cameras of the twentieth century, like the Stereo Realist sold by the David White Company until the 1970s, and the SK-3D7K 3D video camcorders sold by Toshiba in the 1990s.

ACT TWO: JANUARY 2010—CES, LAS VEGAS

As the curtain rises on the Consumer Electronics Show (CES) of 2010, we are presented with the secret that STB makers knew: 3D TVs are everywhere, displayed in all major consumer electronics (CE) booths. Sony, LG, Samsung, and Panasonic all introduced 3D TV sets—putting them front and center at their booths and press conferences, and showing all 3D flavors and technologies. They had active and passive stereoscopy on LCD (liquid crystal display), LED (light-emitting diode), OLED (organic light-emitting diode), plasma, and DLP (digital light processing) displays, as well as upcoming products and research prototypes. For the duration of the show, DirectTV was broadcasting a 3D channel we could see on many receivers in booths all around the floor. Quoting Art Berman, industry analyst with Insight Media: "There is so much interesting and important news related to 3D that it is impossible to pick just one item to report. In a sense, the news is the size and scope of the 3D news!"

FIGURES 1.2A AND 1.2B
The Fuji W1 and W3. In 2009 Fuji introduced the FinePix Real 3D W1, the first digital 3D still camera, followed in 2010 by Fuji's FinePix Real 3D W3.

Users do not buy a technology, they buy the experience that comes from it. Sony announced that they would produce the 2010 FIFA World Cup in 3D and ESPN would broadcast the 25 matches on their new 3D TV channel. Hours after that announcement, "ESPN 3D" was ranked as the number five search on Google. The audience's craving for 3D was established.

CES 2010 also saw the launch of the 3D extension of the Blu-ray format and the presentation of Panasonic's 3D camcorder, the soon-to-be-famous AG-3DA1.

ACT THREE: APRIL 2010—NAB, LAS VEGAS

Once 3D TV had the technology side of consumer display and content distribution covered, it was time to get the independent production industry on board. Strong signals had to be sent to entertainment executives that they could hitch their wagons to the new shining star of 3D TV. Three elements were needed: affordable production equipment, distribution channels, and confidence in the market. The 2010 NAB Show supplied all three.

Affordable production equipment was presented in many booths around the show floor. Newcomers to 3D buying cheap rigs would discover later on that low-cost camera mounts sometimes lead to expensive postproduction sessions. But for now, there is an extravaganza of 3D equipment providers.

Distribution channels were announced by Discovery Communications' Chief Media Technology Officer John Honeycutt. In his keynote at the NAB Digital Cinema Summit, Honeycutt presented Discovery's 3D initiative in partnership with IMAX and Sony. His final stunt was to call 21st Century 3D CEO Jason Goodman onstage to present Sony's prototype of a 3D camcorder, based on a dual-head PMW-EX3.

Sony's booth was all about 3D, with a 3D OB (outside broadcasting) van, a 3D giant screen, 3D rigs from various manufacturers, and the presentation of the production system to be used at the FIFA World Cup, with the Sony MPE-200, a 3D image processing unit dubbed "the 3D Box" by the industry.

Now that leaders in the industry are embracing the 3D trend, smaller players are invited to follow suit. Based on pre-orders alone, Panasonic will sell 800 3D cameras by the next IBC, while 3ality will sell more than 80 of its high-end 3D camera rigs throughout the year.

EPILOGUE: SEPTEMBER 2010—3D SUMMIT, UNIVERSAL CITY

At the annual 3D Entertainment Summit, the industry event hosted in the heart of this entertainment city, the 3D land rush is all the rage. The U.S. 3D TV channels are now on all cable and dish networks, and 3D TV productions are happening all around the world. The preproduction series of the Panasonic AG3D have been shooting actual TV content all summer. In a very short amount of time, we went from "How can you afford to release your next block-buster in 3D?" to "How can you afford *not* to release your next blockbuster in 3D?" As one panelist told the audience: "If you are not in 3D by now, you are stupid. Period."

Main Critics of 3D

In order to give a fair assessment of the current perception of the 3D trend in the general audience, we have to mention the 3D-bashing hype that could be found on the Internet in the summer of 2010. It came from a variety of sources, from inexperienced bloggers to seasoned and respected media journalists. This back-lash was to be expected, both as a natural response to the marketing pressure and as a consequence of new 3D technology shortcomings or inappropriate use by some opportunists. Let's have a look at some key elements mentioned during the summer of 3D bashing and explore whether there is any value in these criticisms.

THE USELESSNESS OF 3D, AND STEREO BLINDNESS

"That 3D stuff is pointless, and, BTW, I can't even see 3D."

Some 3D posts started with the honest statement that the reviewer usually did not enjoy 3D movies at the theater, and that 3D cameras or TVs were there-fore pointless—either too expensive or lacking functions readily available on 2D products. A perfect example is an infamous review of the Fuji FinePix Real 3D W1 camera on a Japanese blog, which claimed that it was an expensive 2D camera, as the reviewer did not see any interest in 3D. Like a color TV review by a colorblind journalist, the piece reminds us that a sizeable part of the audi-ence being visually challenged is actually "3D blind." The industry has to care for their needs as well, providing a way for them to enjoy the 3D content in 2D when it is part of a social event, like a sporting event on TV.

THERE IS EITHER TOO MUCH OR NOT ENOUGH 3D

"Let me tell you and all the studios executives how 3D should be done."

If you make some objects fly into the theater, half the critics will say you are slapping the audience in the face. On the other hand, if you push all your imag-ery behind the screen, the other half will complain there were no 3D effects at all. Do both, and someone will complain that the 3D confused the storytelling. We won't blame the audience for this; interview more than a handful of stereog-raphers, and you are sure to hear the same rants from the creative side. Everyone has his taste for 3D, and there's no rule about how much is enough, how much is too much, and how much is barely enough. It is time for some stereographers to stop pretending they are the only ones holding the holy 3D truth, or that they are the first in the history of cinema to use 3D in a creative way. Someday, one of them will be telling us that Eisenberg shot his 1940 *Crusoe* in 3D with no cinematographic intent whatsoever, besides using twice as much film stock.

THE ACTIVE/PASSIVE 3D FORMAT WAR

"We are in for a new format war between active and passive 3D TV format."

As of 2010, there are two types of 3D glasses: the passive ones and the active ones. Almost all 3D TVs on the market require active glasses, with only a hand-ful of expensive displays, mostly used as professional monitors, that work with passive glasses. Comparing the two is kind of like comparing apples and oranges: they have very different purposes, specifications, and price points.

The first generation of active 3D glasses was vendor-specific, but they can be made compatible with different TVs after some light polarization and synchronization protocol adjustments. However, these adjustments confused reviewers to such an extent that some saw in the glasses the start of a new format war—one based on display technology rather than content distribution.

In early January 2011, as we finalized this book, we introduced the world's first hybrid 3D glasses, which work in both active and passive modes, at the 2011 Consumers Electronics Show in Las Vegas. This new product, designed by Volfoni and called ActivEyes, is for both professional and personal use, allowing directors in OB vans to use passive monitors for camera checks and active 3D TVs for beauty and program monitoring at once.

Here is another lesson for the CE industry: The HD optical support format war that left the HD-DVD dead and the Blu-ray gasping for a 3D defibrillation, actually did hurt the audience confidence in home cinema technologies more than we thought.

THE PROMISED GLASSES-FREE FUTURE

"Don't even think about 3D TV with glasses. Glasses-free 3D is just around the corner."

Some reviewers discovered glasses-free 3D display technologies in 2010 and hailed them as the future of 3D TV, urging readers not to buy any 3D TV unless it is glasses-free. That would be good advice if people in the know had not already waited more than 20 years for glasses-free 3D TVs to reach a decent cost/quality point. Those displays generate 3D viewing by beaming a set of discrete 2D images to specific viewpoints. Since they divide the display resolution, they need to synthetize the additional viewpoints. This means that you start by paying for a 4 K (or quad HD) display, feed it with pristine stereoscopic content, and enjoy 3D conversion artifacts on a less than 720p resolution. For half the price, most people would prefer to wear 3D glasses and enjoy full HD-3D upscaled on a gorgeous 4 K display.

THE 3D BOX OFFICE DOWNTURN

"Studios are on the edge of 3D bankruptcy; they won't say I didn't warn them."

This represents another discovery by the Web's bloggers: the summer of 2010 was supposedly disastrous to the 3D box office (BO). They based this statement on two sets of figures:

- Overall movie BO revenue was declining.
- The ratio of BO revenue coming from 3D screens was down.

What these bloggers did not mention was the fact that six out of the ten top grossing movies were 3D. How does one explain such contradictory figures? First, 3D movies are now released every other week, pushing each other out of the 3D screens. Despite continuous increase in the number of 3D movies, 3D screens are still in insufficient numbers to satisfy the demand. Second, the year started with 3D cinema's biggest monetary success in history, *Avatar*. One cannot break historical records every month. This supposed BO downturn was the poster child of 3D-bashing, where the ripple effects of 3D's groundbreaking success made it look like a short-term failure.

That said, some 2010 releases were rushed 3D conversions of genre movies. As Jeffrey Katzenberg, DreamWorks CEO, said in September at the 3D Summit: "Story is still and will always be the key. 3D will not save a turkey." (His comments on the quality of some of the rushed 3D conversions were even harsher.)

THE LACK OF 3D CONTENT

"Don't spend a dime on a 3D TV; there's no 3D content out there."

For once, this is an accurate statement, but it still is not a fair or meaningful critique. With 3D in its infancy, the current crop of CE products is obviously aimed at early adopters (the politically correct term for "rich geeks"). If you bought an HDTV in the early 2000s, you had to wait a little bit for HD content, typically for over-the-air, cable, dish, or optical support distribution; the same was true for color TV, FM radio, and, in fact, virtually every home media delivery system. Remember that 3D-ready TV sets were introduced in 2007, three full years before 3D TV was mass-marketed at CES 2010. As of late 2010, you can have at least two 3D channels on any dish or cable network across the United States, and in an impressive list of countries around the world.

2011 AND BEYOND: A FORECAST ATTEMPT

Can we confidently assume that recurring questions like "Is 3D a fad or just passing hype?" or "How soon before 3D disappears again, like it did in the 1950s?" are now behind us? Let's consider them to be valid concerns for a couple years, for the sake of revealing interesting information from their evaluation, and let's discuss what we can infer from the recent deployments and activity in 3D.

3D TV Will Be By-Appointment Entertainment

Although it won't last long, you may initially have to plan for 3D viewing more than you do for regular broadcasting, just as you plan to go out to see 3D cinema. This is a common effect of new media deployment, and your home cinema experience will get closer to your theatrical cinema experience, sometimes sharing the type of content you are watching. Similarly, 3D cinema may get closer to home entertainment, with television parties hosted in local theaters that include alternative content like live concerts, sporting events, and even special screenings or world premieres. Fans waiting overnight in line may be a new form of tailgating.

3D TV Will Accelerate Stereoscopic Art Development

In cinema, project development is counted in years, and the turnaround from green light to release is about two to three. *Avatar*, however, took ten years to develop and five years to produce. This is a prohibitive amount of time when it comes to television technologies and storytelling techniques.

In television production, the longest timeframe is one year—and in most cases, it is only a few months between the invention of a storytelling tool and its common use in talk shows and sitcoms. In news, it is weeks, or even days.

As soon as music video TV channels are 3D, stereoscopic creativity will get its ADHD treatment. As soon as nature and animal TV channels are 3D, the "we take you there" shows mixing detailed wildlife close-ups and gorgeous vistas will have their steroid shots. If you want to have the faintest idea of how far 3D sports coverage will evolve in 2011, just have a look at the first and last FIFA 3D matches produced in 2010. Live stereoscopic production will grow up right before our eyes, as we witness camera operators and directors learning and expanding the tools of the trade while producing 2011 sport events in 3D TV.

IS 3D WORTH THE COST?

As we were reminded at the 2010 3D Summit, the burden of going 3D is actually assumed by filmmakers and moviegoers. They are the ones who make the decision to pay for the cost of 3D: the movie maker, because 3D production is more expensive and 3D is known to affect his art; the moviegoer, because he is the one who pays for the 3D price hike out-of-pocket. These two people are crucial for answering the two key questions:

- Does 3D have an added value over 2D?
- Is that 3D added value worth the cost?

So far, there is no doubt that the answer is "Yes"—if 3D is done well on technical, artistic, and commercial levels. A discussion of the commercial viability of 3D is beyond the scope of this book, but let's discuss both the technical and artistic aspects.

Technically, you should:

- *Allow enough time and money for the 3D.* If you don't have additional time, that's okay, because with the right gear, 3D does not require any additional shooting time over 2D. If you don't have a budget extension to get from 2D to 3D production, don't even think about trying. All you'll get is damage to your 2D and eventually killing your 3D. On the other hand, if time is not an issue, you could plan to learn on your own equipment for many weeks.
- *Embrace the learning curve; don't fight it.* Send your crew members to 3D lectures and workshops and have them get trained in their new gear. The art of 3D production involves a set of new practical, intellectual, and aesthetic tools; don't expect people to know it without being taught.

Artistically (and this is most important), you should:

- *Create compelling content.* The 3D version of a broadcast or movie *has* to be more compelling than the 2D version, or why bother?
- *Do 3D with intention.* Do not just throw 3D at your audience's face; do not simply rely on "that 3D shot" to sell 3D. You want to tell a story, but you want to do it better than you would in 2D.

AN OVERVIEW OF TYPICAL 3D PRODUCTIONS

So far, 3D has been applied in three major types of content production: fiction movies, documentaries, and sports broadcasts, both as 3D TV and as alternative content in theaters. In the next chapters, we will take a detailed look at the technical and artistic aspects of these productions.

As a teaser, though, let's have a quick look at the conditions in which such productions occur, that is, how 3D gets involved in these branches of the entertainment industry, and how they are affected by it. As a 3D TV executive once summed it up: live television brings the event to you, HD quality seats you in the stadium, and 3D realism throws you onto the field. How does this affect content production?

3D Broadcasts

A recurrent project for many a broadcast research centers was 3D TV production. We have now entered a new era where 3D TV production has escaped to the entrepreneurial world, which has started to self-finance its projects. Take a look at the following timeline:

- April 14, 2008: First 3D broadcast to NAB, by 3ality
- September 14, 2008: First transatlantic 3D broadcast to IBC, by 3ality
- December 8, 2008: First 3D NFL broadcast to theaters, BCS Championship, by 3ality
- January 8, 2009: First Super Bowl game broadcast in 3D to theaters, by 3ality
- January 31, 2010: First broadcast to U.K. Pubs and Clubs, by BSkyB with 3ality
- March 24, 2010: First 3D cable broadcast to U.S. home subscribers, of Islanders vs. Rangers hockey game at Madison Square Garden, by MSG with 3ality
- April 21, 2010: IPL (Indian Premier League) cricket broadcast in 3D to theaters across India, by 3ality
- May 26, 2010: First over-the-air terrestrial 3D broadcast, State of Origin Rugby Series, Australia, by Nine Network and SBS (Special Broadcasting Service), with 3ality
- June 11, 2010: First ESPN 3D broadcast, FIFA World Cup, by HBS (Host Broadcast Services) with Sony
- September 2, 2010: First fiber-optic 3D broadcast direct to U.S. home subscribers, Patriots vs. Giants from Meadowlands Stadium, New Jersey, by Verizon FiOS with 3ality

It is now possible to put on a live 3D broadcast that equals the quality of what was post-produced only a few years ago. As an example of this progress, refer to Figure 1.3, which shows the production of a Black Eyed Peas concert in 2010 compared to the U23D feature concert shot in 2007.

FIGURES 1.3A AND 1.3B
U23D and 3D Black Eyed Peas. U23D and 3D BEP were produced only three years apart and show tremendous progress in live 3D production.
Images courtesy of 3ality and 21st Century 3D. Steadicam operator, Phillip Martinez; photography by Jason Goodman.

Now that 3D broadcast technology is mature with regards to acquisition and contribution, the battle has shifted to graphics, direction, and getting to the premium camera positions—which sometimes means finding a way to share them with 2D production.

FIGURE 1.4
The Pace 3D Shadow Rig. This rig was designed to mount on a regular 2D camera unit in stadiums in order to share camera positions with regular HD production.
Image © 2011 PACE.

The front line is now in editorial, with the search for the perfect blending of good old 2D storytelling and new 3D images, effects, and points of view. To give an overly simplistic example, long lens shots tend to be hard to accomplish in 3D, whereas wide angle lens shots almost always look great. In a large shot, the whole stadium feels like a scale model, whereas in a long shot, the players look like cardboard puppets that seem about to collide into each other.

This is not to say that there is no place for long lens shots in a 3D broadcast. In the creation of compelling content, the most important thing is that the story be told, even if it is the "story" of a game. Not every shot needs to be a 3D "wow" shot, as long as there is a fair mix of great 3D shots and the story is told successfully.

The following is a list of 3D TV channels around the world:

- Japan: The satellite BS11 (airs 3D content four times a day)
- South Korea: Sky 3D

- United Kingdom: BSkyB Channel 3D, Virgin Media VoD
- United States: New York Network Cablevision, Discovery 3D, ESPN 3D, DirecTV VoD service
- Australia: Fox Sports
- Russia: PlatformHD in partnership with Samsung
- Brazil: RedeTV
- France: 3D broadcasts by Orange, Numericable, and Canal+
- Spain: Canal+ 3D

Alternative 3D Content

While watching 3D mature and experiencing the major production paradigm shift currently happening, the experts in the know were on the lookout for the "CinemaScope" of the 2000s. What was the new media technology that would kill 3D, just as widescreen viewing ended the golden age of 3D in the 1950s? Alternative content (AC), like live sports or musical events, was seen as the most serious contender, with dynamic seats and multiplayer games far in the distance. As it happened, the 3D wave was so strong that AC itself had to go 3D, as you see now with 3D sports broadcasts in theaters.

Our thesis is that 3D will remain the strongest effect of visual media digitization, even if AC in theaters is another side effect of digitization. In reality, 3D and AC are complementary: the first generation of 3D broadcasts, such as FIFA 3D, have to cope with 3D TV screen scarcity, but by also serving as AC for 3D theaters, they balance their budgets. The current low rate of 3D TV equipment acquisition can make it worthwhile for theaters to show AC events while they are broadcast on 3D TV, and thus host the biggest 3D TV party in town.

3D Documentaries

Stereoscopic displays are used in virtual reality for the enhanced realism and added navigational skills they provide. The purpose of a documentary is to present a vision of reality to its audience—so, with its realistic effect, 3D will soon prove itself to be an excellent tool for that specialized movie genre. Will this effect be the same for social documentaries and nature movies?

It's no wonder that Discovery was the second major U.S. TV franchise to publically commit to a 3D channel (after ESPN). This involvement in new media sparked a whole set of independent 3D documentary productions in the summer of 2010. For better or worse, producers and DPs with no 3D experience are jumping on the boat with low-end 3D rigs.

However, documentary production is not particularly suitable for complex or fragile shooting equipment; its budget does not allow for renting high-end rigs for weeks in the bush, and the shooting environment is often harsh for surface mirrors and micron-accurate motion controls. If there is a branch of 3D production looking for the monopack of 3D, it is the documentary.

3D Feature Films

Since 2005, the number of digital 3D films already released, slated for release, or green-lighted has reached the number of 3D films actually released in the 1950s. Even if the current 3D era were to fade out, it would have generated the same quantity of content as the 1950s golden age. Still, the comparison may end there. First, that golden age lasted only two seasons, 1953 and 1954; and second, the types of movies produced were totally different.

In 2010 we see a relatively varied mix of blockbusters converted to 3D, low-budget movies shot in 3D, and a flock of CGI animation rendered in 3D. After *Avatar*, we have yet to see another major live action blockbuster shot in 3D rather than converted in post, and this should be the case in 2011 as well.

As 3D champion Ray Zone said two years ago: "The train has left the station, the genie is out of the bottle; cinema is going 3D. Where it will go now is not anymore a technologist question. It's a business and art issue."

Despite the 3D screen count continuing to increase by good numbers, feature movies keep facing severe 3D screen scarcity. In 2010, we saw two 3D movies from the same animation studio, *Shrek Forever After* and *How to Train Your Dragon*, fighting for 3D screens. The year 2011 will be no different, with a new 3D film coming out every two weeks.

3D IS A QUEST FOR IMMEDIATE IMAGE PERFECTION

Live 3D is at the crossroads of two very demanding worlds: live production, which requires total obedience to the shooting schedule; and 3D production, which requires perfect camera matching in geometry and photography.

The challenge is to be able to produce a technically perfect and controlled image, often with no lead time or opportunity for a second take, while working in a very tight schedule and sometimes in tough material situations. Does it sound like trying to cook gourmet food while hiking the Himalayas? That would be a fair description.

This book will explain how this tough task is accomplished, detail what tools have been developed for that purpose, and teach you how to put them to use in your own 3D projects. Eventually, you will reach the point where 3D production feels as easy and joyful as 2D filming.

WAS THERE NO SUCH THING AS HDTV?

Was there no such thing as HDTV? This may sound like a bold statement, and your accounting department may want to know where all that investment money went. The answer is, it went into getting ready for 3D. Let's explain this a little bit.

The technology shift that is shaking the motion picture and entertainment industries is the digitization of the audiovisual medium. Digitization changes the life of visual media in two aspects: it can be copied infinitely at a marginal cost, and it can be compressed thousands of times and keep its visual quality. Infinite copy generations gave us compositing, the most modern visual effects, and virtual editing. Compression gave us high-definition TV and illegal downloading, otherwise both of which would be far too expensive to operate and may not even exist. There's no spare bandwidth to be lost in broadcasting analog HD.

Digital technologies had an impact on content production. With CGI images that make any visual effect or stunt digitally possible, they extended the domain of suspension of disbelief and led us into a world where we just couldn't believe our eyes. This affected story and image realism, but it did not affect the visual art in the same way as motion or sound, or even color, did. Digital 2D brought us minor changes in visual storytelling.

HD provided increased resolution, but it did not change the audience experience. As for the audience's sensory experience, the gain from over-the-air analog TV to digital TV is much more noticeable than from standard definition (SD) to HD. Similarly, there's much more of a difference between VHS and DVD than DVD and Blu-ray. If digitization changed our visual world to some extent, HD did not change the visual rules; artistically, there was no HD. Many HD production trucks still have 4/3 markers on their preview monitors.

Technologically, 3D is a sibling of HD, an offspring of digitization. If it were not for the digital revolution, there would be no 3D; it wasn't until it was possible to tweak images at the subpixel level that 3D postproduction took off in the 1990s. Stereoscopic movies escaped from high-end large-format special venues when digital projectors became available, and that 3D mode was their best sales pitch. Once again: there would have been no digital projection outreach without 3D. The 3D renaissance and digital revolution cannot be separated.

Now consider how, in many cases, the upgrade from HD to 3D is marginal in cost and complexity. Thanks to the computerization of CE and production gear, 3D is often a software upgrade on HD. When it comes to hardware, HD and 3D are twin technologies. Many HD products can be retrofitted into 3D with a simple software update (Sony PlayStation 3 and some Blu-ray Disc players, video switchers and mixers, image encoders, and transport equipment) or a minor electronic upgrade like 120 Hz TVs. Some HD products are 3D-ready with not a single knob to turn on—like RPTVs (rear projection TVs) and DLP projectors or SRW video tape decks.

Technologically, there was no HD; it was just that 3D software was not yet ready when digital hardware was deployed.

Thus, there's a difference between 3D and HD: 3D is changing the audience experience, and 3D will eventually change the way we make movies and the way we produce live sports on TV—like color or electronic news gathering (ENG) did in their time. It's not an issue of technology and skills; it is about art and direction, like camera positions and editorial pacing. HD did not impact the visual arts as much as 3D will. Artistically, there was no HD, but 3D is waiting to hatch.

The original cause of the revolution is digitization, and the end result is 3D. HD was a transitional byproduct, which barely lived for a decade, almost never found its packaged media, and did not influence the art.

Still, thanks are due to HD for paving the way for 3D and taking care of the upgrade costs from analog, SD, and 2D television.

3D Means Getting the Most Perfect Picture Twice

When you are looking at 3D content, your visual system combines the images produced on both retinas and fuses them into a single 3D image. This process is called *stereopsis* and generates the experience of a single 3D vision, also called *cyclopean vision*. Comfortable 3D vision comes from meaningful differences between the two views, without any visual clues that do not match what our eyes would see in a natural environment.

Our visual system, which is comprised of our eyes, optical nerves, and visual areas in the rear cortex, runs a cross-view quality check to extract the information pertinent to 3D reconstruction. Differences between the left and right views are called *retinal disparities*, and, when they adversely affect 3D perception, *retinal rivalries*.

If the images are not correctly aligned, our eyes will be forced to aim at unnatural convergence positions, leading to muscular fatigue and eventually pain. For this reason, there's no room for less than perfect 3D in entertainment, unless hurting your audience is part of your plan. (We sincerely doubt your legal department would enjoy this for long.)

Michael Bergeron provided reference numbers that he found in the research literature for the maximum sustainable retinal rivalry. You'll obviously want to stay as far away as possible from these numbers in your productions, for they set the bar for half your audience leaving the room in tears.

Maximum Sustainable Retinal Rivalry:

- Vertical = <.8%
- Rotation = <.8%
- Zoom = <1.2%

If you bring some visual effects or graphics into your picture, your accuracy requirements get much higher. If you want to credibly match stereoscopic content and CG images, you'll need to match practical and virtual camera angles much more accurately than in 2D. This means that if your 3D footage is not "clean," you'll have to ask the FX team to match its roughness.

Current 3D productions will most likely be shown on large screens, as cinema, or as alternative content. Planning for 3D TV releases may not make 3D products any easier to produce, as shorter viewing distance and higher light level make 3D TV imagery at least as demanding as 3D cinema.

Live and Movie Production Means Fast Setup

Concerts and sporting events usually share the same kind of large public venues that are rented at a very high cost. This means that the camera positions in stadiums are available one day prior to major sporting events, and at best two to three days before massive music concerts, while the construction crew sets up the stage. TV production's working schedules and procedures have been finessed and optimized for years, and 3D can hardly change anything there. You just can't be slower than 2D. The real world is not waiting for 3D; it's 3D that has to come up to speed.

You will not change that fact in the movie industry either; your 3D camera units must be able to be set up just as fast as 2D. A film crew moves from set to set, from location to location, and shoots as many takes as possible in a single day, so fast setup is even more important in feature films.

On a Cinema Set Every Minute Is a 3000 Dollar Bill

On feature films, any minute spent fixing the 3D rig costs too much money. Major studios estimate that shooting a blockbuster costs an average of $200,000 per hour, $3000 per minute, $50 per second. The time you just spent reading this sentence is more expensive than buying this book. Anyone who delays a shooting schedule gets fired if he can be replaced, or, if not, never gets called again.

Directors do not like to wait, at least not for the camera crew. A stereographer friend on a feature film tells this story: "By the end of the first week, I got the depth set up in under a minute, from the DP (director of photography) handing out the rig, to my 3D being fine. By the end of the second week, I could figure out in advance what 3D look they'd want and I got the IOD [inter-optical distance] and convergence fixed in less than 15 seconds. Still, that was long enough to feel they were wondering why I was still cranking the rig."

And this is just for the technical crew; acting is still the most important job on set. We should never forget that the camera recently spent a century on a set that has belonged to actors for millenniums, not the other way around. Technologies that impede the prevalence of acting usually get dumped quite fast.

Live 3D: You Won't Shoot It Again, You Won't Fix It in Post

With staged 3D, there's no chance to shoot it again. The next president of the United States is not likely to take his pledge twice, the race winner will not cross the finish line again, and that gnu will not resuscitate just to be killed again, even if the lion seems to have had a lot of fun. Live shooting is not only about being ready when it happens; it is also about shooting it the right way, right away. Fixing the convergence in post may be an option, but fixing the inter-optical (IO) distance is not. Just as you can't save an out-of-focus shot, fixing shooting accidents in post is too expensive in 3D. You'll never get a better deal than shooting right.

Of course, in a live 3D broadcast, you won't even have a chance to fix it in post. If it was wrong, it was broadcast anyway, and did hurt the audience. There are many 2D imperfections you can get away with. Not in 3D.

Even some supposedly forgivable 3D imperfections can kill a live broadcast shot; if the camera's vertical alignment is slightly wrong, it may be okay for your eyes to work at realigning the pictures. However, as soon as a graphic is overlaid, it will cause pain to view, for it will reveal the imperfections of the live picture.

Apply the 10 Rules of 3D Instinctively, Automatically

Many stereographers have come up with their 10 rules to produce good 3D, with the most famous list coming from James Cameron. You'll soon create your own list as you develop your 3D style and finesse your procedures. The first two will most likely deal with convergence, inter-optical distance, and monitoring, and the remaining ones should all be about art.

When you're under pressure to set up your 3D shooting, framing, directing, and cutting (whether it is live or staged), you won't have time to think too much about the rules. Your gear has to think for you. The most important parameter should be the big shiny knob on the rig, not that flat screw under the socket. The same is true for monitoring, visual aids, and metadata gathering. Ergonomic design is not a luxury; it is a step toward quality.

LESSONS LEARNED SINCE THE DIGITAL 3D REVOLUTION STARTED

We have seen that digital 3D is a new medium that is just starting to be explored. Some crews have been there, done that, and some even survived and came back to share their experience. They share it sometimes as production tools become available for sale or rent, sometimes as shared advice on mailing lists, almost always as 3D content to be seen again and again in order to learn from it.

What do these 3D veterans have to tell us?

About Cameras, Optics, and Recorders

We all started practicing stereoscopic imaging by putting two cameras side by side, often trying to match the human inter-pupillary distance of 65 mm. It soon became obvious that this 65 mm is meaningless, and what is actually important is the ratio between the IO and the camera-to-subject distances—the full equation involving the background, focal length, sensor size, screen width, and viewing distance. A seasoned 3DP (3D director of photography) adds light, haze, depth of field, music, and story.

Still, there's an iron rule that your camera is most likely too fat to operate in a side-by-side configuration, unless you settle for a pin camera. A mirror rig (MR) is compulsory for most shots, with the IOD averaging from 10 to 50 mm on a typical feature production.

Aligning cameras is a time-consuming, complex, and too-easily-reversed operation. Matching lenses is sometimes possible, making the process more streamlined. To that end, lens makers have started offering 3D-matched zooms. Give them a try; the value is not just in their 3D marketing.

Not all 2D cameras are good 3D cameras. Most broadcast cameras are built to work as a fleet, and it's easy to put them on genlock (generator lock) to remote-control them. On the other hand, digital cinema marvels have a tendency to behave as divas when one tries to force the internal clock or to slave one to another.

Record your footage as a stereoscopic feed, clearly identifying your assets. Color code the tapes, name the files, flag the images. Do whatever it takes, and even more. You'll never have too much left/right identification in your workflow. Recorders that handle this for you will save you time and money in the future.

3D Has Enhanced Photographic Requirements

A good survival rule in 3D is to be wary of anything you can get away with in 2D. Flares, specular effects, and polarized lights are good examples of light effects that range from annoying to artistic in 2D, but they can kill a shot in 3D. For example, since lens flares occur inside the lens, they have huge interocular disparities, up to being present in only one eye.

Subtle errors in color and luminance matching between cameras can create uncomfortable retinal rivalries, and will impede on the image analysis systems. If there's a color gradient in the image you are shooting in 3D, and that gradient happens to be shifted by the color balance in one camera, the image analysis will be tempted to shift the images in space in order to match the colors in both eyes.

STEVE SCHKLAIR

When using image-domain geometry correction in a live production, all camera feeds need to be fixed before they enter the production, not just during the program and preview.

Frame rate is a crucial issue in 3D, and its standards will have to be increased in TV and cinema in the next 5 to 10 years. Currently, we're still struggling with progressive and interlaced standards in 3D, but soon we'll have to face the fact that the brain is more sensible to stroboscopic effects in 3D than in 2D. The deep depth of field that some stereographers recommend for 3D doesn't help either. As such, a lot of sports content would benefit from being produced in 720 at 50p or 60p; right now it is most likely produced in 1080 at 50i and 60i. This is an issue with the current generations of 3D displays that combine the two fields and double flash them at 120 Hz. Instead, the proper process should be to interpolate each field to full resolution separately and flash them once each.

There's a closely related issue with the interlaced-to-progressive converters used in 3D: they should actually generate four images, not just two. But solving this requires a significant redesign of the workflow and tools.

The Best 3D Shots Impede Storytelling

You will likely face the dilemma that your audience wants a good story *and* wow effects. Unfortunately, these two goals are often irreconcilable; it is very difficult to get immersed in a story while also having dramatic 3D effects forced upon you.

As stereographer Eric Deren says: "3D is like FX for sound; if you notice it, they did it wrong."

Or as Phil "Captain 3D" McNally has said: "Wow effects are like sweet candies. Everyone likes chocolate, but we all get sick if we eat too much at once. When you are cooking, you use sugar with caution. There are some meals where you don't want any, there are some cakes that deserve super-sugary frosting; and then, you don't serve them as a starter. Keep this in mind and don't overdose your audience with 3D effects."

STEVE SCHKLAIR

The story is the most important element. Gratuitous wow effects do not move a story along. They do the opposite, and take an audience out of the story. These are shots that are screaming out, "Look at me! Look at me! I'm 3D!" Still, every audience would like a few wow 3D shots, with negative parallax. These have to be carefully scripted in, if used at all. Perhaps the titles in a feature or the graphics in a broadcast are enough. Think of the early days of surround sound, where every soundtrack swirled the sounds around the room in a dizzying fashion. Over time this settled down, and now the surrounds are used creatively, or just to create atmosphere. Eventually, and we hope very soon, 3D visuals will settle down to a mature level and exist solely to add to the filmmaker's craft of storytelling.

Run and Gun Configurations

When John Honeycutt gave his keynote speech at NAB 2010, he invited Bruce Austin on stage to present the Element Technica Neutron-SI2K rig Bruce used to shoot 3D in Amazonia. Here is this 3D warrior's firsthand account of six months of shooting the 3D documentary.

BRUCE AUSTIN

Shooting 3D in Africa is like putting your rig in a washing machine, running a full high-stain cycle, and then checking to see if there's a missing screw.

Despite all its limitations, its long focal length being one, I love the Panasonic AG-3DA1. In real nature documentary situations, rigs just do not work; we have to get rid of them at some point. They are too dust-prone, full of chromatic and geometric aberrations, and heavy and fragile to boot. You feel like you're hurdling around a studio camera in the bush, as though someone in the camera department played a prank on you when packing your stuff. We need cameras 5mm in width to make practical SBS (side-by-side) rigs for animal documentaries.

If you need 15 seconds to set up and 10 seconds to set your IO and convergence, you have to remember that, on average, an animal leaves within 60 seconds. I eventually learned to set up the camera while we were far away from the scene, guesstimating the 3D, and then we would roll up to position. We had to leave the engine on, otherwise the animal would leave, and that created vibrations.

Content Creation Is Affected

Broadcasting a sporting event in 3D involves the same rules as in 2D: let the audience understand the game, and give them the feeling of being in the stadium or on the field. There will be some changes, like framing close-ups with different graphic placements in mind, and reducing camera movement may be needed to prevent visual fatigue for the viewer. Additionally, camera positions have to be selected carefully in order to avoid images of people walking in front of the screen plane.

For the audience, 3D brings a new level of engagement. Even the crew members feel it. As 3D sports broadcast director Derek Manning confesses: "In 3D, every shot is an experience, every cut is an intermission. It's so immersing, so engaging, on the first game I directed in 3D, I found myself watching a shot, totally forgetting I was actually running the show."

FIGURE 1.5
Producing Live 3D Reveals Unexpected Effects. A still camera flash generates a halo of focused imagery in the middle of a tracking blur.
Side-effect catch by Nick Brown, Digital 3ality, during a BSkyB 3D football production.

3D TV Is Very Close to 3D Cinema

One of the unpleasant discoveries of the summer of 2010 was that 3D TV is no less forgiving than 3D cinema. A widespread mix of educated guessing and naïve expectation suggested that the smaller screen size would make the 3D imperfections less noticeable; vertical disparities of a few pixels would be troublesomely big on a theater screen but unnoticed on a TV set. However, experience shows that this is not the case. Is it due to the sharpness and luminance of the image? It's not yet clear, but the lesson of the day is that 3D TV is not cheap 3D.

In addition, the distance between the viewer and the screen reduces the screen size effect. As a result, most of the depth settings are relatively constant, which means it's primarily the depth placement that evolves. Producing for large screens and small screens still dictates different framing and editing—but the differences are not the ones that were expected.

New Opinions on 3D Content

Discussions with fellow stereographers at scientific conferences, industry trade shows, and online forums have brought to our attention a few changes in the general opinion on 3D content production.

The scenario does not need to be 3D. I'd like to correct something I wrote in my previous book, *3D Movie Making*, which said that it was beneficial to think about 3D from the very inception of your project; in fact, this is not accurate. Your story has to be told, be engaging, and make the audience willing to follow it to the end. There's nothing 3D about this. If you feel that your story needs to be filmed in 3D to captivate the audience's attention, you are either engaging in a modern art piece or a very bad movie.

The screen size is not that important. What is important are the angular disparities, and they tend to be relatively constant as the viewing distance increases with the screen width. Add the 1% tolerance in divergence and the diopter effect, as described by stereoscopic 3D expert John Merrit, and you end up with stereoscopic metrics that scale and overlap pretty well from HDTV to cinema. Eventually, the parallax settings will be more influenced by the director's 3D style than the math. Parallax setting is ultimately more artistic than technical, provided you do not get into insane numbers.

Frame rate is more critical than expected. When Digital 3ality produced the New York Rangers game on March 24, 2010, the hockey players' fast-moving action was the biggest challenge. It was eventually solved by producing the show in 720HD and using a different approach than interlaced-to-progressive conversion.

Long lenses are not all that bad in 3D. The IPL cricket competition in India mentioned earlier forced Steve Schklair's team to work with longer lenses than they planned: "We had to search for the best camera position that allowed us to create good 3D—where the players are not 'cardboarded,' where the positive parallax does not get wild, where the framing is coherent and aesthetic, and most of all, where the game makes sense. Camera positions are more crucial than lens choice. Never forget that telling the story the right way is more important than making artistically sculpted pictures."

The Ongoing Invention of 3D TV

The 3D visionaries who believed in stereoscopy ten years ago have not stopped looking forward. What do they have up their sleeves now?

Live integrations of multilayered 3D sources and graphics. Basically, they talk about producing the 3D visual extravaganza of U23D in real time; in other words, replace the good old 2D cross-fades and graphics by mixing multiple 3D views of the same event. On the technology side, this relies on fine depth analysis of the video feed, used to drive the DVE and graphics engines. On the creative side, it's up to you. Crude foresight would suggest stats and graphics following the players and floating above the field, and close-ups of the lead singer overlaid above the dancing crowd.

To get there, we need to get the image analyzers to drive the graphics engines, and we need to rethink our visual relationship to the event—in spatial volume, not just in perspectives or layers. Do not settle for putting graphics and action in respectively separate and safe spaces. Go all the way to have them cooperatively occupy all the 3D space.

The whole science of generating depth metadata and automatically understanding volume will ultimately trickle down to the contribution and distribution channels, and then all the way down to your set-top box that will use this science to merge on-screen graphics, like TV programs or menus, with live images.

Higher in the production chain, we need to get the image processors to run the camera units in auto-convergence modes, based on the director's artistic requests. As Steve Schklair says, "You want to keep the 3D creative positions in truck A, and get rid of all the mechanical positions of convergence pullers in truck B. Everybody in an OB van is at a creative seat; it has to be the same in 3D."

This is the front line battle in 3D. Get rid of the technicians, give the power to the artists.

3D's New Collaborative Landscape

As *Avatar* DP Vince Pace put it in September 2010: "We are in a collaborative market between 3D vendors and channels right now. The investment made in the 3D gear has to be shared, and the created knowledge has to be spread out. We had 20 years to finesse HD, and on some projects, we had 20 weeks to deliver 3D."

Getting the industry to produce quality 3D will not be easy. The economy isn't great, and the investment in 3D has to be recouped. A lot of people need to be trained on new gear and new procedures; directors have to be trained to make new edit decisions, and camera operators have to learn new reflexes.

If we want the audience to embrace 3D broadcasts that disturb its viewing habits, we must make up for the disruption. We need to continue the search for that new 3D camera that will bring us the money shot; the new effect that will make the audience prefer to put glasses on rather that watch in 2D.

Fortunately, the 3D industry seems to get it; we are beginning to see more and more collaborative work, especially in the realm of education.

3D CREWING AND NEW JOB SCOPES

Producing 3D will involve new tasks, new jobs, new skills, and sometimes new people. If you are shooting a single crew independent documentary in the Himalayan mountains, you do all the 3D. If you are on a big-budget feature film, there may be up to a dozen people involved in depth art direction, stereoscopic calculations, and rig manipulation. After the AC (assistant camera) turns the 3D knobs on the rig, you'll have all the TDs (technical directors) fixing it in post, and the supervisors editing and timing your depth. In a live show, the 3D can be set by the camera operators, the convergence pullers (camera assistants who set the 3D parameters while the camera is running), a stereoscopic supervisor, or even a bunch of computers in the OB van racks.

You'll have your say with all these people, but your power will end on the release day, when the theater projectionist will most likely reframe your piece of art and kill your floating windows. Future 3D TV sets may even have a reconvergence button, if not a depth-enhancing mode that changes the IOD.

The Stereographer

The stereographer used to be the jack-of-all-trades of 3D productions, bringing stereoscopic expertise to the project, from development to projection. With 3D production increasing in size, duration, and complexity, the job tends to be shared among a principal photography stereographer, usually assumed by someone with a DP or AC background, and a postproduction stereographer, usually someone with an FX supervisor or compositing background.

In a live TV production, the stereographer is more of an instructor who will teach the ENG team how to use the 3D gear and supervise the pool of convergence pullers or 3D image analyzers that control the depth in real time.

On the movie set, the stereographer sets the depth, sometimes in collaboration with the DP or director, sometimes independently. This will eventually change, with the stereographer role gradually fading out. Setting the depth will then be another artistic tool utilized by the DP—just as it is already the DP who is responsible for the continuity of depth of field, or using depth of field to enhance storytelling (working closely with the director, of course, as is already done). There may or may not be a 3D-AC in charge of actually manipulating the rig.

In *3D Movie Making,* I signaled the paradox that required a stereographer to have experience in 3D and in feature films even though no 3D feature films had been produced for many years. That paradox has now evolved into a new one: Good stereographers are those who will eventually make themselves useless, because in every 3D movie or 3D broadcast, they teach the camera operators, ACs, DPs, and directors how to make good 3D. Eventually, this 3D knowledge will be pervasive in movie crews; everyone will have some general knowledge of 3D, and will also master the specialized skills needed for his or her job position. By then, a stereographer may or may not be useful on set—in the same way that there are no longer color technicians. On the other hand, there are still sound engineers. Time will tell which way the road goes.

It is also possible that all stereographers will eventually be stereo supervisors or VFX supervisors. If 3D is a new visual storytelling tool, then it is the DP who will be responsible for using this tool to tell the story. It is worth noting that the generation of stereographers who worked on the film-era 3D movies had a camera background, while the digital generation comes from visual effects supervision.

Knowing how much 3D is an end-to-end quality issue, more and more stereographers are reluctant to get a job where they do not control 3D quality from shoot to post. As stereographer Eric Deren says, "Someone in post can very easily mess up what you shot, as soon as you are gone. Even worse, you may have to deal in post with the nightmare of fixing dismal 3D that somebody else shot. In both cases, the end result is poor or bad 3D that is reaching the screen with your name on the credits and your reputation at stake. Whether they are the DP or the stereographer, people shouldn't be paid until the post is done."

The Convergence Puller

The second most well-known job in 3D production, the convergence puller (CP), is a camera assistant who sets the 3D parameters while the camera is running, typically tracking a shot. The job here is to keep the screen plane in accordance with the camera movements and scene blocking. This task was compulsory in analog 3D, but it is much less critical with digital 3D, especially when shooting parallel and reconverging in post. In both converged and parallel methods, this 3D-AC job includes tracking the interaxial with the shot motion.

In 3D TV productions, motorized rigs allow you to remotely control the interaxial and convergence; therefore, the convergence puller can work from the OB van. A pool of CPs actually work as team, coordinating the depth of the cameras under the stereographer's command. In some situations, image processors can replace the convergence puller, in which case a 3D vision engineer steps in.

The 3D Vision Engineer

Image processors are complex computers that can automate a lot of functions on a 3D production. Not all convergence pullers know the intricacies of an image processor well enough to use them to their full capabilities. Especially for complex setups involving graphics insertions, multicamera settings, or complex feedback loops with rig motion control, a highly skilled and trained technician is needed. The 3D vision engineer is a computer specialist trained by the vendor, if not directly sent from the engineering team.

The Rig Technician

Low-end rigs can be set up and operated by any clever cameraperson with some basic training. High-end rigs require trained technicians to set up and configure all the automatisms, synchronization, and remote operation boxes and cables. The rig technician is the person responsible for the engineering of the camera systems. This includes confirming accurate sync, building the lens LUTs, and being responsible for the capturing, recording, and accuracy of on-set metadata.

The Stereoscopic Supervisor

The stereo supervisor is in charge of the coherence of the depth treatment in postproduction. He or she will ensure that the depth quality is kept pristine on both a technical and artistic level. In all CG animation stereoscopic movies, the stereo supervisor is the stereographer in charge.

CHAPTER 2

The Stereoscopic Camera Unit

The type of camera or rig you'll need for filming 3D is dictated by various parameters—and for quite a long time, the number one rule was availability. However, this has changed since 3D entered the realm of mainstream entertainment, with the recent increases in vendors of 3D tools, the expanded availability of 3D gear at rental houses, and the global growth of 3D production budgets.

FIGURE 2.1A
Compact 3D Camera.
The JVC GSTD1BUS is a 3D camcorder designed for run-and-gun productions.

One rule of content creation says, "The best tool is the one you love for the job you have to do." Still, we are often asked, "What is the best rig in this price range?" or "Shall I buy this 3D camcorder or get a 3D rig?" There's no one-size-fits-all answer to any of these questions, because there's no one-size-fits-all 3D camera unit. Consider this: Have you ever met a one-size-fits-all 2D camera (besides in the dreams of its salesman)?

You'll choose your 3D camera unit based on the project you are working on, and sometimes on the very shot you will be doing that day. As a stereographer on a feature movie, you'll most likely have to match the DP request to use a 2D camera in your rig. As a DP, you'll have to make sure your choices of camera and lenses can be hosted in a rig that fits the monetary, volume, and weight limits of the production.

FIGURE 2.1B
Portable 3D Camera Unit.
Paul Taylor, stereographer, with a 3D Camera Company rig equipped with Silicon Imaging SI-2K cameras.

There are three optical designs for a 3D camera unit:

1. Lens devices or attachments combining views in a single sensor.
2. Cameras mounted at 90 degrees, looking through a half-mirror angled at 45 degrees.
3. Cameras mounted side by side.

FIGURE 2.1C
Full-Size 3D Camera Unit. 3D cinema camera unit, with two Panavision Genesis cameras on a Binocle Brigger III with 3D monitors and SSD recorders.

Globally, there are three types of stereoscopic camera units:

1. All-in-one 3D camcorders.
2. Small 3D rigs, for a steady cam or shoulder mount, using digital camera heads.
3. Large 3D rigs, hosting full-size digital cinemas, broadcast cameras, or camcorders.

THE 3D CAMERA RIG

A 3D rig is a complex mechanical assembly that puts your cameras where your eyes would want to be, not where the camera's form factor forces you to put them. The 3D camera rig will be the admiral ship of your 3D camera fleet. It's big (sometimes bulky), expensive (sometimes unaffordable), complex (sometimes borderline geeky), and delicate to the point of fragility. Still, it's the air-land-sea multipurpose aircraft carrier that will never fall short and will always pull out the very 3D image you are looking for.

Although a new generation of 3D camcorders is evolving, they are specialized cameras that perform beautifully in a specific setting on their own turf. As such, they will never bring you the versatility of a good old bulky 3D rig—and, to boot, a good 3D rig will host any 2D camera you want or need to use. If the DP, director, or FX supervisor wants a Phantom, a Red One, or an ARRI Alexa, your full-size 3D rig will host it.

Over the next few years, the money spent in 3D camera design will have increased by a hundred- or thousandfold. These numbers aren't surprising, considering how scarce the 3D camera companies were a few years ago. We will soon see a new revolutionary 3D camera system every three months. Most of them will actually offer amazing new features and will be the perfect tool for a specific shoot, angle, project, or budget. However, our understanding is that the 3D rig that hosts regular or specialized 2D cameras, and moves them dynamically behind a beam-splitting optical device, is here to last—even if its form factor, price, and complexity will shrink significantly.

Our main reason for holding this position is the same reason we think 3D glasses are here for good: basically, there's only so much you can do to get away from the laws of physics and optics. Stereoscopic 3D is made of two discrete images describing two points of view: even if we throw thousands of engineers, millions of dollars, and billions of computing cycles at the issue, we will still end up looking at these two viewpoints. If you can record them right away, you do yourself a great favor. As 3D visual effects guru Tim Sassoon says: "Stereoscopic 3D is a visual effect. If you can shoot it, you should shoot it. Period."

Now that we have made the case for 3D rigs, let's acknowledge how complex the system is, and explore how and why it came to that level of complexity. After all, a 3D camera is just a pair of 2D cameras stitched together. Get a wood plank, two screws, and some duct tape, and there you have it. To be honest, that's pretty much how most stereographers started in their younger years. The richer had aluminum plates and the smarter got sliders, but we all started with the basics. And the few of us who pursued the journey all the way to the current state-of-the-art 3D rigs ended up with the same solution: a big bulky camera assembly revolving around a half-mirror, hosting a dreaded number of motion control magic boxes, and most likely connected to an image processing behemoth. How did we all end up at the same point, each one following our very own path? Let's fast-forward 20 years in 3D camera design to understand.

First, there were the film camera rigs designed for theme park movies in the 1980s. Sometimes carved out of a single piece of aluminum, they held together two cameras and the half-mirror splitting the light beam. They were beautiful and accurate, but heavy, expensive, and not that versatile, with no dynamic inter-optical distance.

Change came in the 1990s, with the new wave of electronic imaging announcing the digital revolution. Camera heads could be detached from processing and recording units, and motion control started to demonstrate its capacities. At that point, a few engineers or cinematographers on the planet established the 3D equation:

$$\text{Electronic imaging} + \text{motion control} = \text{perfect 3D images}$$

They started developing what would eventually be the blueprints for the 3D rigs you see today. That design was developed the hard way, by getting back from location late and often exhausted, with less than optimal pictures, and cursing about not having the 3D tools that would make it easier. Remember, producing 3D always starts by putting two cameras together and shooting. In that process one discovers the limitations of the system, builds solutions to circumvent them, and progresses toward higher 3D quality, easier production schedules, and more resilience to deal with the unexpected issues that content production always randomly, yet steadily, generates.

If you had been making 3D movies, and therefore 3D cameras, for the last 20 years, here is what you would have discovered:

Step one: You need to motion control the left and right camera's relative movement to generate good 3D images, because

1. Cameras need perfect alignment, requiring XYZ-axis translation and rotations.
2. One needs to be able to set up the inter-optical distance and convergence almost instantly.
3. On shots where the camera or the action is moving, inter-optical and convergence has to be dynamic.

Step two: You realize that your inter-optical is too wide. In most movies shot in 2010, inter-optical is under half the human inter-pupillary distance, which is about three centimeters. This means that the cameras need to be closer than the lenses' width:

1. Cameras need to shoot through a 45-degrees half-mirror.
2. The mirror has to be a surface mirror.
3. Mirrors are extremely prone to getting dusty.
4. A mirror is not a perfect plane; it bends under its own weight.
5. Surface mirrors have chromatic asymmetry.
6. Most importantly, the mirror's surface is fragile, and hitting it with a lens can scratch it.

Step three: You need to use zoom lenses, because changing lenses is a complex task on a mirror rig. Hopefully, you are already in the late 1990s, and the new HD zooms are sharp enough to be used as adjustable primes. When zooming in with your 3D rig, you discover that

1. Zoom progression is not linear and changes from lens to lens.
2. The optical axis shifts along a progression, and that shift is different with every lens you try.
3. As a result, each lens pair has specific alignment requirements that vary with focal length.

Step four: You have now reached the early 2000s, and computing power is soon to become a commodity. You safely assume you can build zoom look-up-tables (Z-LUTs) that use the XYZ motion controls to align the camera's optical axis. Here comes a new batch of bad news, however:

1. Manually generating the Z-LUT is a time-consuming process.
2. You should manually generate the Z-LUT every time a rig is assembled.

That last point should have you raising your eyebrow. What does this mean? It means that if you take the very same set of equipment and rebuild the very same rig, you won't end up with the very same results. First, assuming you can perfectly repeat procedures in movie and TV production is not such a safe bet. Second, we need to talk numbers here. You want to get to less than a couple of pixels of vertical disparity on your final image. When the sensor has 1080 lines of photosites on a 1/3-inch sensor, one line is 1/1080th of 3.6 mm, close to three microns. The larger digital sensor, the Phase One P65+, with 6732 lines on 40 mm, has a whopping 6 microns per pixel. To give you a comparison base, a human hair is 17 to 180 microns. You cannot build a mechanical assembly with moving parts and expect alignment figures to be predictable within a few microns.

1. The order of magnitude is to move camera and lenses weighing 10 Kg at up to 5 cm/sec.
2. Inertia and momentum effects set a physical limit that your hardware magicians will not be able to break.

You still need an automatic lenses matching tool, and you build your image analysis tools:

1. Automatic Z-LUT creation is a quite complex image processing problem involving coplanar geometry.
2. Over a typical shooting session, thermal dilatation can change a Z-LUT or a camera geometry. Just touching a camera may be enough to change the correction values.

Step five: You have now successfully reached the late 2000s, and you are the inventor of one of the few world-class 3D camera systems. By now, it is obvious that 3D cinema is going mainstream, and 3D TV is right around the corner. Both require that you produce perfect 3D imagery, and both won't cope for long with the idea that every 3D shot is an FX shot that should be groomed in post.

1. Manual depth setting by human operators is not adapted to 3D TV productions.
2. Full frame analysis and correction should be performed in less than 40 ms for live TV.
3. All units involved in a multicamera production should be depth-coordinated.

After reading this list, you may wonder if it's worth it—perhaps we are overdoing it, and the answer may be to start from a simpler place, or to get more "fix it in post" power.

Description and Vocabulary

In Figures 2.2 you can see the main parts of a 3D mirror rig:

- The half-mirror, which splits the light path into two optical axes.
- The transmissive camera, which records the light passing through the mirror.
- The reflective camera, which records the light bouncing on the mirror.
- The hood, which protects the mirror from catching surrounding lights (not shown).
- The inter-optical and convergence motion controllers.
- The zoom, focus, and iris controllers.

Functions and Features

What does a 3D rig do, essentially? As we have seen, it keeps a pair of cameras together and then moves them with microscopic accuracy. It's all about motion control (MC). At a bare minimum, you want a rig to allow for easy camera alignment, which we'll call *mechanical control*. Then you want to be able to move cameras relative to each other by cranking wheels (at the very least) or by running motors (preferably), which we'll call *dynamic control*. Eventually, you want such movements to be automatized, with *intelligent motion control* that takes cares of the lenses' optical shifts, and, ultimately, you want that intelligent rig to obey artistic orders like "more depth in the back" as opposed to technical requests like "converge closer."

These are the three levels of functions a 3D rig should offer: mechanical control, dynamic control, and intelligent MC.

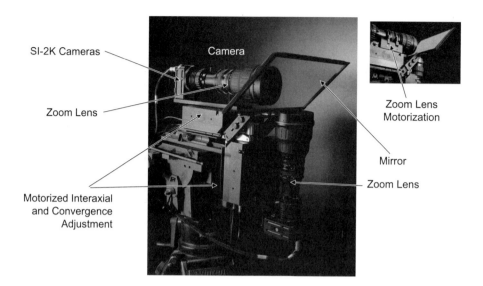

SI-2K Cameras

Zoom Lens

Motorized Interaxial
and Convergence
Adjustment

Camera

Zoom Lens
Motorization

Mirror

Zoom Lens

**FIGURE 2.2
The Main Parts of a
3D Rig.**

3D RIG, LEVEL ONE: MECHANICAL CONTROL AND CAMERA ORIENTATION

Mechanical control of a camera position is a bare minimum requirement for good 3D shooting. This control includes the ability to register cameras together. In theory, this means controlling three axes per camera, in both translation and rotation. This amounts to a total of 12 degrees of freedom. Obviously, only one camera performing all movements would be enough. Out of these six remaining axes, three should be fixed, and three should be adjustable.

The fixed mechanical controls are the camera height, depth position, and roll axis, which are to be fixed only once.

The adjustable mechanical controls are:

- The distances between the cameras, called *inter-axial, inter-ocular, inter-optical,* or *stereo base.*
- The pan, or rotation, along the vertical axis, which is called *convergence, angulation,* or *zero parallax setting.*
- The yaw, or tilt, which is the rotation along the transversal axis and is, used to correct the optical axis vertical angle.

The yaw control is used to compensate for the zoom axis mismatch. Note that this mismatch is in both X and Y directions, so it will affect the convergence angle. As a result, the convergence control is actually used to correct the zoom axes.

When discussing mechanical controls, it makes sense to mention the rolling shutter and camera orientation issue. Most first-generation rigs had the vertical camera with its top facing the set. This meant that if you looked at it through the mirror, it seemed to be upside-down; indeed, that's the way it looked at the scene: upside-down. If your cameras had a rolling shutter, as most CCDs do, it meant that they scanned the image the same way video cameras used to, or the same way a scanner or a Xerox copier does. In the 720p U.S. video standard, short for 720@30p, the norm is to scan the image top to bottom in a little less than a 1/30th of a second. This means that the bottom of the image is read 1/30th of a second later than the top. If your cameras are scanning in opposite directions, it means that the top and bottom parts of the image are desynchronized by up to a 1/30th of a second. Thus, fast-moving objects being imaged at different times appear to be in different positions.

French stereographer Alain Derobe, when teaching 3D shooting, often gets a student to swing a golf club in front of such a 3D rig configuration. This creates motion-depth artifacts with very interesting results: right-handed golfers seem to hit their heads on the way up and miss the ball on the way back, with the club twisting forward as it reaches the ground; left-handed golfers are the other way around, avoiding a head injury but seeming to whack out their own legs. You don't want this in your footage. In order to avoid it, you want the vertical, or reflective, camera to be flipped around; then the image will be scanned right to left instead of left to right, which generates only 1/1000th of the top/bottom desynchronization. A handful of digital cinema cameras have the good grace to offer a socket bolt on both the top and bottom, allowing for adequate orientation even in a wrongly oriented rig.

FIGURE 2.3
Rolling Shutters and Mirror Rig. Using a rolling shutter camera in a mirror rig requires specific camera orientation, as shown on this 3D Film Factory rig.

3D RIG, LEVEL TWO: DYNAMIC CONTROLS AND LINKED FUNCTIONS

You'll soon want to be able to instantly crank up and down the three moving axes (tX, rZ, rY), either because you need fast setup from shot to shot, or because you want to animate inter-optical, convergence, or focal length. After all, not all shots are static. Most, if not all, professional rigs offer the option to animate stereography, which is actually where the name *convergence puller* comes from. And all professional rigs come with motorized controls, some of them with servo-controls that will link functions together. What functions would you want to link? We have seen that zooming in requires that you animate Z and Y rotations together, following a Z-LUT. Considering that, in your mechanical assembly, the gears controlling the rotation angles are not exactly positioned along the optical centers of the lenses, any rotation correction generates a translation error that may need to be corrected. If it's not the case with zoom compensation, it will be the case with the convergence and inter-optical distances affecting each other.

In 3D TV production, the linked functions can include linking convergence to focus and inter-optical to focal length. In this case, shooting 3D really feels like shooting 2D, with the very same control knob on the handlebar. This configuration is efficient with sporting events, especially for remote camera positions where there's no surprise in shot composition. Vince Pace, the 3D cinematographer for *Avatar*, developed the concept by creating a *3D shadow unit* that mounts atop a regular 2D camera. It automatically sets its focus plane, zoom factor, inter-optical distance, and convergence distance based on the 2D settings. This solution has a key selling point: it does not require another camera position in crowded stadiums where real estate is negotiated months in advance.

STEREOGRAPHERS' TIPS ON 3D RIGS

Yves Pupulin: Later we'll see a special case: the steady-cam rig. Although we'll talk about this in more detail later, let's just mention one thing: on such a rig, you want both cameras to move laterally; otherwise, any change of inter-optical distance will change the center of gravity, and the operator will have to balance to compensate for the momentum change.

Eric Deren: While we're discussing the mechanical balance, let's talk about all the gear we end up gripping to a camera: filters, shades, matte boxes, microphones, lamps, monitors, and all sorts of 3D boxes. Make sure you never put one of these magic arms on the cameras, and never use the hot shoe as a docking socket. Every time you do so, you take the chance of affecting the alignment. Tether a control box on the camera body, push a button, and *voilà,* you have potentially messed up your camera alignment.

Max Penner: Last but not least, you never know where your 3D rig will end up: on a crane, on a bike, on a rooftop, on a helicopter . . . the possibilities are endless. You want to be able to fix everything on it, and you want to be able to bolt the rig everywhere that mad director will dream about. To that end, drilling many threaded holes on the rig body will come in very handy.

FIGURE 2.4
ARRI Alexa on a 3D Rig. Note the threaded holes on the sides of the rig, used to fix accessories or to bolt the rig on ad hoc mounts.

3D RIG, LEVEL THREE: IMAGE ANALYSIS AND GEOMETRY CORRECTION

All the whistles and bells of a dynamic rig will not bring you instant camera setup. For one thing, the process of registering the two cameras is complex, and generating Z-LUT is time-consuming. It basically consists of aiming at an alignment pattern and then registering the cameras at both ends of the zoom range and at as many in-between positions as needed to get a smooth Z-LUT. This is a typical task that you'll want to give to the motion-control computer that drives the rig motors.

Then, once you've set up your shot, you'll want to make sure you have the right stereoscopic parameters. If your image is out of focus or underexposed, it's easy, or at least possible, to catch it on your control monitor. If your 3D parameters are wrong, it may not be obvious based on what you see on a small field monitor, especially if you don't have the eye to catch 3D defaults. And even if you have years of experience, you'd rather have a green light blinking on a reliable piece of equipment than rely exclusively on your instinctive understanding of the 3D image. Let's say it again: Some maintain that, ultimately, you must use a full-size screen to evaluate a 3D image. That's a 40-foot screen, if you are shooting for theatrical release. Clearly, you want a computer to help you make that decision.

The next step in assembling the best camera unit is an image-analysis tool that helps you configure and monitor your 3D. What you need is artificial intelligence that computes the corrections that need to be applied to the optical system, so that you can type in the screen metrics or the director's stereoscopic parallax request, and then let the computer set the inter-optical and convergence. All you need to do is look at a monitor with the picture overlaid by red, orange, green, and blue tags showing the 3D parallax. If you're shooting live 3D, the computer can even adjust the inter-optical on the fly, just by tracking the action. On a director's cue, it can also change convergence to match the depth on another camera position. The active depth cuts that were added in post in live movies like U23D, or in CGI movies like *How to Train Your Dragon*, are now available for live broadcasts.

Last, but not least, the system is able to fix the optical geometry errors in the image domain. As we have seen, even the best 3D rigs cannot get a perfect image alignment. Even if they could reach sub-micron accuracy, the lenses' assembly discrepancies would still generate some vertical rivalries—though we are talking about image imperfections that you would most likely not notice, like a faint background noise that is only noticeable once it stops. What's the point of fixing imperceptible 3D alignment, then? First, you have to see such image correction in action to understand what it means. The 3D image has to be experienced—perfect 3D too. Second, that faint white noise eventually builds up as visual fatigue and may give your audience the infamous 3D headache.

Can image processing eventually replace high-end motion control in rigs? That is essentially Sony's approach to 3D, as deployed on the FIFA World Cup 2010 3D broadcasts. The concept is to rely on the image processing stages to take care of 3D pictures that would not be watchable without correction. It's a known fact that software eventually kills the hardware in many aspects of visual effects. The scope and validity of this approach is one of the current debates in the 3D community. There's no question it works—up to a certain point, and at a given computational cost. The question is: Are we at the point where computers can figure out what the lenses did not bring to the sensors?

How to Evaluate the Quality of a 3D TV Vendor

Shooting for 3D TV is one step beyond shooting for 3D cinema in complexity and requirements. You want each camera unit to deliver perfect 3D, and, on top of that, you want the whole 3D experience to be coherent. Think about color. Each camera has to generate a nice color picture, and then a vision engineer has to make sure the color matches from one camera to another. That's exactly the same challenge for 3D. You want nice 3D from all camera positions, and then coherent 3D across camera positions.

When shopping for a 3D solution, here are the questions Steve Schklair suggests you ask your 3D TV vendor, and the answers that you should expect.

Q: What is the setup time, from truck roll-out to shooting?
   A: Two hours is okay, two days is not, and 30 minutes is the standard time for world-class teams.
Q: How is perfect alignment assured?
   A: You need computerized motion control and live post-processing.
Q: How are the spatial differences between cameras handled?
   A: You need a stereographer to coordinate the depth look between the cameras and to ensure depth continuity of the live feed. Remember that there will be no post-correction of your 3D feed once it leaves the truck.
Q: Do you 3D-fix the previews, or only the program?
   A: This is a catch; previews need to be fixed too, for they are recorded in the EVS for instant replays.
Q: How does your stereographer work?
   A: The stereographer acts as the color engineer on the 3D. He adjusts the volume of the scene, not simply the camera on which he is working. This brings us to the concept of "automatic stereoscopic setup," where the camera units obey the image processing stages to generate a coherent 3D interpretation of the live event.

HOW DO YOU EVALUATE THE QUALITY OF A 3D RIG?

If you look at a list of the 3D rigs available as of the summer of 2010, you'll find quite a price range between low-end and high-end rigs. What does a $60 K rig give you that a $3 K rig does not? Some key points are:

1. Stiffness needed to keep heavy cameras aligned in dynamic shots.
2. Compactness and light weight for steady-cam or shoulder operation.
3. Ergonomic design for fast setup and alignment.
4. Embedded motorization for fast camera alignment and shoot setup.
5. Good combination or meaningful balance of items 1 to 4.
6. Size and quality of the half-mirror.
7. Accessories (hood, matte box, connectors).

Side-by-Side or Mirror Rigs?

Not all 3D shots require a mirror rig; there are many shots where the inter-optical distance is larger than the camera. In these cases, it is possible, simpler, and much better to mount the cameras side by side. This eliminates the mirror and all its filters and visual artifacts. This affects a minority of shots, but they are not rare, and the benefits are great. Here is a list of times when you can use a side-by-side rig instead of a mirror rig.

- Faraway shots, high 50 camera in sports 3D TV
- Main camera in soccer and other large-field sports
- Large landscape shots with no foreground
- Cable cams aiming down with shallow depth to record
- Back position shot, framing the whole scene for a concert
- All shots using a miniature point-of-view camera with a small form factor

FIGURE 2.5
Example of Mirror Rig:
the 3ality Digital TS-5.

Some 3D rigs are specially designed for side-by-side (SBS) configuration, and they tend to be much simpler to design and operate than mirror rigs. Because they are used with longer lenses and farther-away subjects, they produce shots less prone to keystone issues.

Some modular rigs can be reconfigured either as side-by-side or beam-splitter rigs. On some rigs, this requires a complete breakdown; on others, it can be done with an easy flip of one of the camera supports.

FIGURE 2.6
Side-by-Side Cameras
for Helicopter Shot.
Helicopter setup in the Makay Desert, Madagascar.
Image courtesy of Binocle/ Gedeon.

More Gear in the Optical Path

On a mirror rig, there are many new objects on the light path from the scene to the sensor: the half-mirror, and its friends the filters and the matte box. There's still some secret craftsmanship here that not all stereographers are willing to share. For this section, special thanks and credit go to stereographers Eric Deren and Max Penner.

THE HALF-MIRROR

The mirror in your 3D rig is not just any mirror: it's a 50/50 surface mirror. This means that exactly half of the light is reflected (*reflected light*) when the other half is let through (*transmitted light*). Reflected light and transmitted light, define the *transmissive camera* and *reflective camera*. The mirror has to be a *surface mirror*, it means that its reflective coating is on top of the glass, not under it. Walk to your bathroom mirror and put your finger on it; you'll see the thickness of the glass between your finger and its reflection (actually, you'll see twice the glass thickness). Now go to the kitchen and grab a brand-new, never-been-scratched stainless steel pot—one you can see yourself in—and put your finger on that. There is no space between your finger and its image. This is because the pot is a surface mirror, and your bathroom mirror is not.

To understand why the 3D mirror has to be a surface mirror, try another hands-on experiment. Get that bathroom mirror to your office video projector and use it to divert the light beam. You'll see a duplicated image, with a secondary picture that is approximately 10% the brightness of the main one. This is because the glass surface of the mirror is not 100% transparent, and thus it is a mirror in itself. If your rig were not fitted with a front surface mirror, the reflective camera would see that double image.

FIGURES 2.7A AND 2.7B
Element Technica Neutron Rig in Both Positions. The Neutron rig can be switched from SBS to mirror rig configurations in a few minutes.
Images courtesy of Element Technica.

Your 3D mirror needs to be 50/50, or as close as possible. Sometimes it is not, and therefore requires adaptations and corrections, which are done by adding filters to fine-tune light balance. (We'll discuss this more in a minute.)

It also needs to be color neutral, and most likely is not. Due to the coating material and its thickness, the mirror will react differently to various wavelengths. The ultimate example is the dichroic prisms in cameras or projectors that split white lights into RGB beams. That color sensitivity is also a function of the light angle of incidence. This means that the color imbalance is a 2D gradient following a circular pattern, and it changes in intensity as you zoom in and out. To some extent, the longer the focal, the less color vignetting.

The mirror will be extremely efficient at catching up unwanted lights from all around the cameras, or from the cameras themselves. Catching light is what you want your mirror to do, but make sure that it doesn't go overboard. As an example, even the red tally light can cast an unpleasant halo on your image. For this reason, the mirror box should be fully hooded, and both camera windows (through which the lenses get their images from the mirror) should be completely blinded around the lens.

Be aware that the mirror can also reflect light into the scene as well; on very tight close-ups, it can even reflect light on the actor's face.

To complete this discussion, we will address the issues with polarized lights, like specular reflections, in the next section, which is dedicated to the filters used to take care of them.

A Few Things to Know About Beam-Splitters

Sébastien Lafoux

Sébastien Lafoux, with 3D Camera Company, did extensive mirror testing when designing his Stereo Tango rig. Here's what he has to say about it.

To begin with, here is a list of common characteristics of beam-splitters:

- Ideal spectral distribution target: 50% transmission, 400 nm to 750 nm; 50% reflection, 400 nm to 750 nm
- Ideal light loss target: 1 stop
- Most common substrate: low-dispersion crown glass (Schott B270 flat glass, Schott N-BK 7 optical glass)
- Most common coating method: vacuum deposit
- Most common pigment: titanium dioxide

There are also a number of common problems with beam-splitters:

- False astigmatism, which is when the horizontal wave front error causes bad focus of the reflected image at long focus distances and lengths.
- Back focus alteration on the reflected images.
- Color temperature disparity between the reflected and transmitted images.
- Polarization effect on the reflected image, causing severe density and saturation disparities between the reflected and transmitted images.
- Different spectral response between reflected and transmitted images, causing disparities in color.
- Achromatic aberrations causing uncorrectable flare discrepancies between reflected and transmitted images.

- Inadequate mounting apparatuses, which causes distortion of the substrate and severe degradation of the reflected images.

It's also important to know how to test a beam-splitter:

- Check if the beam-splitter is mounted right side up by bringing the tip of a pencil to the mirror surface. If you see a double reflection of the pencil tip, the beam-splitter is upside down. If you see a single reflection of the pencil tip, the beam splitter is right side up.
- Check for scratches and defects in the coating.
- Test the difference in focus setting between the reflected and transmitted image at wide open iris.
- Test the focus performance at wide open iris with your longest lens, at a focusing distance greater than 60 feet.
- With the help of a vectorscope and a color chart, check the color and flare disparities between the two images, and compare them against the same target without a beam-splitter. Perform this test under both tungsten and daylight illumination. An overlay histogram will help you visualize the color disparities.

- With the help of an autocollimator, check the collimation of both reflected and transmitted cameras through the beam-splitter.
- Test your rig in the horizontal and tilted down positions to make sure the beam-splitter is properly secured and the focus and optical alignment is not affected when the rig is tilted downwards.
- Check if the beam-splitter and its mounting apparatus can accommodate filtration in front of the lens; you will need it to cut infrared contamination and to cut light levels when using the latest generation of digital cameras.
- Check if the mounting apparatus can accommodate a clear cover to protect the beam-splitter during setup and during special effects. This will extend the useful life of the beam-splitter and save you a significant amount of money.

The average selling price for a good quality beam-splitter is about US$5,000, depending on size and quantity. However, a high price does not guarantee a good beam-splitter.

Happy testing!

_____

Sébastien Laffoux, Laffoux Solutions, www.tangohead.com

FILTERS

If your mirror is not doing a perfect job of splitting light in half, one camera will get more illumination than the other, and the apertures and depth of field will not match. This must be fixed, for eye rivalry in sharpness, details, and texture density is prone to generate visual processing overload and mental fatigue. This is because, first, your brain needs to match two uncorrelated images; and second, it then has to map the finer texture onto your 3D vision, rather than just using whatever each eye sees.

Light levels need to be balanced with neutral density (ND) filters. Stereographer Eric Deren suggests getting some 1/8th to 1/4th stop ND filters that may be on special order at your camera shop. If you cannot get them, use the gain setting to balance the cameras, not the iris. Experience shows that noise discrepancy is less noticeable than depth-of-field mismatch.

Light polarization is an issue too. A reflective surface will polarize the light in a direction defined by the product of the surface's normal and incoming light vectors. A light source beaming onto a glossy wall will bounce polarized. When it reaches the half mirror, it will go through it unaffected, and meanwhile will be filtered out from the bouncing light path. As a result the transmissive camera will receive more light than the reflective one. The disparity is neither persistent nor uniform with camera movement, and can amount to up to two or three full stops in specific conditions. There are two ways to take care of it: linear polarization and circular polarization.

The linear polarization solution places a linear filter in front of the transmissive camera to replicate the light-filtering that the reflective camera experiences. This filter will typically generate a full stop loss, and requires another one placed on the reflective camera to even out the light levels. This solution requires that you put filters inside the mirror box, and consumes one stop on both cameras.

Facing the challenge of a night shot with polarizing surfaces like car hoods, and no stop to lose, Eric Deren came up with a simpler setup using a quarter-wave plate, also known as a *circularizing filter*. By applying this filter in front of the mirror box, the linearly polarized light gets circularized and is much less affected by the half-mirror. Despite being theoretically less perfect than the two linear filters, this method has proven very effective for day shots and much more productive.

One more word from Eric:

> Fix all this filtering gear on the rig, not on the camera; otherwise, any adjustment is likely to misalign them. Remember that the mere use of touchscreen functions on prosumer cameras is enough to mess up your alignment. While you're at it, make sure the lenses are tight. Not perfectly locking them may not even be an issue on a lucky 2D shoot day, because they'll stay stable enough for shooting—but in 3D it's a no-no not to double-check that the lenses are perfectly in position and locked down before aligning the rig. Otherwise they'll slip during the day, and by the time you tighten them up, you'll need a full realignment of the rig.

Remember to have one replacement mirror, at the very least, because they are amazingly fragile and hard to find once on location. Even if you can find a local spare one, you take the chance of getting a lower quality device. Even a comparable one might have different optical characteristics that will force you to reconsider all your fine-tuned light filtering. Put them in a safe box, protected from dust and hard drops—and, while you're at it, put a handful of anaglyph glasses in this save-the-day bag. They'll make themselves handy someday.

Special Case: Steady-Cam Rigs

Steady-cam rigs are a specific breed of 3D rigs. The *steady cam* is an articulated arm mounted on a harness with a whole set of balancing weights and stabilizing springs; it allows the camera operator to walk freely while moving the camera in virtually every position. They are typically used for close-up subjective shots—such as shooting dynamic point-of-view from a character who is either a murderer or a victim of a murderer—which means they need to have a small interaxial, or, in other words, a mirror rig. They need to be quite stiff to hold cameras together while the operator climbs the stairs, and they need to do all this within a very restricted weight limit that also includes the two cameras, batteries, recorders, and 3D image processor. In addition, you need a rig where the left and right cameras move symmetrically to keep the whole mount balanced if the inter-optical changes along a dynamic shot.

Rigs from Around the World

Below is a short selection of 3D rig makers from all around the world. A more up-to-date list, with complete contact and specifications, is available on the book's companion website.

- 21st Century 3D, Jason Goodman
- 3ality Digital
- 3D Film Factory
- 3D Rigs
- Binocle 3D
- Dimension 3, Dan Symmes
- E3D Creative
- Element Technica
- HinesLab StereoCam
- Kerner Optical
- Kronomav
- PACE
- Pacific FX
- Parallax3
- P+S Technik
- Redrock Micro
- Stereoscopic Technologies
- SwissRIG

CAMERAS IN 3D

A very broad range of cameras is used in 3D productions. You'll find that many 2D cameras are suitable for use in 3D rigs, from the consumer camcorder to the very best digital cinema camera. That said, not all cameras will be convenient for 3D. We'll see what a 2D camera needs to fit into a 3D unit.

If there's no rig and camera combination that meets your needs, you may want to have a look at 3D camcorders, or, as a last resort, at 3D lenses that mount on 2D cameras (if you have tight form factor constraints).

Requirements for Filming 3D

GENLOCK

The number one requirement for a 3D camera is the *genlock port,* which is a video input that allows you to force a camera to run on an external clock. This enables all cameras in a studio to run in synchronicity and mix smoothly in analog video switchers. HD tri-level genlock is a must. Whatever wizardry you perform to pull perfect imagery out of a camera, if the left and right images are out of sync, you are either doomed or dead.

The good old video genlock is not quite accurate enough for 3D, because it controls how fast the camera runs, but it does not provide any control over when the camera starts generating a new frame. Actually, vintage video genlocked cameras can be up to almost a frame out of sync; the genlock just makes sure the delay remains stable.

The point in 3D is not only to keep both cameras running together, but also to make sure they actually scan the images at the very same pace. Left and right images have to be scanned at the very same moment, line per line, pixel per pixel (if possible). And that's precisely what the three-level synch provides. This is what makes the Sony PMW-EX3 very popular in the 3D crowd, and what makes the Canon XF105 a 3D-ready camcorder: a genlock-in connector.

MECHANICAL DESIGN

After genlock, the second most important requirement in filming 3D is the mechanical design. You want to be able to fit your camera on your 3D rig. The two key factors are a stiff tripod socket and no protruding microphone. Plastic body cameras tend not to keep alignment when touched, moved, or simply exposed to heat. A long-neck hypercardioid microphone will hit the mirror, especially in reversed mount configuration for rolling shutter cameras. Keeping the camera away from the mirror forces you to shoot with a small field of view.

As an example, the Sony EX3—despite being a great 3D camcorder with a compact design and HD genlock—suffers from its ergonomic design for shoulder operation, which makes it extremely prone to move on the rig and lose its proper lens alignment. Connectors on the back are preferable, for any connector on the side will generate unwanted rotations that are more complex to control practically or post-correct than vertical shifts.

DIGITAL OUT

The third most important feature is a digital out. It is a must for 3D monitoring, and, if needed, recording uncompressed or high bitrate on external DDR (Digital Disk Recorder). SDI out will be the best, with HDMI as an interesting low-cost contender. Many 3D multiplexer boxes now offer HDMI inputs. It is important to understand that until you can get a live full resolution image out of the camera, you do not have a 3D camera. You do not really get into 3D production until you combine the two image sources in one device, whether this device be a monitor, a recorder, or another 3D-aware piece of equipment. Otherwise you are just shooting a pair of 2D movies that may eventually look nice in 3D if you are talented, lucky, and spend enough time to gather and groom the assets.

GLOBAL OR ROLLING SHUTTER

The type of electronic shutter you use will influence your 3D production processes. In digital imaging there are two ways to get the image data out of the electronic sensor. One is to get the entire image at once, with all photosites starting and stopping to grab photons at the same time. This is called a *global shutter*. The other option is to scan along the sensor surface, line by line, pixel by pixel, like good old tube cameras did in the analog dark ages. This way is known as a *rolling shutter,* and the standard is to scan from top to bottom.

This distinction is important when shooting stereo with a down-looking beam-splitter. Because it's looking at the set through a mirror, the reflective camera is seeing the world upside down, and therefore scans it from bottom to top. This is extremely troublesome with 3D. Say you are shooting at a fence through a car window. Because the POV moves while the image is scanned, the fence seems to be skewed and stays to the right. A reflective camera would see the same fence leaning to the left. And, in 3D, the fence would be seen as leaning forward or backward, depending on which camera is left or right. If the fence example isn't convincing enough, imagine shooting sports with fast-moving objects, like a tennis ball. At the bottom of the frame, the time delay is almost one full frame. Each camera registers the ball at a different time, and thus at a different position—so you'll see the ball bouncing a few centimeters above the ground, or, even worse, under the ground.

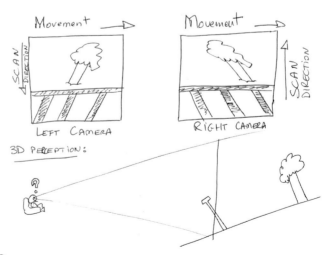

FIGURE 2.8
Rolling Shutter Affects Image Symmetry. In this traveling shot, the image is skewed in opposite directions by the combination of the movement and the scan. When displayed in 3D, the asymmetrical skew generates false depth and geometries, rotating the whole scene toward the audience.

Which cameras have a global shutter, and which cameras have a rolling shutter? There's no definitive rule. In most cases, a CCD is global shutter and a CMOS is rolling—but this is not *always* the case.

http://blog.abelcine
.com/2009/04/15/the-difference-
between-a-global-shutter-and-a-
rolling-shutter/

Legacy 2D Cameras in 3D

BROADCAST AND DIGITAL CINEMA CAMERAS

In terms of image quality and special features, all broadcast cameras are suitable for shooting 3D. Still, some are more comfortable than others to work with.

PROSUMER CAMERAS AND DSLRs

There are many reasons to use a prosumer camera in a 3D production. First, when you're going to need twice as many cameras, it's fair game to try to pay half price for them. Second, a lot of 3D projects are production tryout, crew challenging, learn-as-you-do, low-budget productions. Third, everyone does it in 2D . . . why can't you do it in 3D? Just make sure you don't shoot yourself in the foot by selecting a prosumer camera that doesn't work for 3D. There's a 3D rule that says everything you can get away with in 2D is a potential show killer in 3D—and this includes cutting corners on equipment. Still, it's never a bad idea to know the rules for using camcorders as second units.

Filming with DSLR is a hot topic in cutting-edge technical creativity. With its large sensor, a DSLR behaves like a digital cinema camera for a fraction of the price. Unfortunately, the lack of a genlock port makes them unsuitable for moving pictures. Still, they are a good technical platform for stereoscopic rehearsals, training, or shooting super-ultra-HD 3D background plates to be used later in the VFX process.

REQUIREMENTS FOR PROSUMER CAMERAS

There are some photographic/video requirements for using prosumer cameras, which we list below:

- They must have HD genlock, also known as tri-level synch.
- They must have a digital out. SDI is a great bonus; HDMI can do with converters.
- They must allow remote operation of main functions (start, stop, focus, zoom, iris...).

There are also some form factor and design requirements:

- They must have a compact body that fits into small mirror rigs.
- They must have a narrow body that allows for a small interoptical on SbS rigs.
- They must have a rigid body and frame, with a flat tripod mount or socket.
- They must have connectors on the back or top, rather than on the side.
- They must not have a protruding mike that would hit the mirror.
- They must enable access to batteries and recording support without removing the camera from the rig.
- They must have a flip-out LCD that can be folded back inside-out for image monitoring in the stored position.

The New Generation of 2D Cameras Designed for 3D

As late as 2008, no one was designing a camera for 3D. Still, some 2D cameras were created by 3D enthusiasts who made sure their product would be the best match for a 3D shot. The best example is the Silicon Imaging SI-2K that Ari Presler conceived with 3D in mind. This is where the SI-2K's small form factor—cables on the back and top/bottom socket mounts—comes from. As soon as the camera was on the market for 2D (and used in a future Best Picture Oscar winning movie, to boot), Ari started to include 3D-dedicated functions in the software that drives the cameras and records the images. When the whole system was integrated in an embedded computer, we had all the building blocks for a run-and-gun beam-splitter configuration.

Since those prehistoric times of 2008, big camera names jumped on the stereoscopic train and started finessing their camera design with 3D use in mind—from high-end digital cinema cameras like the ARRI Alexa, to consumer-grade Canon XF105.

SILICON IMAGING SI-2K AND SI-3D

Not only was the SI-2K designed to fit in a 3D rig, but its connectivity and data streams are 3D-centric. Having the camera recording the appropriate picture is only half the job; the second half is to have the pair of cameras seen as one single 3D camera by the operator. As the camera head is connected to its host computer via an ethernet cable, it's cheap and easy to connect both cameras on a single, transportable PC. Now that the heads are basically computer peripherals, it's just a question of software development to get there. At NAB 2009, Silicon Imaging introduced a remote control graphical user interface (GUI) that was able to command both cameras at once, and record both image streams in a single unified data format on the hard drive. The unified GUI included 3D-dedicated visual aids like difference, mix, edge detection, and histograms.

Cinedeck eventually created and integrated it in a custom-design version of its embedded computer-recorder. In 2010, Silicon Imaging presented the Hawkeye, an integrated dual SI-2K head with further reduced interaxial distance. When mounted together, SI-2Ks and the Cinedeck form the SI-3D systems that could qualify as a 3D camcorder.

ARRI ALEXA

http://www.siliconimaging.com/DigitalCinema/

The Alexa is the latest digital cinema camera from ARRI, a renowned German company. It is being used by many cinematographers on 3D projects, including Martin Scorsese on *The Invention of Hugo Cabret*. The clock and timing subsystem was especially tuned for multiple cameras. Because this camera is still a very recent addition to the cinematographer's toolset, you will have to look for more information on the book's companion website.

FIGURE 2.9
SI-3D Rig with Cinedeck. On this small 3D camera unit, images coming from the SI-2K are recorded on the Cinedeck SSD.
Image courtesy of Element Technica.

FIGURE 2.10
The ARRI Alexa. Two ARRI Alexas on a Stereo Tango rig.
Image courtesy of Sébastien Lafoux.

SONY HDCP1

The Sony HDCP1 is a compact point-of-view camera designed to fit into a 3D rig. Its 68 mm narrow form factor is conveniently close to the 65 mm average human interaxial distance. Its top and bottom tripod socket allows this rolling shutter camera to be reverse-mounted as a reflective camera. All the connectors and memory card accesses are on the back of the body, and the lens can be controlled through the camera that passes the commands from the SDI to the lens control connectors. The system is currently extended to send commands to the rig's motors using the Element Technica protocol that has been made public.

CANON XF105 PROFESSIONAL CAMCORDER

Acknowledging the widespread use of compact camcorders in 3D rigs, Canon put a series of features in its XF105 that will appeal to stereographers. First is the genlock input, a definitive must in 3D; the second is the SDI out.

Canon also added lens controls designed for 3D. The first one is the ability to calibrate the image stabilizer in order to fine-tune the optical axis telecentry. In a word, you tell the camera where to zero in when you zoom all the way in. Select a common target point for both left and right camera, and *voilà*, you have a cheap zoom telecentry correction—much cheaper than a 6-axis motorized rig or 4-U rack-mounted image processor. Curb your enthusiasm; this solution has a few limitations. Mainly, zoom tele-decentry is not linear, and tends to be sinusoidal. Two points may not be enough to fix it all.

The second lens control is a *zero reference* in the focal length. At any point along the zoom factor you can set a reference, and from that point on you'll have the relative focal length shown as a numeric value in the LCD control monitor. What's the point in knowing you are plus or minus N millimeters wider than you were ? The answer may come from the third new function.

Canon extended the VLAN port on the camera with a yet undisclosed new set of commands. A *VLAN* is a general purpose command port that was used for years by stereographers to remote control pairs of cameras cheaply. Considering that the XF105 hardware was designed to work well in 3D, it is our understanding that the software is most likely to behave stereoscopically, with either a slave/master mode or a stereoscopic remote controller that can address two cameras and make sure the sensors and lenses works at the same pace.

FIGURES 2.11A AND 2.11B
The Canon XF105. The Canon XF105 was designed for use in 3D rigs. Note the genlock input and HD-SDI output connectors, typically not included in such camcorders yet necessary for 3D filming.

OTHER MINI CAMERAS ADAPTED FOR 3D

Many camera makers work on using their miniature point-of-view products as 3D cameras. Among them, we'll mention the Austrian company Indiecam, which is working on an integrated 3D camera unit with symmetric remote control and dual stream recording.

FIGURES 2.12A AND 2.12B
The Indiecam: Concept Design and First Prototype.

3D Camcorders

Even in 2D, some productions will not use a full-size camera. Some can't afford it, and some don't need it—for whatever reason, they require smaller or cheaper solutions. Even on large budgets, you may want to shoot some B roll, or have a camera you can play with without endangering your carrier if something unfortunate happens. Why would it be different in 3D?

Compact, single-body, all-in-one 3D camcorders have been the holy grail of stereoscopic principal photography for quite a long time. Unfortunately, the more they approach the real world, the better we see their limitations.

The advantages of an integrated 3D camera are obvious. One power switch, one record button, one stereoscopic file. No cables, no mirrors, no screwdriver, no surprises. The drawbacks come with the fact that 3D photography is all about the relationship between the set and the camera metrics. The usual process is to have a scene, and to adapt the camera to it. Recent statistics have shown that most 3D shots, in CGI or live action, have an inter-optical ranging between 5 and 20 mm. All-in-one cameras have either a fixed inter-optical at 70 mm, or a minimum inter-optical larger than 30 mm. As a result, short of adapting the camera to the shot, you'll have to adapt the shot to the camera. You'll want to stay away from the first plane objects, keep the background close enough, or both.

Still, it's easier to stay far away from that lion killing an antelope than asking him to wait until you're done setting up your shot.

The other specialized application for such cameras will be news and talk show studios with close backgrounds. Virtual studios will love them too, because the green screen distance is irrelevant, and the FX guys will love to work with a locked-down camera geometry.

PANASONIC AG-3DA1

When 3D became an established hit in CGI animation movies, 3D aficionados were on the lookout for any sign that live action production tools were being prepared in research labs. We knew that such research would act as a self-fulfilling prophecy: if Sony showed a 3D camera, 3D would be a sure business, other players would have to follow, and Sony would have to make a 3D camera. Indeed, that 3D camera was actually presented by Panasonic at NAB 2009, in an obscure corner of the booth, behind the 3D theater. It was presented as a dual-lens nonfunctional mockup, and was rumored to be a single-imaging system producing alternated stereo. Response from the audience was twofold. "A 3D camera? Great, save one for me." And: "60 Hz alternative 3D? Forget it." How accurate was the single-imaging system rumor? We don't know. And a few months later, a slightly different product was officially introduced as the AG-3DA1.

Michael Bergeron, Strategic Technical Liaison with Panasonic Broadcast

There's an ongoing trend in production equipment: Prices are brought down by higher integration and better chip designs, and more and more components are put together. In 3D, this will lead to a whole range of specialized 3D cameras for as many 3D special shots.

On the production side, the need is to test and try. We need to invent new compelling shots, and each one may require a new camera type. We need that signature shot that will make 3D worthwhile. To find it, just watch 3D and be on the lookout. There are a lot of opportunities for clever individuals and companies, because the all-purpose 3D rig is very far away. The next wave is made of specialized rigs.

Based on this, Panasonic looked at the 3D production landscape and found that the biggest hole in the offerings was the lack of a single-body camera. For us, it was the obvious missing key in the acquisition toolset. There were a lot of 3D rigs of all qualities, prices, and sizes, but there was nothing in the prosumer range. And the

availability of all-in-one cameras has been a key factor for HD deployment in productions. We knew this would repeat itself in 3D. You cannot put the genie back in the bottle: people want to produce with lightweight cameras, and that hole needed to be filled in 3D. We knew it would be easier for us to move up from that point, to offer a greater range of 3D cameras based on a much greater body of experience. Our camera lineup would grow up with our users' 3D business and expertise.

We sold our first production batch on pre-orders, and will likely do the same on the second batch. This shows the same interest from our consumers as for a 2D camera in the same price range.

This camera was used on an all-star game production, along with PACE rigs.

To help identify the streams later in the workflow, the left and right images on the AG-3DA1 are identified with a flag in the HDSDI channels. We are working on exporting more metadata later on, but this is a work in progress, with 3D post-solutions vendors. We are working with virtual studios vendors too, and we integrated specific functions in the camera at their request.

The camera is built around one-fourth-inch CMOS sensors and records AVCam, also known as AVCHD, at 21 to 24 Mb. We opted for recording on two SDHC cards for downstream compatibility with editing suites that used to have a single-image stream per support. The file naming and metadata conventions are worked out with 3D director and DP Tim Dashwood and other partners.

The optical alignment is built atop the existing functions built in 2D cameras. We are running the same procedures to qualify the optical assembly by zooming on targets on a test bench. We adapted the usual corrections to the specific needs of 3D. Basically, the Z-LUTs are coordinated.

FIGURE 2.13
The Panasonic AG-3DA1. The Panasonic AG-3DA1 was the first 3D camera introduced by a major brand. It will remain the seminal 3D camcorder.

SONY

At NAB 2010, John Honeycutt of Discovery Communications briefly presented a Sony 3D camcorder prototype they were working on. Based on Sony's best-selling PMW-EX3, its technology was drawn from Sony Broadcast laboratories (San Jose), Sony Pictures (Culver City), and Sony Atsugi (Japan), with major contributions by 3D consultants at 21st Century 3D. It included two camera heads, two image-processing pipelines, two digital outs, and a live picture beamed on a Sony 4 K 3D SXRD projector. The features list of the camera, as shared by Sony's Peter Ludé, was as follows:

FIGURE 2.14
The Sony 3D Camera Prototype. Sony introduced this prototype at NAB 2010, and the audience dubbed it "the EX-3D," based on its visual similarity with Sony's bestselling 2D camcorder, the PMW-EX3.

- Three CMOS 1/2-inch sensors per eye
- Full 1920x1080 progressive capture
- Interchangeable lens capability
- Adjustable interaxial distance (1.5 to 3.5 inches)
- Adjustable convergence via horizontal lens shift
- Full metadata support

In September 2010, George Joblove, executive vice president of advanced technology for Sony Pictures Technology, presented Sony's vision of the 3D production system that would surround this camera. The core concept is to produce a cheap, lightweight, power-sipping camera, and to be able to process its footage on a personal

computer to finesse the alignment and correct shooting accidents, such as uncomfortable stereoscopy due to inadequate inter-optical. In the proposed design, the computer would generate new viewpoints based on the existing 3D footage.

That prosumer camcorder was not shown at subsequent industry trade shows, but it was followed by the prototype of a larger, more professional camera at IBC 2010. It is not clear yet what 3D camera, if any, Sony will introduce in 2011.

3D-ONE AND FRONTNICHE

Side-by-side monobody cameras with inter-optical equal to human interaxial are not new: they are a staple tool in robotics and remote operation systems, and they are used extensively in deep underwater exploration, the nuclear industry, and military applications like mine sweeping. Make them HD, get them a digital interface, and you've got one of these special-case 3D cameras. According to the press releases, they solve all 3D issues that ever occurred in production. That's almost a fair assessment, provided you realize that they also lock down most potential artistic creativity.

FIGURE 2.15
The 3D-One Camera.

The Dutch company 3D-One offers a 3D camera with fixed inter-optical, the CP31. It records 1080p HD in MJPEG format, wrapped in an AVI container. It has HDMI output for uncompressed recording and 3D monitoring.

The British broadcast reseller Frontniche is announcing its own 3D camera, which is being built by the South Korean company Vision 3 International in 2011. It replicates the 65 mm human interaxial distance using a set of three 2/3-inch CCD sensors, and 18x zooms ranging from 7.6 to 137 mm. It will film HD as 1080i and 1080p at 59.94 and 50 fps, with HDSDI outputs at 3 Gb. It offers the classic frame compatible formats for 3D monitoring.

There's also a few more 720p solutions out there, including one from TDVision Systems and one from the European Space Agency that's qualified to fly on the ISS (International Space Station).

http://www.3d-one.com/
http://www.frontniche.com/

3D Lenses for 2D Cameras

If shooting 3D means shooting two images, it doesn't necessarily mean that you're running two cameras at once; there *is* the option to shoot two pictures with a single camera. The camera resolution will be cut in half, and one can chose between time or space resolution.

Time multiplexing is the process of shooting the left and right views alternately on the full surface of the sensor. There used to be a consumer device called the *NuView* designed to record 25/30 fps alternative 3D on 50/60 Hz inter-laced video systems like PAL or NTSC. Some DIYers have successfully adapted it on HD cameras, but the optical resolution of its cheap lenses made this a dead end for HD-3D. A new system, based on an in-lens aperture shift, is currently being developed by ISee3D. We are yet to see actual pictures generated by them.

A serious single-camera 3D shoot is done with oversized sensors that still deliver HD resolution, even if you slice the original frame. There are not that many cameras that offer super-HD resolution to start with, as the Phantom and Red do. Fortunately, they boast oversized sensors similar in size to 35 and 65 mm film back. This blends perfectly with historical film 3D that many 3D lens adaptors developed in the 1970s and '80s.

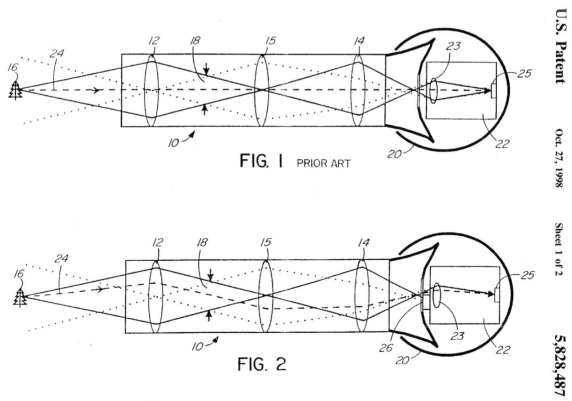

U.S. Patent   Oct. 27, 1998   Sheet 1 of 2   5,828,487

FIGURE 2.16
The ISee3D patent for a single-lens, single-sensor 3D camera.

LOOKING FOR A SCIENCE PROJECT? MAKE YOUR OWN SINGLE-CAMERA MIRROR RIG

If you like learning optical designs the hard way, you can spend some free time on DIY mirror rigs. You can find blueprints and examples on the Internet, with either two or four mirrors. Perry Hobermann, who teaches 3D at the University of Southern California (USC) School of Cinematic Arts, made a simple mount with only two mirrors. Jesse Ferguson on cre.ations.net shares how to make one with four mirrors. The mounts will not squeeze the left and right views, creating 3D in an 8/9th frame format. If you reframe the picture in 16/9th, you'll get a quarter of HD resolution, less than SD.

THE PHANTOM 65 SIDE-BY-SIDE LENSES

The Russian 3D system Stereo-70 is 40 years old and was originally developed for film production. It is built on the recognition that the maximum inter-optical for shooting people or animals is around 30 mm. Otherwise, miniaturization or excessive parallax occurs. The original lens mount has an interaxial distance of 26.4 mm and generates two 35 mm images side by side on 65 mm film. Convergence can be adjusted on the fly by the camera operators. The system has recently been adapted to shoot on Phantom cameras,

http://cre.ations.net/creation/
3d-video-rig

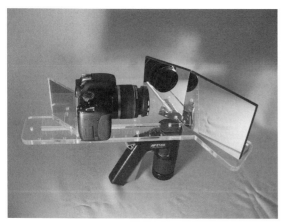

FIGURE 2.17
The Single Camera Mirror Rig Built by Perry Hoberman.
Image courtesy of Perry Hoberman.

FIGURE 2.18
Vision Research Phantom Camera with a 65 mm 3D Lens.

under the Phantom 65 brand name. That camera was used to shoot cable cam sequences for the upcoming *Running with Bulls,* an IMAX 3D stereoscopic movie.

http://www.stereokino.ru/
3dsingle_en.htm

PANASONIC 3D LENS FOR HDC-SDT750

Most readers will wonder why we even mention this product in a professional production book, but at least one of you will someday need a soda-can sized 3D camera to put on a remote controlled car and pull a stunning shot that looks so great nobody even notices the resolution is abysmal. Cheap underwater, jumping over a cliff, who knows? Here's the product: a lens extension that mounts on a regular HD camcorder and turns it into a 3D one. When you see such products sold for high-end broadcast cameras, you'll know about them.

The trouble with this one is mostly the light loss in the conversion. The 2D camera has a 30 mm front lens when each 3D lens is about 7 mm wide. The amount of light getting through it is reduced even further by the additional lenses on the way to the sensor. From a 1lux minimal light, we drop to 28lux.

FIGURE 2.19
The Panasonic HDC-SDT750 with its 3D Lens Adapter.
Image courtesy of Panasonic.

DSLRs IN 3D

What is trendier than shooting art video with DSLR? Shooting 3D. If only there were a way to do both. Unfortunately, current DSLRs have no genlock port. This may be added for 3D, but the cost increase will have to be justified for the majority of 2D users.

The other option is to fit your DSLR with a 3D lens. So far, the only product available is a Loreo lens mount with two issues. The first is the resultant image 8/9th aspect ratio, and the second is the low quality of the optics that show quite a lot of color fringing.

Recently, Panasonic introduced a 3D conversion lens for its Lumix G cameras, the H-FT012.

SINGLE-LENS PARALLAX GENERATION THROUGH APERTURE SHIFTING

The single-lens 3D system is among the magic wands that stereographers are looking for. Fortunately, there's a theoretical path to that 3D treasure: the

FIGURE 2.20
The Panasonic H-FT012 for Lumix G Cameras.
Image courtesy of Panasonic.

aperture shift. If you move the iris in a lens laterally, you move the optical axis around the focal point. If you alternate two equally spaced iris positions in the horizontal axis, you generate two stereoscopic viewpoints with a single camera.

The issue is that you have to include both apertures inside the lens' original maximum aperture. When you increase the stereoscopic base, you do the following:

- Minimize the left and right apertures.
- Minimize the sensitivity.
- Increase the depth of field.
- Maximize the optical aberrations, working with the edges of the lenses.

Furthermore, you are recording alternative stereo, with left and right images shot sequentially. Still, this is an interesting approach, and we had a long interview with ISee3D CEO Dwight Romanica about the topic.

Dwight Romanica, ISee3D CEO

We basically inserted a pair of active glasses between the lens and the sensor. This allows the blocking of the light getting through the left or right half of the lens, virtually turning the front lens width into interaxial. In our actual implementations, we are reaching 55% to 90% of the front lens turned into interaxial.

On high-end products like broadcast cameras, we will implement a mechanical shutter placed in an optical attachment. On low-end products like consumer camcorders, we plan to implement a liquid crystal shutter (LCS) device that costs pennies in mass production, leading to generalized, single-lens, 3D-switchable cameras.

The known advantages are single-camera simplicity, perfect for run-and-gun production, plus the views alignment is persistent, and can even be perfect. Issues are inherent to view-alternated 3D capture, when left and right images are taken one after another. In a 3D rig, great care must be taken to ensure that both images are acquired at exactly the same time. In alternated 3D, you take for granted that the images are not taken in synchronicity. If you do a vertical pan, you have vertical disparities. The solution is to reduce that delay, or to match the display's delay.

In the 1990s there was a 3D lens attachment (NuView) that can be described as a periscope fitted with a see-through mirror and a pair of 3D glasses. The glasses ran at 60 Hz, locked to the camera's video out. As a result, the left and right frames were recorded on odd or even fields of standard interlaced video. Seen on a CRT TV with 60 Hz LCS glasses, a VHS of Hi8 tape would be 3D. It was flickering like hell, but it was still 3D. All the current frame-compatible formats are the brain children of this pre-digital 3D system, whose invention is credited to Lenny Lipton. What was possible when all displays were running the same frame rate (50i or 60i) is not possible now, until a strict frame rate and 3D format conversion policy ensure that the stereo is not messed up by the time it reaches your eyeballs. Still, the current state of the art is to shoot synchronized left and right, even if the majority of displays in theaters or at home have a 144th or 120th of a second left/right delay.

At some point, frame interpolation algorithms can be specialized to fix this, knowing they have to interpolate movement up to the point at which all disparities are horizontal.

The average light loss is announced at one f-stop because only half the exposure time is available per eye. More loss is to be expected in an actual shoot, due to optical system imperfection, transition time between left and right shutter positions, and a potentially smaller aperture.

A simpler approach is to properly flag the alternatively produced 3D and make sure the display actually processes the images and presents them accordingly. On 120 Hz active displays, it's just a question of appropriately up-converting the frame rate. Just as we have interlaced and progressive 2D formats that are taken care of, we would have alternative and synchronous 3D. If such single-lens active stereo gains ground in professional production, we'll then see SMPTE standards describing it. In the analogic world, SD3D (PAL or NTSC) was supposed to be shot alternatively, and film had to be shot synchronously. In the digital era, we may see 3D in 1080ia, 1080pa, 1080is, and 1080ps as combinations of interlaced or progressive frame structure with alternative or synchronous stereo timing.

SINGLE-LENS DEPTH ACQUISITION TECHNIQUES

A single camera generating RGBZ (color and depth) frames coupled to a 2D-3D conversion system would be a great production tool for continuous surfaces or large landscapes used as backdrops. There are currently three technologies that show interesting depth acquisition capability:

- Light detection and ranging (LIDAR)
- Constructed light
- Spatial phase imaging (SPI)

The principle of LIDAR acquisition is to illuminate the scene with a burst of light and shoot the scene at an ultra-high speed. Light rays bouncing on the

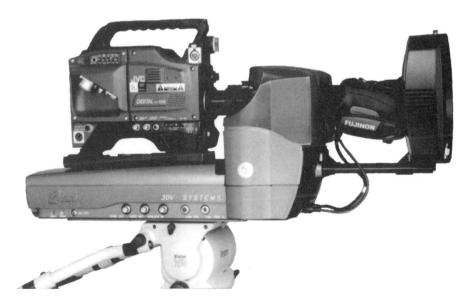

FIGURE 2.21
JVC ZCam. In 2003 JVC introduced this hybrid camera system with a Z sensor on the optical axis.

closest object will illuminate the sensor sooner than ones bouncing on surfaces that are farther away. Consecutive frames describe various depth planes. Illuminating the scene with low intensity radar makes the process compatible with image acquisition in the visible light range.

Advanced Scientific Concepts, Inc.'s LIDAR system is used for docking the space shuttle to the ISS, and they are now working on bringing their technology to the entertainment industry. This technology has a limited resolution, virtually infinite range, and requires relatively low computing power. It is well suited to acquire urban landscape shapes, like the geometry of a stadium for 3D conversion systems.

The constructed light approach uses a test-pattern-like image flashed on the scene. A single image is shot in between two "regular" frame acquisitions and analyzed. From the deformations of the pattern, the depth of the scene is recreated. This technology has a limited range and requires some computing time. It is well suited for close-up still image acquisition, and to generate 3D scans of objects such as actors' faces. Many handheld 3D scanners use structured light. Minolta once produced the Minolta 3D 1500, a consumer digital still camera that shot 3D images.

Advanced Scientific Concepts, Inc.: www.asc3d.com

Research paper on constructed light: http://citeseerx.ist.psu.edu/viewdoc/download?doi=10.1.1.126.6857&rep=rep1&type=pdf

PhotonX: http://www.photon-x.com/

The SPI depth acquisition records the light polarization of each pixel. This describes the orientation of surfaces towards the sensor and the light source. From that point, shapes are reconstructed, based on the assumption that all surfaces are continuous. Of all these three depth acquisition techniques, SPI is the one showing the higher resolution. Photon-X has developed a set of sensors and plans to integrate them with broadcast imagers.

CHAPTER 3

3D Image Processing and Monitoring

Stereoscopic image quality control is more complex than mere 2D monitoring. You want to look at the stereoscopic disparities, more than the image in volume. You want to make sure that all the bad disparities, the vertical ones, are either nonexistent or within the required range. Regarding the good disparities, the horizontal ones, you want to make sure they remain, at the very least, in the comfort envelope. Further inspection will ensure that they match the artistic intent, or depth script. The ultimate judgment should be based on the depth feeling your imagery is gathering. And that's the only one that requires actual 3D vision.

How does the progression of quality assurance in depth acquisition occur? Its science and procedures are presented here in three sections. We'll distinguish

- Image monitoring, a visual evaluation using basic signal formatting.
- Image analysis, an automatic extraction of the stereoscopic descriptors of a picture.
- Image correction, the resultant grooming of a stereoscopic picture.

We built this distinction on our observation of the wide range of implementation complexity and cost of such systems.

Image processing involves only basic 2D image manipulation, like 50% mixes or frame-compatible formatting. Its typical implementation is in stand-alone conversion boxes called *stereoscopic multiplexers* or inclusion in a 3D display. Its application domain is the image monitoring.

Image analysis refers to complex processes involving software, computers, multi-image processing, and, in the most advanced cases, full 3D reconstruction. Some image analyzers provide a feedback loop to motorized rigs.

Image correction can be via a feedback loop on the rig's motion control, or in the image domain, in real time or in batch processing. The latter is a software solution that would run overnight on your laptop, and almost instantly on a render farm. The former may be the very same program, but implemented on dedicated processing hardware, with the ability to correct your live 3D stream as you shoot it, even before it reaches the OB van grid.

MONITORING 3D

The main rule is that you want to see the 3D. Clearly, you need to monitor your work in 3D. You wouldn't monitor a color shoot on a black and white monitor, nor would you record sound without a headset, just by watching the levels. For the same reasons you wouldn't do these things, you shouldn't shoot 3D without being able to see it.

That being said, this does not mean it has to be in stereoscopic 3D. To start with, not everybody needs to monitor the 3D on a 3D display, and there's even a debate on the importance of running dailies in theater to check 3D in its final screen size. As we'll see, the best monitoring for stereoscopic images is sometimes on a 2D display. This requires the images to be adequately formatted into a structure that will reveal their potential defaults.

Stereoscopic Image Processing for 3D Monitoring

Once again, let's refer back to our color analogy. There are three levels of color monitoring: basic control is watching lowlights and highlights, making sure your images are not burned out; intermediate color control just requires an all-purpose monitor; and advanced color control requires a color-calibrated monitor, light-controlled environment, or the trained eyes of an expert colorist or DP. Otherwise, reference patterns and a vectorscope would do the job, even with a colorblind technician. Beyond this, onset LUT management will allow the crew to make sure the tweaked image will match the desired artistic effect.

BASIC 3D MONITORING

Basic stereoscopic control can be done with a 50% mix on a regular 2D monitor. Vertical disparities should be unnoticeable on a small field monitor; otherwise they'll be uncomfortable on full-size screens.

Side-by-side and over/under modes can also be used, but they are less efficient in detecting horizontal or vertical disparities and rotations. Anaglyphic 3D is often preferred for previews and is best enjoyed without glasses. The red and blue fringes act as disparity enhancers on the display.

INTERMEDIATE 3D MONITORING

Intermediate level quality control is done using a difference view that clearly shows the disparities and makes them much more noticeable, even measurable.

Basic and average controls can be supplemented with markers showing reference parallaxes on the monitor. One can use simple Post-its or tape applied on the screen. Some professional displays can electronically insert visual helpers,

FIGURE 3.1
50% Mix Monitoring. Example of basic 3D monitoring; 50% mix of left and right eye.

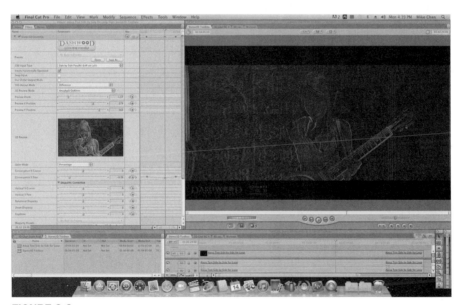

FIGURE 3.2
Difference Preview. Example of intermediate 3D monitoring; difference between left and right eye.

like gridlines, bars, or checkerboards. If you are shooting with no target screen size, 1% and 2% of the screen width are the regular landmarks. If you are shooting for a defined screen size, the size of the reference grid unit can be the equivalent of one or two human inter-optical distances. On a feature, the reference maximum positive parallax will be chosen during the preproduction. Obviously, specific parallax references for FX shots will be enforced with even more caution.

ADVANCED 3D MONITORING

Advanced controls for specific image default detection—like rotations, keystones, and various geometry mismatches—can be performed with the naked eye and years of experience, or with specialized tools. Alignment patterns are one option. Image analysis is another. Combining the two is a great approach.

More complex image processing can be performed on a stereoscopic feed, without going all the way to the complexity of a full 3D analysis. Digital disk recorders built around a computer offer some advanced monitoring tools, such as

- Edge detection, for focus matching
- Interactive digital zoom, for fine alignment and convergence
- Alignment grid overlays, for parallax control
- False color zebras
- Spot meters
- Dual histograms, for color balance
- Parallax shifts, to adequately monitor parallel footage
- Anaglyph mixing, to be used with and without glasses
- Wiggle displays, to quickly switch between views

Identifying 3D Image Defaults

Most 3D-related headaches come from bad 3D images, a generic term under which stereographers include all pictures that suffered, at any stage of their life, from lack of caution, knowledge, experience, or luck. Mistakes occur very easily in 3D production and should be noticed and corrected at once, for some of them may be extremely costly to fix later on in the production process. This is one of the reasons why you should always check your work in 3D, and on the biggest screen available.

You may be feeling that this "watch your 3D, every time you can, and on a big screen" advice is printed on every other page of this book. That may be the case, and it would be a good thing. There are probably fewer than five directors or DPs on earth who are able to put together a 3D shot without needing to check it in 3D—but even these geniuses would never do such a thing; they will always visually check the 3D, one way or another.

In the next sections, fixes and tricks are sometimes suggested for low-end configurations using prosumer cameras. Obviously, the readers using high-end rigs and digital cinema cameras are invited to refer to their manuals to find the proper course of action to apply the proper fix to the image default.

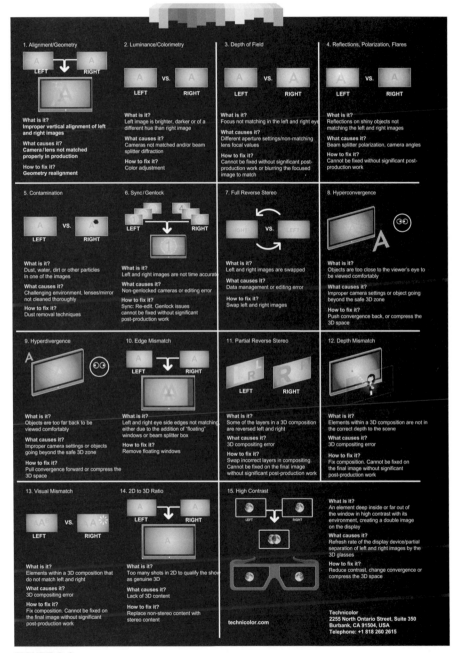

FIGURE 3.3
The Technicolor Stereoscopic Certifi3D Chart. Another visual representation of the most common stereoscopic defaults.
Courtesy of Technicolor.

INTER-OPTICAL DISTANCE

Cause: The distance between the cameras is not adequate.

Consequence: In cases of excessive IO, the 3D effect is too strong: the close-up elements are too close *AND* the far away elements are too far away. In cases of insufficient IO, the 3D effect is too weak: the difference between close-up and far away elements is too small, and the overall scene looks shallow. If 3D is too strong, it will prevent the audience from enjoying it, generating excessive positive and negative parallaxes, painful divergence, and toe-in.

Catch it: This is the reason why on-set 3D monitoring is a must. To make it safer and easier, compute your absolute maximum parallax in screen percentage, based on your final screen size. Then compute your monitoring screen relative maximum parallax, in inches or centimeters, based on its resolution and size. Eventually, draw a rule on a strip of adhesive tape and overlay it on the picture. Check it, or have it checked as often as needed. If you are using a computer-based recording or monitoring system, you can get the same results using digital overlays.

Correct it on set: On set, bring the camera to the right interaxial. If you have reached the limits of your rig, change the camera placement, focal length, or consider changing the rig. Get a beam-splitter rig for smaller inter-optical distances, or get a wider base on a parallel rig.

Cure it in post: Inter-optical errors are the most expensive to correct, for one of the eyes has to be regenerated in CG using 2D/3D conversions, or view-synthesis techniques.

CONVERGENCE

Cause: Cameras were converged on the wrong point, or one eye was excessively horizontally shifted.

FIGURE 3.4
Simulated IOD Default.
Image courtesy of Steve Schklair, 3ality Digital.

Consequence: The whole scene is either too far away *or* too close to the viewer.

Catch it: As usual, you can catch this by visually checking your 3D, and, if needed, relying on the visual helpers you draw on the monitoring screen.

Correct it on set: Turn the convergence knob on the rig. If you have reached its limits, you are shooting under a very strange configuration. Please send me a picture of the set. If you are sure you need more convergence, shoot with a huge over-scan, and you'll reconverge in post.

Cure it in post: This is the easiest, cheapest, and most common 3D correction. It's actually a mundane task in 3D to reconverge footage, from on-set to final grading and packaging. A 3D TV remote should even include a reconvergence button to let viewers fine-tune the image to their preferences, which is done by shifting one or two eyes sideways. However, this will most likely bring the image edge inside the visible frame, creating an undesired floating window that virtually moves the perceived screen in or out the theater space. In order to avoid this, a slight zoom in and crop should be applied to both eyes.

FIGURE 3.5
Simulated Convergence Default.
Image courtesy of Steve Schklair, 3ality Digital.

VERTICAL ALIGNMENT

Cause: On set, one camera is most likely pointing up or down, or a zoom is off-axis. In post, one eye has been vertically shifted.

Consequence: One of the views is uniformly higher or lower than the other. This affects the readability of the 3D, not its strength or depth placement.

Catch it: During monitoring, apply horizontal stripes of tape or show guides in your digital recorder or compositing GUI. Check that left and right images of objects, shown in anaglyph, 50% mix or difference, are horizontally aligned.

Correct it on set: If the vertical parallax is more than half a percent of the picture on a high-end rig, the camera's geometry should be fixed. On low-end and makeshift rigs, it may be useless to spend too much time fixing it. This glitch is easy to fix in post, at the cost of a slight zoom and crop of both eyes.

Cure it in post: Another easy fix: shift the images, just as in a convergence correction, but this time along the vertical axis. Zoom and crop are to be expected.

FIGURE 3.6
Simulated Vertical Alignment Default.
Image courtesy of Steve Schklair, 3ality Digital.

KEYSTONE

Cause: Keystone appears when the optical axes are not parallel, due to convergence or, less often, strong vertical misalignment.

Consequence: As seen in Figure 3.7, which presents the effects of toe-in convergence, keystone generates asymmetric zooming in the sides of the pictures, generating vertical misalignment in the four corners. According to stereographic director Brian Gardner, minor keystone is acceptable and may even help in perceiving 3D, to the extent that our visual system, being itself a toed-in converged system, experiences and uses keystone as a natural binocular vision byproduct. This unconventional take on 3D obviously applies to infinitesimal deformations, not to the huge and painful image distortions that have to be fixed.

Catch it: Using the 50% mix and the horizontal lines, you'll see a picture that is okay in the center, but is symmetrically skewed in the corners. The top and bottom of the center third of the picture are okay.

Correct it on set: Maybe you should not converge on that shot. Shoot parallel, get a huge over-scan, and set the convergence in post.

Cure it in post: Fixing a keystone in postproduction is not an easy task, but a small correction is easy to set up and will be efficient. Apply a perspective distortion in the direction of the offending keystone, and then zoom and crop as usual. A significant amount of keystone requires complex depth warping and falls into the expensive fixes one should avoid. For shots that will be mixed with CG images, stereoscopic supervisors tend to prefer to work with footage shot parallel and then reconverge in postproduction.

FIGURE 3.7
Simulated Keystone Default.
Image by Bernard Mendiburu, based on Steve Schklair, 3ality Digital.

ROTATION

Cause: Image rotation appears when the camera's optical axis is rotated along the Z axis.

Consequence: Horizontal alignment is progressively lost from the center to the four corners of the image. It generates painful vertical parallaxes on the sides and depth artifact in the center top and bottom areas.

Catch it: On the monitoring screen, the image is okay in the center and gets worse as you approach the edges. All four edges of the frame are off, in asymmetrical directions.

Correct it on set: There's something wrong with the rig, most likely a rigidity issue on a makeshift rig. If it's significant, it may be the sign of a mechanical default in the rig mechanical integrity, and therefore should be addressed as a safety warning. Sometimes, tension on a cable or momentum on an attachment changes the balance of one camera.

Cure it in post: Image rotation can efficiently be fixed in post, at the cost of a crop and resizing.

FIGURE 3.8
Simulated Rotation Default.
Image courtesy of Steve Schklair, 3ality Digital.

FOCAL LENGTH

Cause: Prime lenses are not always matched and zoom lenses are almost never matched, and therefore it is difficult to get two cameras zooming symmetrically. If you zoomed with a low-end rig using prosumer cameras, you will likely have to fix it in post.

Consequence: One image is bigger than another, the center is okay, and the 3D gets worse at the edges, with asymmetrical depth artifacts in the mid-high left and right areas.

Catch it: The 50% mix shows a picture matching in the center but not on the edges. The misalignments are radially symmetrical, from the image center into the four directions.

Correct it on set: Correct the focal length on one camera. If you are using a low-end camera with motor-only control of the zoom, you'd better save the trouble and plan to fix it in post.

Cure it in post: This is another glitch that's easy to cure in post. Because most other corrections include a resize of the images, focal length adjustment usually comes for free in the touch-up package.

FIGURE 3.9
Simulated Focal Length Default.
Image courtesy of Steve Schklair, 3ality Digital.

FOCUS MISMATCH

Cause: Low-end cameras have poor manual control on focus distance, and autofocus modes may disagree on the subject distance. Despite the efficiency of our visual system at pasting sharpness from one eye to the other, we eventually notice it when focus asymmetry gets too big. In CG imagery, it sometimes happens that one eye has no motion blur pass. This causes a strange feeling and adversely affects the fusion of the images. Focus matching is a visual quality element to be taken care of in 3D. The relation between the focus distance and focal length with zooms is another point of concern.

Consequence: One image is sharp, the other is blurry. Only certain depth ranges of the pictures are affected.

Catch it: Focus asymmetry is really hard to catch on a 50% mix and is better seen on a side-by-side view. On a 3D display, you will have to alternately close each eye and compare the images.

Correct it on set: High-end rigs with professional lenses and remote focus should never give you this trouble. On low-end rigs, this is much more common, and there's no real cure if your cameras have no focus ring. In this case, you have one more reason to get more light and an infinite focus rather than a shallow focus.

Cure it in post: Obviously, this has to be taken care of on set. In postproduction it is close to impossible to regenerate sharpness; the sharper eye would have to be blurred to match the other one. A 2D/3D conversion may be the only solution.

FIGURE 3.10
Simulated Focus Mismatch Default. Looking at known sharp textures like human faces helps detect focus mismatch.
Image courtesy of Steve Schklair, 3ality Digital.

DESYNCHRONIZED STEREO

Cause: The two cameras are not running in perfect synchronism. If both left and right images are shot without paying great attention to time synchronization, issues will definitely occur. The faster the camera or the action moves, the higher the timing requirements. If your image is motion blurred, you need an extremely accurate genlock, down to the line or pixel clock, or the motion blurs will have vertical parallaxes.

Consequence: The slightest time delay will transpose camera and actor movements into unwanted parallaxes. If you took care of every mismatch listed earlier in this section, but missed the time synchronization, you will get shots with all the defects you tried so hard to control.

Catch it: Objects that have a cyclic movement, like a waving hand, are the best cues for incorrect timing. They show inconsistent parallax; the action in one picture is constantly catching up with the other.

Correct it on set: Check this with the director of photography, the camera technician, or the first, second, or third assistant—whoever is in charge of the genlock. If you are the person in charge, check the clock distribution and check that everything is perfectly symmetrical, down to the quality and the length of the cables.

There are some cameras that can be genlocked at video frame rates, like 25 or 30 fps, but not at the digital cinema 24 fps. The Sony PMW-EX3 has this reputation.

Cure it in post: Try retiming software, or some time warp filters from your favorite FX suite. While you are computing optical flows, you may give a chance to 2D/3D conversion too.

**FIGURE 3.11
Simulated Synchronization Default.**
Fast movement can generate vertical mismatch, as on the waving hand, plus fake depth, as on the jumping dog.
Image by Bernard Mendiburu, based on a set from Steve Schklair, 3ality Digital.

ROLLING SHUTTER ORIENTATION ERROR

Cause: You shoot some fast action with a mirror rig and the rolling shutter camera in the reflective position is not upside down.

Consequence: Both cameras are scanning the vertical axis in opposite directions, and the frame delay is up to one full frame from the top to bottom of the picture.

Catch it: This one is quite hard to catch visually. Pan the camera laterally and see the horizontal disparities build up asymmetrically between the top and the bottom of the picture. Spin a scale model windmill in front of the camera and see the wings bend toward or backward upon the rotation direction. You don't have your scale model windmill with you? The director is likely searching for you with a baseball bat. Try to secure it and have someone swing in front of the camera. That should do the trick.

Correct it on set: Turn one of the cameras upside down.

Cure it in post: Same as synchronization mismatch, besides the fact that you need to apply a vertical gradient to the retiming. However, we are not aware of such a feature in correction tools.

Beware: Active display of passive stereo and vice versa can interfere with this issue.

FIGURES 3.12A AND 3.12B
Simulated Rolling Shutter Default. Rolling shutter scanning orientation [S] mismatch will skew objects moving [M] in opposite directions.
Images by Bernard Mendiburu, based on Steve Schklair, 3ality Digital.

ERRORS INDUCED BY THE HALF-MIRROR, AND OTHER ERRORS

The half-mirror in the rig may not be perfectly 50/50. In this case, some image asymmetry can be the direct or indirect effect of the asymmetry of the light beams.

Depth of field mismatch: Asymmetrical depth of field is generated by unequal apertures. First, check the camera settings: the gain, the shutter speed, the ND filters. On a low-budget production, the second possibility is that the cameras are on "auto" and the computers figured out two different sets of numbers. In any case, depth-of-field asymmetry will then come with lightness, contrast, and motion blur asymmetries.

Colorimetric mismatch: Colorimetric asymmetry is a staple default of the half-mirror. Even on a clean side-by-side rig, you'll have a hard time matching the white balances. Our brain will do a great job at hiding such color mismatch. When you're setting on a white reference, control that the camera agrees on the color temperature. Advanced cameras have complex presets, sometimes on memory cards. Make sure they match too.

Lightness mismatch: Uneven exposure will generate asymmetries and give or take texture in the highlights or shadows, creating an unpleasant binocular High Dynamic Range (HDR) experience. The interesting thing with lightness asymmetry and 3D, is that it actually generates a time delay in the obscured eye. This delay will generate unwanted parallaxes in every direction the camera or subjects would be moving. On a dolly, or horizontal pan, it'll tweak the depth. On action or vertical camera movement, it will affect the 3D perception.

3D Monitoring Tools

We are turning a corner, moving from makeshift 3D monitoring into professional gear. Not long ago, monitoring 3D required processing left and right images with a dedicated computer and plugging it in on one of the very few 3D displays available. Rear projection DLP TV came first, and passive polarized monitors followed more recently. The situation is now totally different with the following new products:

FIGURE 3.12C Simulated Iris Mismatch Error. Detecting lightness mismatch requires a side-by-side display and a very sharp eye. *Image courtesy of Steve Schklair, 3ality Digital.*

- Consumer 3D displays with no dual input and image processing.
- Professional 3D displays with integrated dual input and some 3D processing.
- Simple 3D multiplexers that get two images into a 3D format.
- Complex 3D processors with some image-manipulation capabilities.

CONSUMER 3D DISPLAYS

Consumer 3D displays have the ability to show 3D, but they were not designed to be used on set or on location. They cannot run on batteries, and most likely require the 3D images to be processed for display. They all cost from $1000 to $5000, with the plasmas, full HD projectors, and passive TVs in the upper margin.

If you are using these displays, remember to thoroughly investigate the setup menus to disable any image enhancement features like smooth motion and other cinema colors. The frame interpolation, which adapts the 24 fps input into the display's 120 Hz refresh rate, is a known culprit. It is usually built around a modernized 3:2 pull-down to generate a pair of 60p video streams.

Commonly Available Consumer 3D Displays		
Display	**Input Format**	**Glasses**
Rear projection DLP TVs	Checkerboard FC	Actives with DLP link or IR with transmitter
3D-compatible projectors	120 Hz active stereo	Actives with DLP link or IR with transmitter
Active 3D TV like plasma or LCD	Most FC formats	Actives, brand-compatible
Passive 3D TV	Most FC formats	Passives, most likely compatible with RealD cinema glasses

PROFESSIONALS 3D DISPLAYS

Professional 3D displays were specially designed for use on set and on location. Most of them run on batteries and have left and right input and SDI and HDMI connectors. Some have image-processing features for monitoring 3D, such as 50% mix, left/right difference, and reconvergence. Some monitors offer flip and flop image inversion to monitor 3D coming live from a mirror rig. Another useful function is an overlaid grid with variable pitch that allows for a quick check of excessive disparities.

Transvideo was the first company to offer a field monitor. The CineMonitorHD12 3DView is a classic 12-inch with left and right SDI inputs, and anaglyphic and active stereo modes.

The second generation of professional 3D field monitors use passive 3D displays, with polarizing filters that rotate each line in opposite directions. One can look at the 3D picture with low-end disposable 3D cinema glasses, or with high-end designer glasses that offer a much better contrast.

Panasonic has a 25.5-inch 3D monitor, the BT-3DL2550, with dual SDI and DVI-D inputs and a 1920x1200 resolution. It displays 720p, 1080i, and 1080p video in 10 bits color depth.

Panasonic plasmas are to be considered too. They offer full resolution, thanks to active 3D, high brightness, saturation, and contrast. The stereo separation is great, with no ghosting or sweet spot effect. Professional models for field use are not yet in catalogs.

Sony offers the LMD2451TD, a 24-inch monitor with the same 1920 × 1200 resolution. The LMD4251TD is a 42-inch version.

JVC has a 46-inch monitor, the GD-463D10U, and at NAB 2009 presented a 4 K 3D monitor prototype.

Assembling two monitors in a beam-splitter mount will give you a full-resolution passive display. Cinetronic, among many others, offers such a system. It was used in the production of *Pirates of the Caribbean 4*.

FIGURE 3.13
Panasonic 3D Monitor.

3D MULTIPLEXERS AND IMAGE PROCESSORS

All 3D multiplexers are signal converters used to convert the image stream initiated at the camera into a format that a 3D display or a 3D recorder will understand and process adequately. Their main uses include:

- Getting the signal from a pair of (DS) 2D cameras into a (FC) 3D monitoring or recording device.
- Converting bit streams between consumer and professional connectivity standards.

- Retrofitting a legacy 2008 3D-ready display into a modern 2010 3D-capable device.

Bit stream conversions include:

- Converting dual-stream (DS) 3D into frame-compatible (FC) 3D, with two inputs and one output.
- Converting FC 3D into DS 3D, with one input and two outputs.
- Digital format conversion, to and from DVI, HDMI, and HD-SDI.
- Active/passive stereo conversion to and from 120 and 144 fps.
- Sometimes digital/analog conversion, DVI/VGA.

FIGURE 3.14
Cinetronic 3D Monitor.

Image manipulations include:

- Image axis permutation, called *flip* or *flop*, for mirror rig live monitoring.
- Horizontal image translation (HIT), used when shooting parallel material.
- 50% mix, left/right difference, and anaglyph image encoding for basic 3D monitoring.

http://cinetronic.com/en/stereohd

There are several types of models:

- Miranda DVI-Ramp 2 (a dual-channel genlockable DVI/SDI converter)
- Cine-tal Davio
- Inition StereoBrain
- Doremi Dimension3D (designed to connect PCs to DCI projectors)
- AJA Hi5-3D, aka the Keith Box (a pocket-sized camera companion device)
- Matrox (developing a 3D multiplexer with Tim Dashwood for NAB 2011)
- Blackmagic Design (introduced its conversion box, the HDLink Pro 3D at IBC 2010)
- SpecSoft 3D Live (sold as hardware or software, with a free version available for download at http://www.spectsoft.com/)

STEREOSCOPIC IMAGE ANALYSIS

As a digital art, stereoscopy benefits from image processing applications. For live production or shot setup, new gear is arriving to the market, with a new set of tools that can be described under the umbrella name of *computer-aided monitoring*. These tools go far beyond the passive image processing we are used to, involving a lot of genuine science and bits of artificial intelligence in the process.

The purpose of image analysis is to understand the relationship between a left and right image: how the cameras are positioned, and how the lenses tweak the light toward the sensors. Where, in 3D, are the objects in the field of view, what do they look like, what are they made of, and how do they move? Basic image analysis will provide correspondence points, whereas complex analysis will generate a significant amount of metadata describing the scene. The results can then be used just as monitoring helpers, or to control the rig's actuators and eventually to correct the 3D in the image domain.

State of the Art in Stereoscopic Image Analysis

Stereoscopic image analysis is a complex science; it takes a PhD just to understand the jargon. And to be totally honest with you, we are still on our way there. Still, we consider it to be a central piece of the science and future of stereoscopy, with applications in every production and postproduction phase.

The purpose of image analysis is to understand, down to the subpixel level, the relationship between the left and right images. This means identifying visual features in images and pairing them perfectly. It is a binocular artificial-vision process. When enough points have been found and matched, it is possible to figure out precisely what's wrong with your camera alignment and how to fix it—with a speed and accuracy you'll never match. Nobody can estimate the amount of a rotation, down to subpixel accuracy, just looking at a pair of pictures for one second. The real-time correction systems presented in the next section are based on such analysis, followed by various types of image manipulation that produce perfect stereoscopic images. Even if it is a complex multidimensional mathematical resolution, we, simple artists, can describe the process as 2D. See it as a Photoshop layer manipulation, not a Maya object rendering.

There are two big challenges in the field: one is to filter out the false pairs of homologous points, which is when the computer puts together two unrelated features. You want as many couples as possible, with the best accuracy ratio, and these are antonymic expectations. How you sort them out and where you draw the line are the factors in the secret recipe that determines the value of an image analysis system. The second challenge is to run the whole process in real time, and to generate a smooth correction—which is especially important in live 3D, when one cannot delay images. At the very best, your computer will always be working on a frame that has already gone on air by the time it has figured it out.

Both domains are quite crowded when you look at the science side of it, with a respectable amount of publications on the topics. On the other hand, it's quite a desert when you search for actually available solutions. To our knowledge, there were only two companies in the world with actual products on their shelves back in 2008, when this book was first planned: 3ality Digital in the United States and Binocle in France. Since then, three contenders have presented their solutions: the Fraunhofer Heinrich Hertz Institute (HHI), with its STAN (STereoscopic ANalyzer), codeveloped with the German production company, KUK; Sony, with its MPE-200, brought to fame by the FIFA 2010 World Cup coverage in 3D; and, in Spain, Kronomav, with its rigs and analyzers. They are working at interfacing their computers with other vendors' motion controls.

Applications of Stereoscopic Image Analysis

A stereoscopic image analyzer is like a new crew member with an incredibly acute visual system and a very crude understanding of what entertaining pictures are. What would you do with such a trainee? Here are a few examples of ideal tasks:

1. Providing stereographers, DPs, ACs, or directors with enhanced monitoring tools.
2. Accelerating 3D rig setup, with alignment suggestions, on screen, or via motion control.
3. Automatizing a 3D camera unit's interaxial and convergence based on depth settings.
4. Coordinating a 3D camera fleet, with shared depth settings.
5. Automatically screening 3D content for stereoscopic defaults.

COMPUTER-AIDED MONITORING

Stereoscopic image analysis makes it easier to live with the truth that one has to see 3D to make 3D. The problem is, of course, that you may not always, if ever, have a good enough 3D display on set. Let's talk size: even the best professional 3D displays will not give you the finesse you need to evaluate an image that'll be seen on a 40-foot screen. Current 3D monitors come in 10-inch, 22-inch, and 46-inch sizes, on which evaluating parallax, divergence, and vertical disparities is quite a challenge. Experienced stereographer Vince Pace explains that a 46-inch 3D screen is all he needs to evaluate 3D imagery. Before you get to that level of experience and confidence, however, you will benefit from the help of dedicated 3D vision computers.

Another problem with field 3D monitoring is brightness. 3D visualization systems have an overall efficiency ranging in the 15% to 20% range, which means that with your 3D glasses on, you'll get a picture five to six times dimmer than you'll get on an equivalent 2D display. Here are the visual modes you'll find on a typical 3D-Computer Aided Monitoring:

1. Show accurate parallax, vectors.
2. Identify screen plane, foreground, and background using color-coded tags.
3. Show the depth bracket of the shot on depth histograms.
4. Compare the measured parallax against the target screen size.
5. Run various 2D image quality controls in a 3D mode.

Disparity Vectors

In this mode, homologous points are shown with an arrow linking them. This mode allows for evaluating the parallax and pinpointing most geometric defaults, such as rotation and the causes of various vertical disparities, including zoom mismatch.

**FIGURE 3.15
Disparity Vector
Monitoring.** Disparity
vector monitoring on
disparity tagger.
*The Slava Snow Show;
image courtesy of Binocle
and La Compagnie des
Indes.*

Disparity Tags

In this mode, homologous points are shown with false color points or icons showing the amount and direction of parallax. A cross-vendor color-code convention settled on blue tags for out-of-screen elements, green tags for the screen plane, and red tags for the infinity plane. Elements placed in the spaces between these arbitrary planes are in shades of cyan and yellow. Purple is sometimes used for flagging objects with a negative parallax stronger than the desired maximum foreground.

**FIGURE 3.16
Disparity Tag Moni-
toring, with Depth
Bracket.** In addition to
discrete disparity tagging,
this monitoring mode
displays, on the lower
third, a global depth
placement of the scene.
*The Slava Snow Show;
image courtesy of Binocle
and La Compagnie des
Indes.*

The threshold is computed upon dialed-in screen size, and sometimes additional factors including viewing distance and divergence limit. If you prefer, you can type in your reference positive and negative parallax values in pixels or percentage of image width.

Binocle's Disparity Tagger displays geometric shapes that enhance visual information. Strong positive or negative parallaxes are shown with triangles pointing upwards or downwards. Screen plane is tagged with squares. Vertical misalignment is shown by rotating the shapes to align their base with the corresponding vector they represent. The size of the shapes represents the confidence of the computation. The areas of best efficiency happen to be the subject of interest, with sharp and detailed textures. In other words, your hero is more likely to be strongly tagged than the background—how convenient!

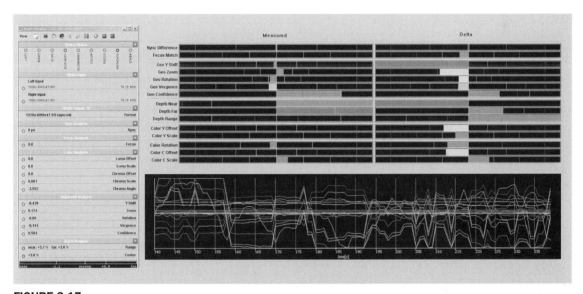

FIGURE 3.17
Depth Analysis on 3ality SIP. In this monitoring mode, many parameters are tracked, and a visual representation of the "depth budget" is shown in the lower third.
Image courtesy of 3ality Digital.

All vendors include a depth histogram to evaluate the depth composition of your shot. When an image must be corrected in post, it has to be rescaled. The image processor can infer the correction, the amount of resizing, and the resultant framing. That final active image can be shown on the monitor.

FIGURE 3.18
Corrected Frame
Monitoring on Binocle
Disparity Tagger.

Comparative 2D Analysis

All the image analysis tools you used in 2D will be needed in 3D too, not only to analyze the 2D images for defaults, but sometimes to check for 3D coherency. Typically, sharpness or edge detection is useful to check the focus and iris match between cameras. Overlaid vector graph and RGB histograms are useful tools for matching the light level and color balance on cameras.

FIGURE 3.19
Dual-Channel Color
Histogram and 3D
Vectorscope on 3ality
SIP.

COMPUTER-AIDED 3D CAMERA UNIT SETUP

During the shot preparation, once you have put your cameras and lenses into the 3D rig, you want to align them, including matching the lenses and camera electronics. Intelligent disparities analysis will streamline that process.

Optical Axis Alignment

You can always align your cameras visually, and then check it out by getting the disparity vectors computed. What about the other way around? Run a computing pass and rely on the vector map to align your rig. This way you don't have to guess how much rotation and translation you should correct first. You do still have to figure out which knob to turn in what direction, and how much—and remember that all of them influence the others, so you're in for a good deal of trial and error. This is one of the reasons why stereographers have a personal relationship to their rigs. After a while, you learn to do it quickly. Soon, image analyzers will work with CAD models of rigs, cameras, and lenses, and will be able to suggest lists of alignment steps and values for the very setup you are working on.

On a motion-controlled rig, it's even simpler. The computer will automatically align the cameras and run another image analysis until the optical axes match each other.

Color Matching, White Balance, Aperture, and Gain

Every camera has its very own color behavior, and even if your cameras are perfectly matched, the half-mirror is shifting them unevenly. Visually balancing whites and levels can be a harassing task; just shoot at your reference white and let the computer tell you the RGB values it gets. Alternatively, you can match the color histograms on the 3D image processor. Image analysis can do all that in a single pass by analyzing a reference chart, or a real image of the lighted set. Some software suites in development can generate color setups to be loaded in the cameras.

The aperture and gain are trickier. Asymmetric apertures will generate asymmetric focus depth. Image analysis can check out images for sharpness and match them, but the exposure levels on the sensors may not match. On a beam-splitter, it will not. From that point you have two options: add filters, or set gain.

LENS PAIRING

Lenses, mirrors, filters—there are many elements on the light path that are not digital, and therefore may never be perfectly matched. Quantifying the discrepancies on set will give you a chance to correct for as much as possible before the raw picture gets recorded and the stereo balancing has to be done in post. Do a favor to the FX team: get the most you can from the lens pairing. After that point, all corrections are time, money, computers, and long nights.

Z-LUT Generation

Once the rig is aligned, it's time to take care of the lenses. Some lens vendors offer matched zooms sold by pairs. At some point, lenses may even have their LUTs computed at the factory and embedded somewhere in an on-board memory. In the meantime, you'll be working with lenses that do not match, and you'll have to take care of that, in shoot preparation and in postproduction. Just like color matching, you'd have a much better time in post if you did it well in prep.

Before image analyzers stepped in, Z-LUTs were generated by zooming all the way in and out on an alignment chart. Because zoom telecentry follows various sinusoidal curves, you need to realign the cameras at as many in-between points as needed, until the motion-control system tracks it closely enough. Automatic Z-LUT is a great tool that shrinks this process from 30 minutes to a handful of seconds.

Ongoing improvements in technology will soon allow you to get rid of alignments patterns. This is important for live productions, when the zooms are known to drift away and their LUTs may have to be recalibrated. Thermal dilatations are the most obvious issues, for example, following nightfall during soccer matches or heat generation by dancing crowds in a concert location.

REAL-TIME RIG CONTROL

If you have a fully motion-controlled rig and a powerful image-analysis system, the benefits of linking them are obvious. You'll be able to compensate for the optical defaults, thermal dilatations, and even automatically set depth on your shots.

Based on Pre-Established Decision Rules

This basic function is the most popular and easiest to apply. It can be performed by semi-intelligent control units added to a basic rig, or, alternatively, can be part of a high-end rig. Binocle integrates them inside the camera socket that encloses the motion-control actuators, and 3ality has a control unit mounted on the side of the rig. Sony added remote control of rig motion to version 1.2 of its 3D Processor Box.

Based on Real-Time Computation

This advanced function is the most advanced of all. At the time of this writing, only Binocle and 3ality offer fast enough image analysis systems to interactively set the depth on a camera.

3D Rig Motion-Control Command Protocol

Until 2010, image analyzers and motion-controlled rigs were produced together in single vendor solutions. With the Sony 3D Box and the STAN, the situation is changing. Sony is using an Element Technica protocol that has been made public to this end. For the European Project 2020 3D, Jordi Alonso of MediaPro is working with Kronomav to develop a universal rig interface.

FUTURE APPLICATIONS

At the moment, the industry is only scratching the surface of the potential benefits of image analysis. With the increase in computing power and finessing of the software, more tools will soon come to fruition.

Roundness Evaluation

On a 2D TV, all balls are round. In a 3D TV program, some are spherical, flat, or elongated, all depending upon the screen size, viewing distance, depth position, and inter-optical distance. Because of the effect of the viewing distance, it is not easy to set the inter-optical and convergence solely based on a visual check on a small screen. At some point, image analysis will be able to communicate to you an evaluation of the "roundness" of a shot by identifying known objects like human faces, and comparing their 2D on-screen size with their depth range.

Depth Chart Generation

With 3D TV channels opening around the world and 3D crews shooting and editing on the same scope, at some point the contents will be shared over contribution feeds, bought at festivals, or advertised in catalogs. Chief Technical Officers will be asked for a solution to ensure the legal department that no bad 3D is reaching the audience's eyes, and image-analysis robots will deliver the depth chart of any program that is run through them.

Breakout Circuit on Networks Operations Center

How can you make sure that no uncomfortable 3D reaches the audience? Set an image analyzer on the program feed, and make it fall back on 2D if it detects disparities that may hurt your legal standing. Have it log the average and maximum disparity at all times, and back up the data with your legal department for the day someone brings your channel to court for having damaged his 3D vision.

Surface Mirror Optical Description

We have mentioned the defaults of surface mirrors many times, and knowing exactly the default of a system brings you halfway to overcoming that default. An image analyzer coupled with adequate test charts and procedures can describe the very optical behavior of a mirror. That signature can then be injected into the VFX suite to match it.

Limits of Image Analysis

Like many computer-based magic boxes, there's some discrepancy between the sales pitch and the actual delivery of automated image analysis. So far, artificial intelligence is still an oxymoron. There are two well-known issues in image analysis: the impossibility of finding homologous points that don't exist, and the importance of input quality.

EDGES OF THE FRAME

On the lateral edges of the frame, we have asymmetrically occluded image areas. Whatever is seen by only one camera, in front of or behind the stereoscopic window, cannot be matched to the other point of view. This is especially unfortunate, because this is the place where you'll have the most disturbing invasion of the viewer's space; it is the area where people and objects enter the frame and generate 3D-impairing window violations.

You'll want the image analyzer to detect these and fix them by reconverging the cameras or automatically setting a floating window. Unfortunately, these are precisely the points an image analyzer cannot figure out, and for a good reason: such surfaces do not have homologous areas. And that's the very problem, of course.

The solution would be to shoot and analyze an oversized picture and frame in. There are many reasons to do that in 3D, and image analysis is just another one.

IMPERFECT INPUT, IMPERFECT OUTPUT

The system does with 3D feeds what your brain does with your retina's neuron streams; it looks for identifiable details that repeat in each view and translates their angular distance into estimated depth. This process relies on the assumptions that the two images are equivalent in all characteristics but the point of view, and all the disparity vectors are horizontal. If this were right, it would mean you may not even need to correct your images.

The point is, because the photography of two cameras is not perfectly matched in illumination and color, feature matching is impaired. Consider a situation in which you are trying to match a surface that has a luminance gradient and one of the cameras has a higher light level. The same luminance vector (getting darker) can be associated with both photographic mismatches and depth mismatches. How to decide which is which when you are just a processing unit?

Furthermore, there's a feedback loop here. Fixing the photographic parameter will influence the depth computation, and vice versa.

- Photographic mismatch shifts the light and color of feature points.
- To perfectly fix photography mismatch, one needs to identify homologous points.
- To perfectly identity homologous points, one needs to fix photography mismatch.

Among the source quality impairments affecting stereoscopic analysis, we'll mention low light conditions, motion blur, genlock inaccuracy, and rolling shutter orientation.

Existing Products

There are currently four high-end products on the market, from 3ality, Binocle, Sony, and HHI/KUK. (We will discuss this more in the next section, on image correction.)

Recently, word came out that various lower-end projects built on video acquisition dongles and software image analysis are on their way to NAB 2011. It is to be expected that all video acquisition or format conversion hardware vendors (Gefen, Matrox, Blackmagic, Miranda, etc.) will come up with some sort of 3D software tool to complement their hardware offerings.

Cel-Scope3D is an example of a hardware-independent image analyzer: http://www.cel-soft.com/celscope3d/
Hamlet Video VidScope-3D: http://www.hamlet.co.uk/products/software/vidscope-3d/

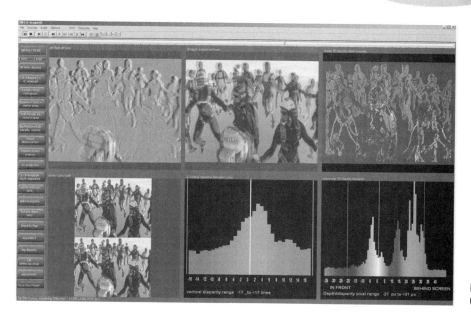

FIGURE 3.20
Cel-Scope3D Analyzer.

STEREOSCOPIC IMAGE GEOMETRY CORRECTION

The next step, when you have a robust, fast, and accurate image-analysis system, is to have it take care of fixing whatever disparities were not fixable in the camera at shoot time. We are not talking of colorimetric correction, but geometric corrections. All mechanical systems have a finite accuracy, and no rig will move a full-size digital cinema camera within a micrometer precision. This includes rotation, magnification, and optical center shift—everything that is not fixable down to the subpixel, or that can shift during the shot session or live event.

When one has a chance to see 3D correction demonstrated, it's almost like looking through newly cleaned glasses for the first time—as if there were a blurry curtain we didn't pay attention to, until we wiped our glasses and all of a sudden the world was crystal clear. The uncorrected image feels strangely okay, until the correction system kicks in and you feel like someone turned the light on while you were reading in dim light.

It may seem like overkill to correct what appears as nothing more than visual background noise—but, in reality, there's no such a thing as visual noise in 3D. What you get are retinal disparities, increasing the audience's visual system workload. Making sense of this imperfect 3D requires physical realignment at the eye level, and additional fusion complexity in the visual cortex. This means causing visual fatigue for the fittest, and headaches for the masses—not a good selling point for your 3D content. You may think that a couple pixels of offset are not enough to generate real discomfort, but you'd be incorrect.

In addition, as soon as you mix graphics with your images, you mix perfect geometry—the CGI—with imperfect geometry—the live feed. In a post-produced feature, it means hours of labor to fine-tune it, to make the blue-screened actors match the CG backgrounds and stick on the floor. In a live 3D feed, like a sporting event, it means that the audience has to choose between looking at the scores or at the players.

Post tools will be presented in Chapter 4, and live correction tools are listed hereafter.

State of the Art in Image Correction

Stereoscopic image correction used to be called *stereo balancing,* or, when it was manually done, *stereo grooming.* It involved a little bit of vertical, a chip of rotation, two bits of zoom, and a lot of time. Its automatic counterpart consists in taking the disparity vector map from the image analysis, and figuring out a way to make all the vectors horizontal. In most cases, a 4-point transformation is enough, the very same operation you do in Photoshop when you independently ALT-move the four corners of your selection.

The challenge is to make sure that you keep the screen plane consistent, that you do not rotate the scene in any direction by skewing one view, and that you do all this smoothly. The current analyzers are not yet computing at full frame rate, but the correctors do. You have to interpolate the analysis results, based on a frame that's already gone in the pipeline, on a handful of frames, waiting for the next batch of vectors. Some systems use the motion-control metadata to help that guessing stay on track with the camera movements.

More optical defaults like nonlinear distortions (for example, barrel, pin cushion, or moustache) are actually not significant on broadcast and digital cinema lenses. They could be fixed if needed when postproduction requires it. So far, it has made no sense to implement them in stereoscopic geometric correction tools.

Applications of Stereoscopic Image Geometry Correction

The ultimate goal of image correction is to get from the premise that "any 3D shot is an FX shot that needs to be aligned and corrected" to the premise that "any 3D camera unit produces good 3D, in accordance with a director's depth request." In a comparison already mentioned, the U23D concert movie was in postproduction for over a year in 2007, and then in 2010, just a few years later, the Black Eyed Peas 3D show was a live broadcast.

This was accomplished by having a device instantly and automatically do what a stereographer would do: detect, identify, qualify, and fix the image disparities, from geometric errors to colorimetric mismatch—in short, all of them.

EXTEND HIGH-END RIG ACCURACY

When you just drop your cameras into your 3D rig, you get misaligned pictures by tens of pixels. Mechanically registering your cameras will bring you within a few pixels of accuracy. A good monitoring tool, patience, and experience will drop the vertical errors under three pixels.

Image analysis will allow you to drop to a pixel of accuracy, and motion control will make the process faster. That's as long as you do not change the shot, move the rig, or follow fast action. Then your accuracy drops, and the disparities get noticeable again. There will surely be vendors claiming that their rigs are stiff enough and that their motion-control systems are strong enough, so image correction is not needed. They basically claim that the laws of physics do not apply to their products. For those who believe in gravity and inertia, and plan to broadcast what they shoot, image correction is the way to get sustained subpixel image registration.

REPLACE MOTION CONTROL ON LOW-END RIGS

At the 2010 NAB, Sony introduced the 3D solution they would use to produce the FIFA World Cup a few month later. They surprised the industry by selecting rigs that would not offer dynamic vertical registration, and instead would rely on their image-processing systems to fix it. The existing state of the art was to control one camera pitch to compensate for the vertical component of the zoom optical axis shift. Sony has since introduced the ability to motion control rigs in later software versions.

LIVE CORRECTION OF DEPTH ACCIDENTS ON BROADCASTS

Who can say nothing will ever go wrong in his live broadcasts? Maybe someone who set up a 3D image correction system on its NOC delivery chain. Set your limits, and leave it to the disparity detector to decide if it can fix the shot, rather than suffering a fallback to 2D.

FUTURE APPLICATIONS OF IMAGE CORRECTION

The current state of the art is only to generate an optically accurate image, as it would have been produced by a camera placed at the perfect position needed for the shot. Other renderings are possible, in the continuation of what is currently done in stereoscopic CGI animation under the name of *multi-rigging*. Two options seem feasible in the very near future: scene depth compression, and object depth extension.

Scene depth compression would deal with excessive IOD by bringing backgrounds and foregrounds toward the screen plane. This is possible because there's no occlusion revelation. Still, the edge detection needs to be perfected.

Object depth extension would deal with insufficient IOD by inflating the volume of objects. This would require increasing the accuracy and resolution of depth maps generated from the disparity vectors.

Limits of Stereoscopic Image Geometric Correction

In our imperfect world, magic boxes can only get you so far. Whatever light that did not reach the sensors will be quite hard to synthesize on a computer. Furthermore, image geometry correction inherits some of its limits from the image analysis it relies on, as well as from later interaction issues with post-processing tools.

GEOMETRIC CORRECTION IS NOT VIEWPOINT SYNTHESIS

Image correction takes care of two potential camera position errors: the origin and destination point of the optical axis. Changing the aiming point of a camera is quite easy: just shift the image, as we do when we reconverge stereoscopic footage. Changing the sensor position is another story. That's what we do when we interpolate viewpoints in postproduction.

Image correction can only correct what the camera is aiming at, not where it is. You still need to get to perfect camera elevation. Horizontal misplacement will generate inappropriate amounts of IOD and convergence angle. That's wrong, but it is not as much of an issue as vertical misplacement generating unresolvable retinal disparities. Claiming to be able to fix vertical shift is just as bold as claiming to fix incorrect IOD.

GEOMETRIC CORRECTION AFFECTS VISUAL EFFECTS WORKFLOW

There's no sensible sharpness loss in image correction; bicubic interpolation does not really show up once you have applied a couple of video compressions along the distribution channel.

The issues come with match-moving software that may not be able to understand images whose optical center is not in the middle of the frame. Pixel Farm's 3D tracker gets its stereoscopic fame partly from the fact that it can work with corrected images. Otherwise, the process is to record raw images with image-analysis results, or corrected images with image-correction parameters. In any case, always flag images that have been tweaked at shoot time.

Existing Gear

3ALITY

The first to market was 3ality Digital, with its SIP 2100 and the upper-scale, multicamera unit, the SIP 2900. It offers extensive monitoring modes, DVI and SDI connectivity, frame-compatible format conversions, and Web remote control. It also drives the rig motors and corrects geometries. It does all this using two PowerPCs and four Xilinx Spartans, for a total processing power of a teraflop. It uses mostly 2D image analysis to control the cameras and make sure the best image is produced from the start, while 3D geometries are computed and corrected in non-Euclidian spaces.

This piece of equipment has been under development for many years and is used on 3D live productions like BSkyB Sports, and on movie sets. Even though it was designed to work with 3ality rigs, it is often used with other systems, especially on feature productions.

The 3ality approach is to put the quality burden on the rigs and cameras, and to minimize the amount of corrections to be applied afterwards. These quality expectations are to correct "mechanical shifts" that will always occur during the production of a live show. When you keep zooming in and out, and pan the camera side to side for hours, you apply momentum on cameras, rigs, and lenses. Experience shows that your mechanical registration will not last until the end of the show. To that end, the image has to be analyzed and corrections have to be sent to the rig.

BINOCLE

Binocle is a French company that has been doing stereoscopic research and productions for more than ten years. They have teamed with the French National Institute for Research in Computer Science and Control (INRIA), known for creating the RealViz FX suite. At NAB 2009, Binocle introduced its image processing system, the Disparity Tagger. It is a regular Windows computer with SDI in and out capabilities. At NAB 2010, the first generation of real-time geometric correction was presented. Binocle's philosophy is to embed the rig's motion control and computing resources inside an all-in-one socket that holds the camera. As a result, the image analyzing system is totally independent and does not interact with rig automation.

KUK

The STAN is the result of collaboration between the Fraunhofer Heinrich Hertz Institute (HHI) and KUK productions. It was presented at NAB 2009 and has since been adapted for P + S Technik rigs. It is now available.

The STAN approach is to use information coming from the rig's motion control to help with the time extrapolation part of the geometric correction. It's also a software solution that runs on a PC platform. It has a simplistic but intuitive user interface.

SONY

Sony's product is composed of a multipurpose digital production system, the MPE-200, and a 3D acquisition specialized software, the MPES-3D01. The hardware is based on the Cell BE2 engine, with four HD inputs and outputs, and the software is developed in the United States.

Sony's approach is to assume that all stereoscopic defaults can be corrected in the image domain, and that therefore a powerful enough image processor can replace a complex rig. The current version of 3D software does not use any image analysis or motion control; all the geometric and colorimetric corrections have to be entered manually during the system setup. The MPE communicates with the lenses via the camera's HD/SDI interface to receive focal length and focus distance information.

Sony has announced a new version that will be able to communicate with rigs using Element Technica's command protocol.

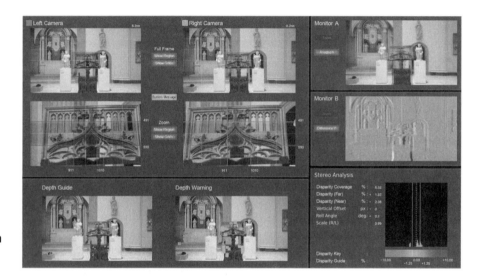

FIGURE 3.21
Camera Alignment on Sony MPE-200 with MPES-3D01.

KRONOMAV AND MEDIAPRO

Kronomav presented its 3D rigs at NAB and CES and developed the first image analyzer, which is already for sale. The Spanish company has now teamed up with the TV producer MediaPro to create a full 3D TV production platform. This includes a new version of the analyzer that will be introduced at NAB 2011, which works both at controlling the rig motion and correcting the pictures in the image domain.

The project manager for MediaPro, Jordi Alonso, is currently working at developing a standardized communication protocol between rigs and image analyzers. Doremi, StereoTec, and Element Technica have shown interest in the ongoing preliminary work. The hardware implementation is on CUDA processors on a regular PC.

CHAPTER 4

Shooting 3D for Broadcast or Editing

Stereoscopic production is currently experiencing a fast-paced evolutionary process. On a typical show, we'll see an expert stereographer collaborating with a set crew that has little or no experience in 3D. Major 3D movies currently in production are directed by filmmakers doing their first 3D story. If the camera rig is not a prototype, it was most likely adapted for the show, received a microcode update, or runs on new image-analysis software. It is a safe assumption that no 3D unit has ever been used in the same configuration on two movies—and this will be the trend for years to come. On a tent-pole 3D movie set, you are likely to find technicians or engineers sent by the rig maker to analyze the situation and improve the equipment efficiency and sturdiness. From this point of view, best practices and gear are an ever-changing reality in 3D production.

At the same time, 3D is leaving the research domain to enter real production universes. Most small and medium productions have no money to spend in researching movie-making theory. Productions for 3D TV and documentaries have no time to experiment, and a very different cost structure. Everybody in an OB truck is a creative. There's no money to fly out a technician for every 3D rig. A 3D TV production wants to get rid of the 3D technicians as soon as possible; the objective is to replace them with adequate gear, like the artificial vision computers discussed in the previous chapter. There is a need for automated 3D camera units, whether it be for sports or as studio cameras for talk shows. This is a relatively modest technical evolution, relative to the overall evolution in production processes generated by the conversion to 3D.

As an example of such processes, the battle is now to get access to premium camera positions. Real estate in sporting venues is too expensive to duplicate all camera positions—it's just not possible either to replace 2D cameras by 3D units or to send a flat view to the 2D director. Not only does it pose framing and storytelling issues, but it also raises a diplomatic issue: who will the camera operators report to, the 2D or the 3D director?

SETTING UP THE 3D CAMERA UNIT
Beam-Splitter Configurations

According to Stephen Pizzo of Element Technica, the typical rig configuration is not the same in TV and movie productions. Rig configurations are referred to as *over through* (OT) or *under through* (UT). Cinema crews tend to prefer to set in OT, with the reflective camera on top, whereas 3D TV crews prefer to set in UT, with reflective on the bottom. The main cause of this is the relationship to the camera itself. On set, the DP is used to standing by a high camera with the film rolls blocking the view. On a TV show, the cameraman stands behind the camera and watches the action with his peripheral vision while controlling the frame on the monitor.

Another thing to consider is that the rig configuration must not block the view of nearby seats in a stadium; in other words, it must *minimize the seat kills*. This may sound like a nonissue until you do the math: a big bulky camera can block the view of up to 20 people behind it. When a seat costs $600, as for a FIFA half final, nobody wants to miss any part of the action just because the game is on 3D TV, and 20 seats amount to $12K. In 25 matches at FIFA, it would accumulate to more than a million dollars spent in paying for the various camera positions.

Another point to take into consideration when filming on location is the need to get to a point of view that is as close to the cellar, or as close to the ground, as possible. As mentioned by stereographer Celine Tricart, this fact dictates whether you mount the rig *looking up* or *looking down*. Changing the whole configuration for a shot is much more complex than just setting a new inter-optical; it is tens of minutes, rather than a handful, and it impacts the shooting schedule. At the very least, group the up and down shots together, and set them at the beginning or end of the day.

FIGURE 4.1
Camera Unit on *Derrière les Murs* (*Behind the Walls*). In this picture the rig is in a "looking up" configuration, freeing the operator's line of sight.

The last point to consider is the dust. On a down-looking rig, dust can fall on the mirror and adversely affect the image. On a 3D TV show or documentary, the depolarization filters will help protect the mirror from environmental hazards.

Color-Coding the Camera Units

The duplication of the camera on every position calls for strict identification. Left/right footage or stream inversion is a staple mistake all along the 3D production process. Color-coding cameras, cables, control boxes, and record supports is a must. Stereographers who don't have their own set or color of adhesive tapes are unusual (unless they've got ACs or rig assistants who take care of it).

Shades of red and blue are universally agreed-upon colors, but there's a cultural divide between U.S. and European productions. In the United States, you'll see "red is right" signs in rig shops. In Europe, "rouge est a gauche" ("red is left"). Don't blame the stereographers for that! As it happens, one will find the very same color inversion in stereophonic sound, or in maritime navigation, when it regards the fixed lights marking channel entrances. Still, the international conventions on boats and airplanes set red on the left.

Whatever decision you make for left and right identification, make sure everybody on your team is on the same page, especially for international events with multiple crews from around the world.

Registering the Cameras

The camera should be calibrated in colorimetric and geometric spaces. This operation is much easier on a side-by-side rig, for the optical mirror will never be color neutral and requires more attention in spatial alignment of the cameras. When learning the process, it is better to start with an SBS rig and then get into mirror rigs when you feel at ease with the process.

SEAN FAIRBURN REGISTRATION CHART

Veteran cinematographer B. Sean Fairburn produced a 3D chart with DSC labs to help in aligning cameras. This chart is loaded with features and details useful to stereographic production, simplifying camera registration.

When Sean is done with the camera alignment, he sets the rig to its maximum interaxial and records some footage of the chart; the left and right cameras shoot mostly the left or right half of the chart, showing "L" or "R" tags. This will be very useful for future reference in postproduction, or for feed identification at the OB truck.

STEREO TANGO ALIGNMENT PROCEDURE

Every rig and every stereographer has his or her own registration procedure. They all include the same list of items, with subtle variations in the order due to personal taste, experience, or a rig's mechanical design. For example, here is the alignment procedure from the 3D Camera Company.

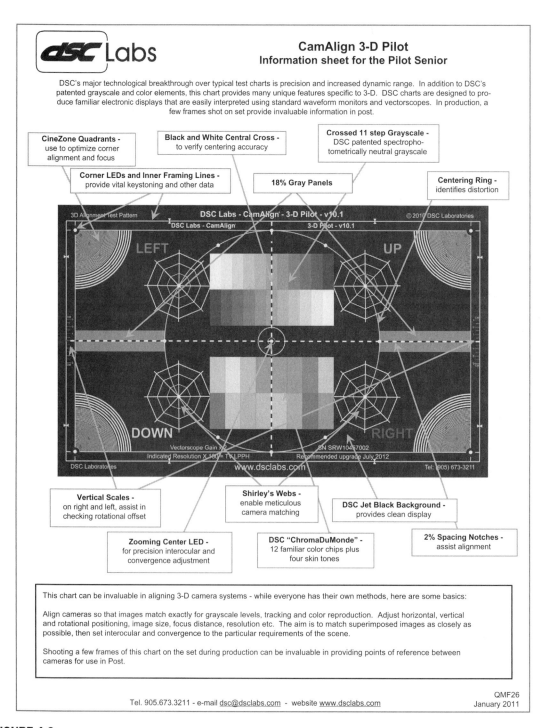

FIGURE 4.2
The DSC Labs CamAlign 3-D Pilot. This chart was designed in collaboration with Sean Fairburn to help align cameras and correct geometries in postproduction.

Use a 3D monitor in anaglyph viewing mode to perform fast and precise alignment. The anaglyph viewing mode is a robust tool to monitor all stereoscopic parameters during shooting.

1. *Check camera orientation*. In order for the rolling shutters of the two digital cameras to operate in the same direction, make sure one of the cameras is mounted upside down. Tango provides dedicated inverter blocks for the Mini 2K SI, the Red One, the Sony HDC-P1, the Sony F23 and F35, and the ARRI Alexa.
2. *Install and lock both cameras with lenses onto the 3D Stereo Tango rig*, and set the interaxial distance to zero. Keep the interaxial at zero during the entire alignment checklist.
3. *Check the distance between the beam-splitter and the two cameras*. Set the adjustable stop blocks at the same value for both the left and right eyes, and make sure each camera is pushed against its respective stopping block.
4. *Check the vertical alignment of the optical centers*. Look into the matte box straight through the beam-splitter with one eye only; the two lenses should overlap, and there should be no vertical offset. If there is a vertical offset, use the large silver thumbwheel behind the top camera to move it up or down until the two lenses overlap perfectly along the vertical axis.
5. *Check tilt alignment*. Looking at a distant landmark on the 3D monitor, use the tilt adjustment knob on the bottom camera to make the left and right images overlap perfectly on the vertical axis. Then check this alignment looking at an object five feet away from the rig. If there is now a vertical offset between the left and right images, adjust the optical centers as described in Step 4, and re-do Step 5.
6. *Check roll alignment*. Look at the horizontal structures on the 3D monitor. If on the left side of the picture a red border above light-toned elements appears, it means the bottom camera (left) leans to the left. Using the two silver knobs located on either side of the roll stage under the bottom camera, adjust the roll until the left and right images overlap perfectly across the frame on the vertical axis.
7. *Check convergence alignment*. Look into the matte box straight through the beam-splitter with one eye only; the two lenses should overlap, and there should be no horizontal offset. If there is a horizontal offset, use the convergence knob beside the bottom camera to adjust the angle until the two lenses overlap perfectly along the horizontal axis. Then look at a distant background object on the 3D monitor, and turn the convergence knob until you make the left and right images overlap perfectly on the horizontal axis. The left and right cameras are now parallel.
8. *Check viewing angle alignment*. If you're not using perfectly matching prime lenses, you may notice a slight magnification disparity on the 3D monitor. Point the rig at a round object: the object will appear slightly larger in one eye than in the other. This is a magnification disparity, which translates into a disparity of viewing angles between the two lenses. To suppress this disparity, move the bottom camera closer or farther away from the beam-splitter until, on the 3D monitor, the magnification is the same for both eyes.

Note: For fine-tuning purposes, all of the adjustments described above can also be applied to the top camera. The 3D Stereo Tango provides six independent axes of alignment for the top and bottom cameras.

The roll, tilt, and convergence adjustments all pivot on the beam-splitter at the intersecting points of the optical axes of the left and right cameras. The roll, tilt, and convergence adjustments can be done manually, or they can be motorized.

FIGURE 4.3
Stereo Tango Mirror Rig.

Calibrating the Cameras

In VFX (visual effects), the rule is to shoot all sorts of calibration footage for later reference: clean background plates, light references, and so on. Considering that all 3D shots are a potential FX shot (if correction is needed), it is always advisable to consider shooting some reference when using a mirror rig.

When calibrating your cameras, always use the transmissive camera as the master, and adjust the reflective camera. The transmissive camera gets a much less damaged light beam; this is because the reflective camera suffers from all the defaults of the mirror, optical, and chromatic aberrations being generated by the uneven light reflection. Obviously, when you are shooting 3D for cinema, you keep all the color adjustments as metadata and record raw imagery. For broadcast 3D, you'll apply the correction in the camera unless otherwise stated by the image analyzer you're using.

Setting the white reference requires much finer work than in 2D. If the color shifts on a 2D cut, it's not a big issue. However, in 3D, you want to avoid this retinal rivalry, where the left and right eye do not see the same colors. Optimally balanced white balance is done with image analyzers; in a perfect world, the settings are sent to the camera via the SDI control channel, or by programming setting cards. Dual-channel vectorscopes or RGB histograms will get you great calibration too. If you have no other resource, encode your stereo into a frame-compatible 3D image, like a side-by-side, and feed it to a regular 2D color-timed display. You'll have both your left and right images on screen to compare them.

Setting the Depth

The art of stereoscopic photography lies mostly in mastering interaxial and convergence. As you know, the interaxial distance will set the overall volume of your scene, whereas the convergence will move it along the depth axis. If these are new concepts to you, we refer you to other books that introduce these concepts and explain their application in 3D production.

Regarding 3D TV and cinema production, one important discriminating factor is the screen size. The *magnification factor*, defined as the ratio of the screen size to the viewing distance, makes them two different 3D mediums. They are compatible—it is technically possible to watch a 3D movie on a TV set and, to a lesser extent, to shoot 3D TV content that will be watchable in a theater. Still, the mathematical overlap is small, and the experiences are not optimal.

On set, you'll generally have two chances at setting the depth. A first artistic pass sets the interaxial and convergence according to the set metrics and artistic intent. A second pass is a technical rehearsal, with a convergence puller to follow the action if needed.

There are many approaches to getting the first pass quick and nice. You can set the interaxial first, and then the convergence, assuming that the few pixels that push back at convergence will not affect the overall volume perception. Or, as explained by stereographer Alain Derobe in his "Natural Depth" method, you can set the convergence based on an arbitrary interaxial, and then fine-tune that interaxial, assuming that the interaxial change will not affect the convergence plane.

TRANSPORTING 3D TO THE VISION MIXER OR RECORDER

Virtually all 3D camera units are quite big, with their dual heads, lenses, mirrors, and motion controls. Everything that cannot be miniaturized has to be tethered as far away as practically possible. The possibility of deporting the image processing from the camera heads was a seminal feature of the Sony cameras used for the first motion-control 3D rigs created at PACE HD. Linking the rig to the OB van or the recorder deck can be done high-end style with two full-resolution HD links, or by using a cheaper and more resilient process: the frame-compatible formats.

> ### NOTE ON WIRELESS CAMERAS IN 3D
>
> If you have a wireless camera, you need to re-sync its left and right signals, and then delay all the other cameras on the field to match it. In most cases, simple Time Code sync is not that helpful, for image delay can be less than a frame—sometimes just a few lines—and that causes drops later in the line.

> ### ABOUT THE CABLES
>
> A general comment on cables: It is advised that you get them with the rig if they are available from the vendor. You want to be absolutely sure that you'll have all your cables in pairs, with exactly the same length and electrical characteristics. A faulty cable or connection in 3D is much more prone to turning into a nightmare than in 2D. Furthermore, vendor cables are custom-made to have the very length you'll need on that rig, for the very camera you plan to put on it. A 3D rig is already loaded with enough cables; don't add loops on top of it. While you're on the industry show floor, take a minute to look at an empty rig, and then compare it to its functional counterpart on the demo area. Try to count the cables—remote controls, genlocks, power supplies, motion controls, lens controls—and try to figure out what they do. Actually, this is a good indicator of the quality of a rig design. A good rig is like a boat: there should be no loose cables or unnecessary loops lying around.

Stereoscopic HD-SDI

"Duplicate everything" is the basic modus operandi of stereoscopic productions. Cables are no exception to this rule, with the complexity one can imagine. However, in some cases, especially for remote camera positions, you'll want to run single cables.

As a reminder, we'll describe the serial digital interface family of standards at HD resolutions:

- SMPTE 292M: the legacy HD-SDI, 720p and 1080i resolutions
- SMPTE 372M: the dual-link HD-SDI for 4:4:4 encodings and 1080p resolutions
- SMPTE 424M: the 3G HD-SDI, basically two SMPTE 372M on a single cable

Although 3G SDI can be used to actually transport stereoscopic streams, it has not been standardized yet and has been dubbed 3D over 3G. Still higher bitrates are needed, and they will be standardized by SMPTE for stereoscopic 4:4:4 encoding, RGB color space, 12-bits color depth, and higher frame rates in progressive modes. In the meantime, we rely on vendor solutions to multiplex image streams on single links.

Stereoscopic production was an early adopter of fiberglass cabling for signal transport. At IBC 2010, Telecast Corporation presented a fiber converter that

can transport up to three 3G streams on a single thread. This device allows the sending of
two signals at full color depth to the image-
processing units, as well as the receipt of a
stereoscopic image that includes motion-control commands in the ancillary data.

Telecast Corporation:
http://www.telecast-fiber.com/
copperhead-3400-3D/

Frame-Compatible Formats

Stereoscopic production reuses a lot of 2D gear and setups. In some cases, 2D
tools have enough bandwidth and connectors to process two HD steams, and
a clever configuration or a software update makes them 3D. Sometimes two of
them are synched and used in parallel; sometimes you must deal with a single
HD channel capacity to transport or process 3D. In these cases, the 3D will be
encoded in a 2D frame-compatible format (FCF).

BASIC FCF

The basic process of frame-compatible formatting is to drop half the resolution
and pack the remaining anamorphic versions of the left and right images into
a single 2D image. Most basic FCFs have the self-explanatory side-by-side (SBS)
and top-and-bottom (TAB) image arrangement. A third format is the *line interleaved* form, with horizontal lines alternately describing the left or right images.
This is the display format of the current generation of passive 3D TV, which
uses Arizawa pattern polarizers. This was also used in analog TV to record left
and right views on separated fields. For this reason, you'll see interleaved FCF
3D referred to as "passive" in recent display literature, and "active" in older
material. Both are equally inaccurate.

The main problem with FCF is obviously the loss of resolution, and the value
of each format results from the direction of the resolution decimation. The
side-by-side seems to be preferred for many reasons; for example, experienced
stereographers can watch it in 3D using the "free viewing" technique that consists in voluntarily converging or diverging their eyesight until the left and right
images overlap and the stereoscopic images fuse into a 3D one.

For interlaced 1080i video, SBS is better than TAB, for each frame still has
540 lines rather than 270. For progressive 720p video, TAB is better than SBS,
because the 2D horizontal resolution actually defines the depth resolution.

Various standardization groups explicitly recommend or impose SBS as the
1080i format and TAB for 720p, with the left image on the left or top part of
the frame, respectively. This rough process is especially efficient for recording
and transporting 3D. A frame-compatible formatted 3D can be routed through
thousands of types of 2D equipment and will never get out of sync.

The FCFs are transition formats that are expected to disappear from the professional universe as the 3D transition progresses. They are likely to have a longer
life in consumer electronics, where their main application is the HDMI 1.3a
standard that embeds 3D signals into a single HD link from the Blu-ray Disc

player to the TV. The 3D conversion lenses generate SBS FCF that is captured and recorded as it is on the support, and eventually sent to the TV accordingly.

The main concern with FCFs is the danger of seeing them stacked atop one another. If an SBS and an TAB FCF are used consecutively, the resulting signal is a quarter HD, marginally better than SD.

FIGURES 4.4 AND 4.5
Basic Frame-Compatible Format. In the side-by-side frame compatible format, left and right images are squeezed together inside a single 2D image file.
Image courtesy of Enrique Criado.

ADVANCED FCF

Frame-compatible format quality can be optimized with a smarter decimation scheme: the *quincunx* or *checkerboard* format, also called the *mesh* format.

A quincunx (Qx) 3D image is composed of pixels alternately taken from left and right images in a checkerboard pattern. This format is also known as *DLP*, because it has been used in 3D-capable RPTVs since 2007. It exists in two types: native Qx, with left and right images composed together, and rebuilt Qx, with left and right images reconstructed on the left and right parts of the frame. A native Qx looks like a 50% mix, and a rebuilt Qx looks like a side-by-side picture. Both present high frequencies. A native Qx is barely compatible with any digital compression, whereas a rebuilt Qx will just require a higher bit stream than a regular side-by-side to preserve its additional visual resolution. This subsampling allows for a much better image reconstruction, because each missing pixel can be rebuilt from four neighbors, rather than only two, and aliasing artifacts are less noticeable.

A proprietary version of the checkerboard was patented by Sensio. Their process relies on pre-filtering the images and post-processing them to regenerate even more visual resolution. The claim is that 90% of the resolution is preserved. The Sensio encoding is recognized as the most advanced and efficient FCF format by the transport industry, and is deployed in most transport providers' facilities offering 3D services.

FRAME PACKING

The two streams of 30fps stereoscopic content can be stacked together into single 60fps monoscopic format. That's what Digital Cinema Initiatives (DCI), the joint venture of the major Hollywood studios, does with 3D movies encoded and transported as 48fps content. It is crucial to properly flag the frames in ancillary metadata, so that the left and right images are properly restituted. Otherwise they'll be out of sync by one frame.

DIRECTING LIVE 3D

Most of the experience in live 3D production is in sporting events, which clearly lead the industry, with concerts following behind. Sports broadcasts follow a ritualized storytelling process, with the main cameras on high ground doing up to 80% of the air time, as well as close-ups on some actions, and a lot of replays and graphics. A 3D production tries to revisit the TV sports liturgy, bringing its own wow shots without breaking the magic and the story.

> If the audience says "The 3D was great, but we didn't get the game," we failed.
>
> **Vince Pace**

Directing Live 3D Sports

Interview with Derek Manning

Finding the Right Balance Between Showing Off and Game Presentation

Derek Manning directed 3D TV football and baseball games for Fox. Here's what he shared with us during an interview.

Camera Positions Are Key to Good 3D Sports Finding the best camera positions is key in doing good 3D sports. If you're too high, you won't get a good 3D shot—and if you're too tight, you'll get great 3D, but you won't get the best views for showing the strategy of the game. For the high and wide play-by-play shots, you want the cameras to get lower and closer to the field, in a medium-high shot position.

You Have to Slow Down Directing There are many more traps in 3D than in 2D. In 2D, I can just see a shot that is good, even if it's down in a corner on a black and white monitor, and I can take it: Go! On a 2D football game, cutting is quite hectic.

You can't do that in 3D, or it's going to be hard on the audience's eyes. You don't want to do it for two reasons: first, because you should preview that shot. Ask for, say, "ready seven," and the TD will preview it for you on the 3D monitor, allowing you to check it in 3D before you take it.

Second, because every shot is an experience in 3D. There's so much more in a good 3D image—you don't need to cut as much as in 2D. I remember watching one 3D shot during a show, and I was so drawn into it that I started to watch it like TV, almost forgetting I was actually directing.

Camera Operators Have a Learning Curve Too Plan for longer camera meetings, because your crew will need to learn new things; they are experiencing the learning process too, just as we are in the truck.

You want them to show off the 3D; you want the higher, wider camera to shoot a little tighter than normal, and the lower camera on the ground to shoot wider. Normally, these cameras would be right on the guy's face, but you may need to ask for a head-to-toe or waist-up shot—because without the background behind the player, it's not really possible to see the 3D. Additionally, it's hard on stereographers to get their 3D correct when you are shooting that tightly.

Teach them to watch out for edge violations, like people entering the frame, or bright objects on the sides of the frame. They have to get rid of that, one way or another. Get it in the frame, or get it out—but deal with it. You may also need their help with this for some camera positions; for example, on a low-end zone shot in a football game, if a player is coming up the field, he will cross the frame, which is going to be hard on your eyes. The cameraman can see this in advance, and alert the director on the intercom so he can get off that shot.

The Shots You Want in Your Show Nice 3D shots have many layers of depth, with people or objects filling the space. This is especially true in baseball fields, where each player has a separate position and they are spread out, with the crowd behind them. In American football, they are more packed together. Still, there are touchdown shots with a player holding the ball at the camera, the other players running toward the cameras, and the stadium in the background. This kind of shot has layers of depth—foreground, middle ground, and background—making for gorgeous 3D shots.

On the other hand, tight shots like those we often do in sports will not come out great. In 2D, it's common to do a close-up on the quarterback's eyes. In 3D, you won't get any depth effect from that shot. However, it's a compelling image that you want, no matter what; this is where you need balance between the 3D show and the game. I remember the stereographer would warn me some shots would not make good 3D. He came with a movie perspective, which was his background. I was doing those head shots, and he was shaking his head. I told him, "I have to do that, that's capturing where the game is—on his face."

Tools for Live 3D Production

SWITCHERS

It is our understanding that most large HD switchers will see a 3D upgrade option as a software update. The situation is less clear for mid-range products, but Panasonic, Sony, and FOR-A have already presented various solutions.

At NAB 2010, Panasonic introduced the AG-HMX100, a stereoscopic video switcher, along with its stereoscopic camera and display. The video switcher is based on a to-be-released 4-channel product that received software modifications allowing it to run as a stereoscopic 2-channel. If you really need the four channels, you can link two mixers together, and you'll get a 4x3D switcher. Panasonic considers that small mixer to be mostly a useful tool for onset monitoring and FX previewing. At IBC 2010, FOR-A presented a video switcher with 3G and 3D capabilities, the HVS-4,000HS. Sony offers the MVS-8,000G switcher.

STEREOSCOPIC REPLAYS AND SLOW MOTION

Instant replays and slow motion are key assets in sports broadcasting. You can't just run them two-by-two and hope for the best. You need them to be natively stereoscopic, with dual-channel input, record, replay, and output. Fortunately, digital recorders used in 2D were already multichannel when 3D arrived in the game. Multiple cameras would be ingested, recorded, and replayed according to cues set by the replay technician. The 3D upgrade consists in linking inputs and outputs together, and duplicating EDL from one eye to another.

You need to feed your instant replay DDRs with corrected imagery so that you get perfect 3D on slow motion and stills. Otherwise, 3D imperfections will be too obvious in slow motion, especially with the graphics (such as the updated score or player statistics) that are typically added on screen.

3D CONVERSION

Real-time 3D conversion is making great progress in field use. Part of its success comes from the scarcity of 3D camera positions, or the inability to pull good 3D from specific shots. Along with being driven by demand, real-time 3D conversion benefits from the current audience's forgiveness for poor 3D.

Following the mantra that "the show must go on," let's see three cases where real-time 3D conversion can be used with acceptable results. The quality of the conversion will be inversely related to the intensity of the generated depth.

- Large landscape with little or no discernable depth features.
- Medium landscape with known geometry.
- Deterministic 3D conversion following known "world rules."

Case 1: Large Landscapes

When properly shooting a very large landscape in 3D, you'll have to choose between a small interaxial and no-depth details, or a large interaxial that generates nice depth features at the cost of a miniaturizing effect on the scene. Basically, if you shoot a tennis court, you'll end up with what looks like table tennis. But if you try to avoid this, all you get is a mostly flat picture, placed in the distance upon the convergence angle of your camera rig. Why bother running two cameras to get this? Instead, get it done by a computer.

For a quick and cheap 3D conversion of a city landscape, use simple DVE (digital video effects) to push the image behind the screen, and bend or orient it if you want to give a little twist to the general orientation of the ground. An experienced stereographer working with a talented visual effects technician can even roughly shape the view in 3D using 2D deformations on a single eye.

Case 2: Known Geometries

When you shoot the inside of a stadium, sporting arena, or concert venue in 3D, most of the discernable depth features are generated by the architecture, not by the hosts or patrons. Players, artists, fans, and supporters 100 meters away from the camera do not generate any occlusion revelation, and therefore they appear in the same depth as the ground or seat they are on. A properly acquired 3D shape of an empty venue that is then fed into a conversion system will generate good stereoscopy.

The only issue with this technique is that there isn't currently a vendor offering this as a turnkey solution. Still, it's not a complex effect to put together, and it can be simplified by generating a depth map and using it as a displacement map source. If you can synchronize the depth map to the camera movements, either via motion control or via point tracking in the image domain, you'll get a dynamic 3D conversion. More advanced processes, including depth-acquisition devices and CG modeling and projection techniques, will perfect it.

Case 3: Known World Rules

The issue with real-time 3D conversion is its attempt to be universal in a trade where nothing is. We use plenty of different cameras, lenses, cranes, converters, and visual effects boxes, because no show is the same as the next one. Converting to 3D implies that you understand the 2D, and that's years and years away from the current artificial intelligence you can put in a VFX computer. That said, if you reduce the complexity of the universe, you want the converter to be able to deal with it.

At IBC 2010, SterGen (Stereo Sports Video Generator) presented the first real-time converter that looks like it may provide acceptable results. The system is loaded with game rules that allow it to understand what's happening on screen. It knows that there's a flat green field with players running on it, and that the field is surrounded by an arena of seats—it even knows that there's a ball. This system produces decent real-time conversion, and will be extended to other field games like soccer, rugby, tennis, and basketball. All these new sports will be available as add-ons to the original product. However, if you try to use SterGen's real-time converter to convert a concert, car race, or documentary, you'll get awful results, just like you would from the "universal" 3D converters.

SterGen:
http://www.stergen.tv/

FUTURE TOOLS FOR DEPTH CONTINUITY

There's hardly a 3D movie that does not use *active depth cuts*, also known as *cut cushioning*. ADC reconverges in and out shots to bring them in a common depth space at the cut time, but that visual effect has not yet reached the live broadcast 3D toolset. If its usefulness is not in question, the reality of its actual implementation is still not decided.

Reconvergence can be done in the image domain, in the 3D image processor, or at the camera unit, via remote control. It will generate a delay between the cut order and its execution, and rely on the interconnection of the video mixer, image-analysis tools, and camera motion controls. If it is done in the image domain, it will generate some magnification and cropping. The most probable implementation we'll see will be in the video switcher, using depth metadata embedded by image analyzers in the ancillary channel, which will mostly reconverge the out shot for faster execution.

3D OUTSIDE BROADCAST

Prepping an HDTV OB vehicle for 3D production is technically easy. You have three options:

- Keep it pristine, walk in, and produce frame-compatible 3D.
- Temporarily retrofit an existing HD van for 3D production.
- Rent one of the brand-new 3D/HD trucks.

Your main problem may be to find the place for the stereo staff: typically the stereographer in the main truck, and the so-called convergence pullers grooming the 3D feeds in a second truck.

Producing Frame-Compatible 3D

If you have no choice other than using an HD truck with no budget to convert to 3D, you'll have to go the FCF route. First, select the FCF you want to use— most likely SBS, for its better compatibility with interlaced video; or quincunx for higher reconstructed resolution. Encode all your sources, including graphics and titles, in that FC format. Run your camera feeds through 3D multiplexers and process them as 2D. If you work in quincunx, make sure there are no issues or artifacts with video compression, encoding, or processing, as you would do in instant replay systems.

Select transitions that process the images in a way that is compatible with the FCF you have selected. The raw quincunx has the good grace to be compatible with most transitions. (Sensio is among the very few companies that has developed a real knowledge in such "soft retrofitting" processes.) Most 3D displays will be able to decode the FCF on the fly for your program and preview monitoring, but some may need an external decoder, especially for quincunx encoding.

Converting an OB Van to 3D

If you have access to your truck and some time and money to spare, converting an OB truck to 3D is a relatively easy task. You need to do the following:

- Bring in 3D monitors with a bare minimum of two, one for program and one for preview.
- Spend some time in the patch area, duplicating all links.
- Reprogram the video switcher for 3D processing, that is, running the two High Definition streams in parallel.
- Reprogram the EVSes to process the dual streams.
- Upgrade the DVR or DDR to dual stream capability, as with the Sony SRW-5,000.

Existing Fleets of 3D Vans

On the 300 HD trucks available in the United States, there are approximately 10 that are 3D. Historically, the first companies to deploy 3D trucks were AMV (All Mobile Video) and Telegesic in Europe, and NHK CosmoMedia America in the United States.

Graphics in 3D

Using 3D graphics may seem to be a no-brainer, for all TV shows are now complemented with full CG graphics that are based on 3D models, and could very easily be rendered on two channels and included in 3D inside the volumetric live picture. However, in feature animation postproduction, this is among the harder jobs done today—so there's no reason the TV crews would have it easy. For one, it's really easy to render CG 3D; the hard part is ensuring that it makes sense with your real, live picture. Your eyes need both image geometries to be perfectly stable in regards to each other, and your brain needs both 3D universes to be coherent in regards to the optical world you're used to living in. This second requirement is not an easy one at all.

Consider a situation where we have a stereoscopic problem and a 3D problem. The stereoscopic problem is that you need to be able to look at the two left and right pictures, and the 3D problem is that you want the two worlds—the CGI and the live action—to be plausible when you look at them.

Comfortable 3D Placement in a Coherent Space with Live Picture

When you shoot live 3D, you are in the "good enough" side of stereoscopic imagery; image geometry and photography are matched to the point that you can enjoy the show without eyestrain or headache. When you generate CG 3D, you are at the perfect end of image quality. CG cameras have the good grace to stay stable even if you shake your keyboard.

When you mix both, however, the imperfection of the live images turns into sheer ugliness, because they can't stand comparison with the CG. Inconsistent keystone effect is a good example. Shoot some wide angle converged 3D, and the images in the corners drift away in opposite directions. Now add a 3D logo in a corner. Which geometry should your visual system stick with? This is just the beginning. Now assume that you ran your 3D through an image processor that makes it perfect (certainly, this is the way to go). In this case, you are introducing your CG graphics. In 2D, they are accepted as unrelated to the scenery, and read as an additional layer. In 3D, they interfere with our cognitive process that rebuilds the geometries as well as the sizes and scales of the characters.

The biggest issue with stereoscopic graphics is the occlusion conflict. If you display a scoreboard in front of the screen, and someone unexpectedly approaches the camera and gets closer to the audience than the graphics position, pure logic dictates that that person should occlude the graphics. Because this is not the case with the current generation of CG titles, you'll have an unpleasant 3D experience.

In 2D TV, the *safe area* convention was agreed upon to ensure that no graphic or action would be displayed in the unsafe borders of the picture. That could always be cut out by various under-scan processes. In 3D, the same concept can be extrapolated into *safe volumes* for graphics.

Set Safe Volumes for Graphics

Where to place your graphics is going to be an interesting debate. For sheer readability, you want to place them in the screen plane. They will be more comfortable to look at, with no focus/convergence decoupling, and they will be accessible to anyone not wearing glasses. It may sound like a strange requirement, but 3D TV will not always be a per-appointment media. You can expect your audience to wear glasses, but you cannot assume they are. Beyond that simple "just like 2D" graphics placement, what are your options?

PASSIVE VOLUME SEGMENTATION

There's superbly simple space segmentation for safe stereoscopic graphics: Keep the action behind the screen plane and all the graphics in front of it. It may not be creative, but it is infallible. Get a wide view of the stadium and float the flags and scores in front of your audience's faces. Technically, you can't really go wrong. Creatively, you'll pretty soon feel frustrated.

If you feel like playing the game more aggressively, cut your scenic box in adjacent volumes, in a more complex layout than successive layers. Create spaces where you push your graphics inside the screen, like on top of the frame, and use them on head-to-toe shots with space above the players. Or float the team flag by a player, trusting your camera operators to keep the empty space free from any intrusion. Tricky, but stunning.

FUTURE TOOLS: ACTIVE OCCLUSION PROCESSING

Image processors can detect edges and disparities, and, within a few years, interactive 3D alpha channels will be generated from such systems. The graphic keyer will be able to cut out that CG flag floating by the player if the player happens to wave his arm, using the same depth information inserted in ancillary data for active cuts. Other options are possible, using the depth acquisition techniques that were presented in Chapter 2.

Designing and Applying Graphics in 3D

When you meet the artists who will design your 3D graphics, make sure they have some basic understanding of depth perception. They should at least be aware of the impact of color on depth perception. Basically, warm colors proceed and cold colors recede, just as with bright and dark surfaces.

Have some consideration for the members of your audience who will see the show in public places, like pubs. They will watch it on passive televisions, with half the vertical resolution. Some sort of anti-aliasing pass will be welcomed.

For the members of the audience enjoying the show in active stereo, beware of the effect of display delay on moving logos. Because one eye sees an image with a slight delay, it is interpreted at a different depth. Depending upon which image, left or right, is shown first, the movement will be perceived differently: a title moving leftward or rightward will be perceived either closer or farther away than expected. On which side of the window will the title be pushed? There's no way to predict it until the frame order is standardized in 3D TV.

When you insert a logo, branding, or advertisement for another show, be careful not to do it on a 3D scene that reaches out of the screen. An obvious solution is to place such images in front of the screen plane, which looks good and will provide wow 3D. Still, until you can rely on embedded depth metadata, you have to figure out how much you should pull them.

Another interesting stereoscopic endeavor will be the *picture in picture* journey into 3D. If you need to merge a flat source inside a 3D feed—typically a distant reporter who has no 3D camera—surrounding his image by a frame that is pulled forward by a few pixels of parallax will go a long way in creating 3D illusion. If you have a stereoscopic source from a distant studio, give it a key-in try; you should be able to pull a nice holographic videophone effect.

Gerhard Lang, Vizrt

Gerhard Lang is the CTO of Vizrt and has provided stereoscopic graphics for ESPN and BSkyB live 3D sports productions. He shares with us the lessons learned on these productions.

Interview with Gerhard Lang

The Vizrt Stereoscopic Solution All 3D TV projects are high-profile productions. They work one HD-SDI channel for each left and right camera, all the way through the vision mixer, and then either apply a multiplexer to carry the images in side by side, or offer a top-and-bottom frame-compatible format for distribution.

When using the vision mixer, we ought to deliver two separate fill and key signals for the left and right eye. Because everything we've ever done since the beginning of Vizrt has always been openGL-based, it was already 3D. The evolution from a 2D product into a 3D stereoscopic operation was very simple.

Synchronization Requirements When ESPN and BSkyB started producing S3D content, they used their existing graphics. This made a lot of sense, because everything was already CG-3D.

For us, that meant doubling the rendering speed. Quad buffer stereo would be too slow, because it could only deliver half the performance that people are used to. Therefore we doubled the rendering stages (as shown in Figure 4.7).

It is extremely important that these two instances are 100% in sync, because if one starts the animation

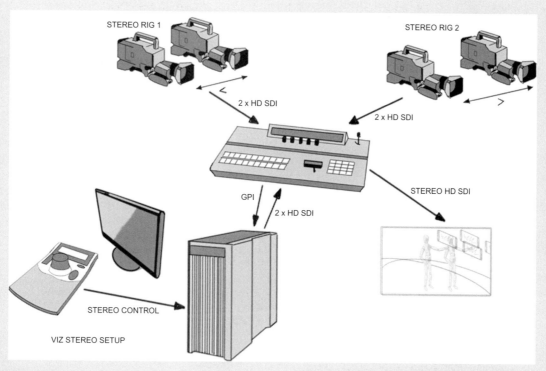

FIGURE 4.6
Stereoscopic Graphic in OB Van Environment. The vision mixer gets two HD-SDI from each camera. The graphics engine receives GPI signaling and sends back two fill and key HD-SDI.

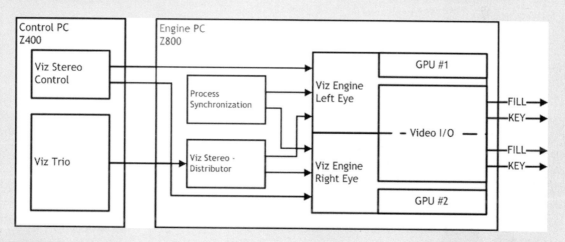

FIGURE 4.7
Stereoscopic Graphic System. The control application sends animation orders to the stereo controller that distributes the two rendering GPUs. A synchronization engine ensures the genlock and frame-lock of the S3D fill and key signal sent to the production matrix via four HD-SDI links.

earlier or later, it's very disturbing to the human brain. We created a stereo distributor, which receives the commands that are usually meant for a single engine and distributes them equally to the left and right engines. We also have a synchronization processor, which ensures that both GPUs are always rendering the exact same field. Those are the two mechanisms making sure animations start at the same time, and that once the animations are running, the fields are always rendered for the exact same timestamp on the left and the right eye.

Setting Graphics in Depth In the Vizrt engine, we have three independent graphics layers: back, middle, and front. The back layer is very rarely used in sports production, where most of the stereo productions are happening right now. Usually the middle layer is used to show lower-third graphics, like tables, analytical graphics, and starting grids. The front layer is used for boxes, such as scoring or clock boxes. Each layer can have its own camera, and therefore can have its own stereo parameters. Even if we don't get the best information from the rigs or from the pixel processors, we can correct the cameras.

The stereographer usually goes through all cameras prior to the production, adjusting the stereo parameters for the three layers for every single camera. When the director selects, say, camera one, on the vision switcher, we get a signal indicating that we're now looking at the video that is filmed by rig number one. We get that information via GPI, and render the graphics according to that camera's settings.

On the main layer, we would have the lower-third graphics. Most of the time these would sit just a bit in front of the screen, and normally they're short. Now, let's say the stereo rig number one is the main camera in the sports production; it is over the grandstands, looking onto the playing fields and over to the other grandstands (a common scenario). This would give us quite a bit of room for the lower third to be placed in front, or almost at the level of the screen.

People are used to seeing the clock in the upper-right corner: that's where they would look for the score and the clock. However, in stereo production, your eyes cannot follow the usual flow. If you look for the score and the clock, you would just go to the upper-right corner from wherever you're looking. Let's say you're looking at the ball right now, and then you move to the upper-right corner to see how many minutes are left. When you do that while viewing a stereo image, your eyes would converge on the playing field, then probably on the grandstand, and then they'd have to converge again to see the score and clock that sits up at the window—which is a very troublesome experience. To avoid this, you should virtually push back the 3D score-and-clock element 150 meters, so it's near the grandstand. This makes the viewing experience a lot more comfortable, because you can follow whatever is in the scene to find your way to the information you need.

However, this positioning may not work if you go to stereo rig number two. Let's say, for example, that the steady-cam is located at the border of the playing field, and its convergence parameters are set so that the players get out of the screen as they come closer. (This is fairly common.) In this case, what you should do is take the score all the way out and let it sit in front of the monitor by half a meter. You'd do the same, with a more subtle change, on the lower third.

You can also disable the front layer so that the back does not get displayed when you use a camera that is very close to the ground, which allows you to avoid having the graphics puncture the players, or any subject on the field. This is currently the common practice.

Adapting Existing Graphics for Stereo You may have a client who gets into S3D and wants to use whatever footage they had before in stereoscopic production. In order to do this, they must check the design to see if it will generate mistakes. For example, a common mistake is to misplace objects and then rescale them. Any object that is 100 meters away but is scaled up by a factor of 5 will have the same screen size as an object that is very close to you but scaled down by 0.5. If you look at this in stereoscopy, it looks completely wrong. This kind of thing must be tested beforehand, such as on the graphics station, where the user interface is 2D but the render context is in full openGL quad-buffering 3D. You can also check it in stereo while you correct what has been done wrong. In addition, you can see if any of the auto-animations are touching the borders, making the viewing experience unpleasant. To that end, the control PC uses a S3D display and a CG-3D mouse with six degrees of freedom to adjust position and orientation of the graphic elements.

Virtual Studios in 3D The interaxial and convergence parameters in a studio do not really change during a production, because it's a very confined space. When you shoot internally, you're not re-focusing dynamically; you basically set it up once and then let it go. You can adjust parameters such as eye separation and convergence dynamically to match the position of the presenter against the virtual studio.

Calibrating Cameras for Stereoscopic Virtual Studios Studio calibration is a two-step process, and you calibrate the lenses as an entity. Basically, you establish the following:

- The relation between the zoom and focus on the lens.
- The field of few of the virtual camera in X and Y.
- The center shift of the lens.
- The deformation parameter of K1 and K2 for this lens.

Lens distortions are especially important between the right and left eyes. In order to be very accurate, you need to distort the image according to the distortion of the lens. If you film a checkerboard, for example, you will see that a wide shot results in the lines at the edges being curved. To fix this, you should render the virtual studio with a 20% larger size, and then use this result as a texture and re-render it on a grid that has been distorted to replicate the lens aberrations. This ensures that you don't see all the artifacts that occur in a distorted image when you try to create two pixels out of one.

Tracking Cameras for Stereoscopic Virtual Studios Stereoscopic camera tracking is exactly the same as

camera tracking for a classic camera. If you're using infrared tracking or motion analysis, position the target so that the center of the virtual camera is in between the two real cameras. There are then many parameters inside the software that are used to calibrate a studio. You can apply rotations and translations around all three axes to match the cameras to the target, and with those parameters you can make sure that the virtual cameras for the left eye and the right eye match the positions of the real cameras. Overall, it's a very complex setup.

Faking the 3D Camera in a Stereoscopic Virtual Studio If you want to use your existing virtual studio infrastructure and you only have one anchor presenting, there is a very simple method of generating a 3D stereoscopic virtual studio: by feeding the single video into the Vizrt engines. Then you offset it in horizontal direction, matching the distance from the anchor to the virtual camera.

You can do that and keep the anchor moving around in a closed environment, less than one meter back and forth. Alternatively, you can measure the position of the anchor by installing surveillance cameras looking down from the lighting grid. This will give the depth position of the anchor.

The really interesting part about this is that you can make the anchor stand at the exact location that you want him or her to stand—but what's even more interesting is that, for most people, the anchor does not appear flat. This is because the human brain takes a lot more hints when it tries to reconstruct a 3D image than just the separation of the left and right eyes.

When we did this experiment the first time, the subject standing inside the green screen environment didn't know about the technology at all. Because she knew it was in 3D, she reached out her hand to create a wow effect. The audience, expecting her hand to come out of the screen, actually moved back. This happened in a few seconds only, and she quickly brought her hand back in. The audience didn't know whether the hand was reaching out or not, but they reacted as if they did.

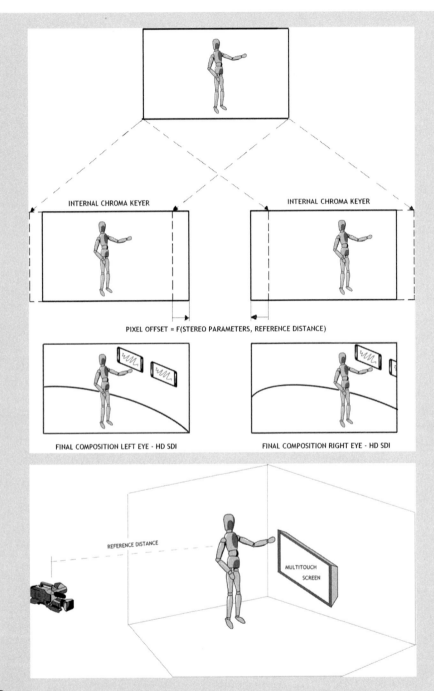

INTERNAL CHROMA KEYER

INTERNAL CHROMA KEYER

PIXEL OFFSET = F(STEREO PARAMETERS, REFERENCE DISTANCE)

FINAL COMPOSITION LEFT EYE - HD SDI

FINAL COMPOSITION RIGHT EYE - HD SDI

REFERENCE DISTANCE

MULTITOUCH
SCREEN

FIGURE 4.8
Using a 2D Camera in a 3D Virtual Studio. If the 2D camera is appropriately placed in depth using X-shift, the presenter is
perceived in 3D.

RECORDING 3D

Most 3D takes are recorded for post-edition or postproduction, rather than aired live. Just as in 2D, the recorded quality and resulting amount of data is set upon the eventual use of the pictures.

The procedures in stereoscopic recording vary depending upon the final product. For a heavy-FX feature, you'll want to keep all available metadata and ancillary data you may get. This can include depth information from image analyzers, rig geometry from motion-control commands and readouts, and clean plates and helper images. Images intended for heavy VFX treatment will be recorded at full color resolution with no compression or lossless compression.

Footage destined to be directly cut into an indie movie or TV documentary can be recorded in compressed 4:2:2 format. This will maximize recording duration, allowing for the use of solid state drives rather than fragile magnetic tapes or drives.

In between, for feature documentaries or low-budget, low FX movies, there are many workflows based on the raw recording of single-sensor Bayer-filter cameras.

Functions You Can Expect from a 3D Recorder

Obviously, old-time 3D recording with two recorders at once is over. A modern stereoscopic recorder boasts twice the 2D bandwidth and records 3D streams at once. What really counts, though, are the invisible functions: the ability to coordinate with both cameras, to record the metadata, and to do some stereoscopic asset management. Actually, there is one 3D recorder that does all of that, and still records on two separate supports: the Panasonic AG-3D. Almost all recorders are built around generic computer hardware, and some run DI or on-set previsualization software.

In the file-based universe, there are many possible recording modes for stereo footage:

- Still frames in folders, each eye in a separate folder.
- Still frames in folders, both eyes in the same folder.
- Video files, eyes in separate folders.
- Video files, eyes in the same folder.
- Video files, eyes multiplexed together.
- Video files, eyes on separated supports.

The basic functions for a recorder are:

- Names files as the same scene/shot/take for each camera.
- Starts and stops both recordings in sync.
- Provides synchronous replay of 3D takes.

The optional functions for a recorder are:

- Reacts to the camera record trigger, sensed via the SDI, and starts both recordings.
- Provides warnings if the cameras are out of sync.
- Provides output in FCF for previews or proxies.
- Harnesses any available GPU for previsualization, 3D formatting, or color timing.

Interview with Bruce Austin

Hands-on Experience With the Cinedeck

Bruce walked on stage at the 2010 NAB 3D conference holding the camera unit he had been using just one week earlier in the Amazonian jungle, two Silicon Imaging SI-2Ks on an Element Technica Neutron rig with the Cinedeck recorder. Here are his comments on the system:

> The Cinedeck is one of the most amazing pieces of gear I've had my hands on lately. We were in a place that was 40 degrees Celsius, with 100% humidity and rain, dust, and wind—but the gear still worked. You can see the 3D on-screen, even if it's not bright enough to do anaglyph in broad light. It does file naming, and you even have a "play 3D" button; there's no other proprietary recorder on the Red or the Phantom that gives you that. That's the reason why SDI output is crucial on 3D gear: until you can feed the two image streams into any 3D-aware piece of gear, you are just producing a sluggish pair of flat content. It's only when you have a 3D recorder, monitor, or multiplexer that you start doing 3D. And remember to only put on tape that you know is good stereo; otherwise, it goes in the rough edit in 2D, and has to be fixed in post or re-edit, both of which will cause great frustration.

Recording Metadata

Metadata recording is a very important issue in 3D, but not one with a solution. Vendors' solutions still rule the show, with no standardization or even coordination announced yet. As of today, rig geometry metadata is recorded with dedicated devices, on independent supports like USB thumb drives. Considering all the efforts the industry has been through to record left and right streams for consistency and coherency, it seems clear that metadata should be recorded along with the image. The closest we get now is to record it in one audio channel.

There are three types of metadata available on set to be recorded:

- Orders sent to the cameras and rig concerning zoom, focus, interaxial, and convergence.
- Values read from the cameras and rig, like interaxial and convergence from motion-control encoders, as well as values read from the lenses with digital encoders like Cooke 5/i.
- Computation results from image analyzers, like suggested geometric corrections.

Examples of 3D Recorders

Recording 3D requires twice the bandwidth of 2D. Solid state disk (SSD) recorders offer such high data throughput that they can record 3D natively. It is just as easy and transparent to the system to increase the number of hard disk drive (HDD) disks. Such disks can be stacked up to aggregate their bandwidth. On a tape recorder, one needs to increase the tape speed or recording density, which is not something you can do by buying equipment at your regular computer shop. For these reasons, most 3D recorders are either SSD recorders or high-end HDD recorders using RAID subsystems, with only one 3D tape recorder in the high-end range.

On location, we use flash drives for their shock, head, and extreme temperature resistance. Because of their limited capacity (about 40 minutes), they are handled like film rolls, with a dedicated technician in charge of the backup and recycling procedures. This includes creating two copies of the footage and sometimes a Frame Compatible 3D proxy. The recycling can be a simple erase, but some generations of SSD need to be reformatted to keep their optimal performance level.

On set or in studio, we use RAID disks for their large capacity. If the disks have to be moved, it is advised that you select a device that has shock-absorbing trays. You may be aware that disk failures are not uncommon; on high-end systems, ultra-high value data, such as your latest take, is actually intelligently spread over many disks, so that a single failure would not compromise the record.

When it comes to backing up and storing data, nothing beats the cost and density of tape support. If you plan to shoot for hours and hours, don't rely on drives: you'll soon need a truck to move them.

Embedded and Onboard 3D Recorders

Both embedded and onboard 3D recorders mount directly on a rig and record on SSD drives. They are a must for untethered steady-cam shots or shoulder rig cameras.

Those recorders built around an embedded PC allow for 2D and 3D previews, and some allow you to control the cameras via a touch-screen interface (for example, by integrating the SiliconDVR software from Silicon Imaging for the SI-2K cameras).

There are several types of onboard recorders:

- Convergent Design nano3D: http://www.convergent-design.com/
- Codex Onboard: http://www.codexdigital.com/stereoscopic/
- S.two OB-1 (records 18 inches of uncompressed 4:4:4 3D on flash drives that are backed up and recycled on the FlashDock): http://www.stwo-corp.com/
- Panavision SSR-1 (needs its docking station to record 3D): http://www.panavision.com/

There are several types of embedded recorders:

- Cinedeck: http://www.cinedeck.com
- 1 Beyond Wrangler Mini3D: http://www.1beyond.com

SOFTWARE 3D RECORDERS

Using specialized acquisition software, you can build your own 3D recorder, or buy it all configured from the integrators. Most of them run on a desktop and record full-frame 3D via AJA Kona 3 or Blackmagic DeckLink cars. Some of them can run on a laptop, and will record FC-3D via a Matrox MOX2 or Blackmagic HDLink encoders. Note that you'll need an FC-3D multiplexer to convert the 3D format.

- SiliconDVR (runs on Microsoft Windows): http://www.siliconimaging.com/
- SpecSoft Rave (runs on Linux Ubuntu): http://www.spectsoft.com/
- QtakeHD (runs on Apple OSsX): http://www.qtakehd.com/

There are several types of ingest hardware:

- AJA Kona 3: http://www.aja.com
- Matrox MXO2 Mini and LE: http://www.matrox.com/
- Blackmagic Design: http://www.blackmagic-design.com

FIGURE 4.9
Qtake Software Stereoscopic Recorder.

TAPE AND DISK RECORDER

Tape and HDD recorders are high-end 2D products capable of dual-stream recording. The RaveDuo, built around commodity hardware, can be integrated in your network operation center (NOC) as a video device, and also serves as a stereoscopic multiplexer for monitoring on set. The codex recorders are used in top-level productions, where they interface with rendering farms and data centers to generate deliverables. Here are some examples of tape and HDD recorders:

- Codex portable and studio recorders: http://www.codexdigital.com/stereoscopic/
- SpecSoft RaveDuo HDD recorder: http://www.spectsoft.com/
- Sony SRW-5,000 and SRW-1 CineAlta tape recorders: http://pro.sony.com/

EDITING AND POSTING 3D

Whereas the tools for shooting 3D have benefited from a lot of research and the practice has generated a good amount of knowledge, the art of editing 3D still involves very crude tools and has generated very few new artistic statements. For those willing to explore the art of 3D editing, we invite you to jump to Chapter 6, where you'll find contributions from experimental stereographic cinema directors, producers, and historians.

We will offer only a quick overview of post procedures here, as this book is mainly focused on event acquisition and live broadcasting. (Stereoscopic postproduction deserves an entire book dedicated to this complex and engaging subject.)

Our discussion involves brief coverage of the subjects that are related to 3D editing, a presentation of the available tools, an exploration of the issues related to tracking 3D cameras, and a look at the controversial subject of 3D conversions.

Editing 3D

There are three types of products available for 3D editing:

- 3D plug-ins for 2D edit suites (like the CineForm codec or Stereo3D Toolbox)
- 3D editing suites (like Avid or Sony Vegas)
- Digital intermediate suites (like Assimilate's Scratch, Iridas' Speedgrade, or Quantel's Pablo)

All these tools take care of the four most important tasks of 3D editing:

1. The coherent ingest of the left and right footage into the edit station.
2. The coherent processing of the left and right footage in the edit.
3. The immediate visualization in 3D of the edit decisions.
4. The rendering of transitions and deliverables in real-time batch processing.

Your requirements for the edit suite reactivity and final render's image quality will drive you towards one solution or another, budget permitting.

The CineForm Neo3D codec interfaces itself between the assets, the displays, and the editing software. When stereoscopic footage is ingested, Neo3D links them together and presents only a single 2D image to the editing suite. That 2D image can be a flat-eye or a frame-compatible 3D, depending upon your selection on a small on-screen controller. If you use a dual-stream-capable hardware card like the AJA Kona 3, the codec will make sure it plays full-frame 3D. What's important to remember is that the edit suite does not have to be aware that it actually manipulates stereoscopic content.

The left and right assets are linked together with metadata, called *live metadata*, because they describe operations on the images that are applied in real time. This is more than classic 2D operations like color correction or color look; 3D operations like image flip and flop, geometric corrections, frame synchronization, and depth balancing are also possible. These operations are controlled from a helper application, CineForm's First Light, which can access the footage from a remote station to fix shots while they are edited.

Transitions and plug-ins can be written for the Neo3D system, and will access both streams of the 3D footage. This allows for 3D-specific image manipulations, like depth transitions or depth effects.

If your edit system of choice is Apple Final Cut Pro, you may be concerned that, so far, there's no support for 3D in any Apple product. Hopefully, you can plug in the Stereo3D Roolbox plug-in that retrofits FCP into a 3D edit suite. This follows the same philosophy as Neo3D, with a simpler approach and a lighter price tag.

Sony has a consumer-level edit suite, Vegas Pro, which has been upgraded with stereoscopic functions in its version 10. Sony's presentation at the SMPTE conference on 3D production suggested that version 11 will be released with upcoming Sony 3D camcorders, and that it will have 3D balancing and viewpoint interpolation functions. We'll see at NAB 2011 whether this is really the case.

FIGURE 4.10
The Stereo3D Toolbox.
Image courtesy of Tim Dashwood.

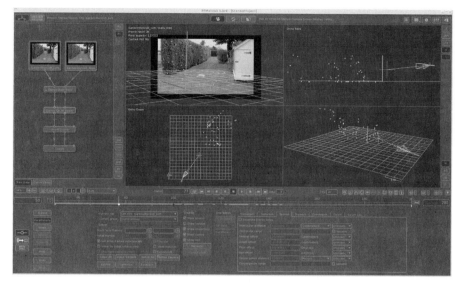

FIGURE 4.11
PFMatchit Stereo Node.
Image courtesy of Pixel Farm.

All the Avid edit systems can handle stereoscopic content. The high-end suites will ingest and play both streams at once, whereas the smaller nonlinear editors (NLE) will rely on frame-compatible proxies to do "off-line stereoscopic" edits.

In 2002, Iridas created its first stereoscopic applications, and eventually applied dual-stream technology to its entire catalog. SpeedGrade and FrameCycler are now totally stereoscopic.

Tracking 3D Cameras

Tracking stereoscopic cameras in 3D is not an easy task, because it requires much greater accuracy than in 2D. Simon Gibson is the creator of PFTrack and PFMatchit, two recent and already renowned 3D tracking tools from the Pixel Factory. Here's his expert opinion on tracking in 3D:

Interview with Simon Gibson, Pixel Farm

What specifically makes PFTrack and PFMatchit 3D-capable?

It is the stereo camera model. This ensures that the same tracking points are used to calculate the position of both cameras at the same time, and can ensure that parameters like the interocular distance are constant throughout the shot, which is unlikely to happen if the two cameras are tracked independently.

The left and right eye views of the scene can be tracked independently of each other, but because of noise and other errors, the two cameras obtained may not exactly match the actual camera positions in the stereo rig when the relationship between them is ignored. Tracking a stereo camera can ensure that the interocular distance is held constant (assuming this is required).

The second virtual camera can be generated synthetically by translating the position of the first, but this becomes problematic if the convergence distance is changing throughout the shot, because the second camera would need to be animated by hand to match the change in convergence.

Also, for monoscopic shots captured from a fixed location in space (e.g., a tripod), the distance of each tracking point from the camera cannot be estimated due to a lack of parallax in the shot. Because there is always parallax between the left and right eyes of a stereoscopic shot, the 3D position of each tracking point can still be estimated.

Finally, tracking both cameras at the same time using a stereoscopic camera model ensures that they appear at the correct scale and orientation relative to each other in the virtual scene. If each camera was tracked independently without the use of survey data, one is likely to need re-positioning manually to bring it into the correct position relative to the other.

Is it easier to track parallel shots than converged 3D?

That depends on whether the distance of the convergence point from the cameras is known. If not, then this value must be estimated by the solver, which introduces another "unknown" into the system. Tracking with a known, fixed, and finite convergence distance is not really any different from tracking parallel cameras, where the convergence distance is known to be infinite.

If the convergence distance is changing, the tracking problem becomes more complicated; now there is an extra unknown for each frame, rather than one unknown

for the entire shot. This is a similar issue to tracking shots where the focal length changes.

Is there anything to take care of on set to help stereo 3D track?

Just measure and record as much data as possible regarding the parameters of the stereo rig and the position of items on set. If all else fails, having a set of surveyed tracker positions available will help out, as with monoscopic camera tracking.

Do you track the two cameras independently, or do you share some of the computation parameters like feature points identification or matching pair confirmation?

We provide mechanisms for both, mainly because no one approach is going to work in every situation. Tracking the cameras independently raises issues such as keeping the distance between the cameras fixed, or ensuring that the convergence distance changes smoothly throughout the shot if it is not locked off.

Tracking points that are identified automatically are also transferred from one eye to the other automatically. For manually placed tracking points, the position in the other eye can either be specified automatically or manually.

Do you generate some sort of depth map after the reconstruction?

Not from stereo cameras, although this is something we are looking into.

What do you foresee in the field in terms of future tools and future procedures?

From a tracking point of view, we will be trying to support whatever the production community is using to shoot stereo. Having a secondary stereoscopic camera on set may become more common from a VFX point of view—even if the final show is not stereoscopic—because the stereo camera allows a wider range of data to be captured for various VFX tasks, such as motion capture and set reconstruction.

A final note on tracking stereoscopic images: When you correct an image geometry by shifting images, you bring the center of the image away from the center of the frame. This can be very confusing for image computations that assume that the optical center is at the center of the frame. When you track

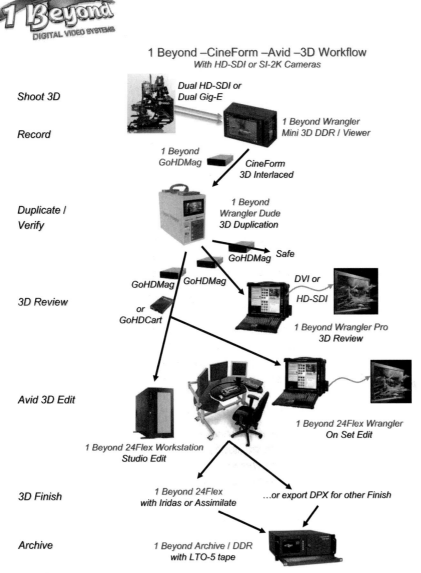

FIGURE 4.12
Synoptic of a Stereoscopic Postproduction Workflow.
Image courtesy of 1 Beyond.

your images, that's most likely to composite them with CG elements. You have two options: one is to correct the image geometry, and apply CG images on warped live footage. You'll need a good tracker to do this. The second option is to match the CG to the imperfect live image, and correct the composited shot based on the analysis of the pre-comp imagery.

3D Conversion

3D conversion is gaining a lot of coverage and controversy in the entertainment press, and most commentators do not seem to understand what they're talking about. The industry paved the way to this sea of nonsense by endorsing ludicrous real-time 3D conversion in 3D TV sets, or daring to release 3D-butchered movies.

Conversion is not a good or a bad thing by itself; it is a visual effects tool—nothing more, nothing less. The quality of a visual effect is a direct function of the time and money you put into it. As Jeffrey Katzenberg put it, "Quality is in the painter, not in the paintbrush."

In the following years, there'll be a demand and an offer for bad 3D conversion; distributors will profit on 3D saving a lame movie, some TV channels will be in desperate need of 3D content, and documentaries will need cheap 3D stock shoots. The sharks are in the water, but serious producers and filmmakers will do their best to stay out of the fray.

On the other end of the spectrum, specialized post houses can deliver such quality conversions that it takes a trained eye to identify them. They'll work with directors who consider conversion to be part of their creative work, and not an afterthought.

In short, conversion as a tool is okay, but conversion as a means is not.

Here are a few key points you should keep in mind:

- Forget about universal solutions for real-time conversion. This is science fiction.
- 2D/3D conversion is a full FX job and requires time and money.
- Solutions with some "babysitting" may be okay.

BARRY SANDREW, CEO, LEGEND FILMS

You should not antagonize 3D conversion versus shooting stereoscopic; the camera captures the depth when the conversion creates it. In the movie business, we create a lot of fake reality, in CG or by other means—and that's okay with the audience and the artists. Ultimately, it's really about who does it: Is it an intelligent machine, or a human artist? When you face that question, just remember who is in the credits for the CGI and the visual effects: the artists are, not the CPUs. And eventually, who is the audience who pays for it all? Humans, not machines.

Good 3D conversion goes much further than repurposing assets or simplifying shooting. It can be used for:

1. Inter-ocular adaptation to match in and out shots during editing:
   - Depth compression if the interaxial was too narrow.
   - Depth extension if the interaxial was too wide.

This is sometimes called *linear depth compression*, to fit into the available depth budget.

2. Scene volume modification to affect a whole scene's depth feeling:
- Volume compression if the objects feel "bulgy."
- Volume extrusion if the objects feel flat.

These are also nonlinear depth functions, also called *depth warping*:

3. Object (or character) volume modification:
- Extrude a single character to make him seem more powerful.
- Compress a single character to make him seem weaker.

This is a new technique not yet employed; it may be named *HDR-Z*.

4. 3D generation in heavy FX shots, which is sometimes used:
- For cost control on shooting.
- Because some shots are just impossible to shoot in 3D.

5. Generating depth maps from 3D footage.

6. Saving 3D shots when one eye is damaged (3D-3D conversion).

MASTERING, CONTRIBUTING, AND DISTRIBUTING 3D

Getting your 3D program sent all the way to your audience is mostly the same business as in 2D. You could reach theaters, just as with alternative content, or send contribution feeds from your network operation center to your affiliates and then to your subscribers.

For the years ahead, distributed content will have to make its way through 2D channels, until the industry agrees on 3D standards and upgrades equipment. This transition will start very soon at event locations and broadcast facilities, and will take up to ten years to deploy to all contribution and distribution channels (with the exception of the packaged content that is already full 3D on Blu-ray).

Formatting 3D

There is a saying about distributing 3D: "Resolution, synchronization, and cost: Pick two." As we know, synchronization is not negotiable in 3D; a lost frame is a lost 3D broadcast. And because sync is the costliest to maintain, resolution is what is commonly left aside in this equation.

COMPRESSING 3D

Before we get into the intricacies of formatting and packaging 3D, let's say a word about compression. All 3D requires more bandwidth. This is obvious for full-frame 3D, where one sends two pictures instead of one, but it's even more true for frame-compatible 3D. Anamorphic compression of the images increases the density of information—in other words, the frequencies. Each macrobloc in a FC3D hosts twice as much information as its counterpart in 2D. Just to get to the same level of quantization (geek slang for washing out pictures), you'll need to allocate more bit stream at the encoder's output.

There are two additional factors. First, compression artifacts adversely affect image matching in the visual cortex. Second, lost definition in the blurred areas eliminates matching features, and echoes on sharp transitions create retinal rivalries. This applies to full resolution 3D too. Here again, 3D is more than twice 2D. At contribution levels, it is advised to allocate 20Mb to each 3D channel; at the final stage, 15Mb is required for a frame-compatible 3D channel on cable.

Most MPEG encoders can process 3D content with a slight software upgrade. Beware of frame mis-sync between channels, especially with free-running encoders. Adaptive group of pictures (GOP) can get them into incoherent I-frames.

LETTER BOXING 3D

In frame-compatible formats, letter boxing has to be equally applied on left-eye and right-eye images. On a top-and-bottom image, the total black area is sliced into ¼, ½, and ¼ parts, as shown in Figure 4.13. Otherwise, the rebuilt images will not overlap properly on the 3D displays.

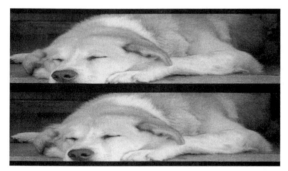 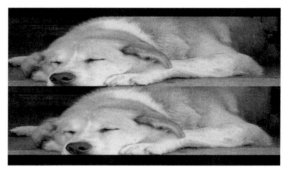

FIGURES 4.13A AND 4.13B
Correct and Incorrect Letter Boxing. Letter boxing should affect symmetrically the left and right images.

THE SMPTE 3D HOME MASTER

As early as 2008, the SMPTE started working on the standardization of 3D with a task force that was followed by genuine working groups in 2009. Don't let the name of the initiative, *Home Master*, confuse you: the SMPTE is working on avoiding the current 3D cinema situation where tens of masters have to be created for every distribution format and market. The objective is to define a set of 3D formats and conventions that will be usable for exchanging content, and that will eventually generate all the subsequent products needed by distribution channels. This Home Master should be understood as the "universal professional master to provide for all home distribution formats that may be invented."

The set of conventions will cover the image description (geometry, definition, frame rate), format signaling, and transport streams.

Contributing 3D with Peers

So far, there has been no real peer exchange of 3D content, for most live 3D productions are managed end-to-end by the network distributing it (or by international consortia, in the case of FIFA). However, these operations give us a glimpse of what will soon be the modus operandi, when 3D content starts to be produced and distributed by new 3D channel operators on various continents.

3D FORMATS IN CONTRIBUTION

You don't really know how many times your program will have been re-encoded and re-framed by the time it reaches its audience. Conversions between top-and-bottom or side-by-side, 720 or 1080, interlaced or progressive, will add up with all the frame rate interpolations occurring in international events NOC and eventually at the display level. The perfect catastrophic combination will bring you such a damaged 3D picture that it'll make analog NTSC look good. The longer you keep your 3D in pristine full frames, the better. Working with two streams that cannot drift by one frame is not easy, mostly because it was not a compulsory issue until now.

As a result, the current state of the art is to preserve the 3D at its full resolution for as long as you control the quality of the signal, and then fall back on frame-compatible 3D. Satellite links are the usual threshold. During the summer of 2010, the FIFA World Cup 3D signal was sent as separate left and right signals in JGPEG 2,000, from stadiums to the International Broadcast Centre (IBC), and then uplinked as side-by-side frame-compatible 3D in MPEG2 HDTV.

ESPN 3D sends its 3D as full-frame 3D from the event venues to its network operations center in Bristol, Connecticut, and then encodes it in frame-compatible 3D for the distribution networks.

RESYNCHRONIZING 3D

Stream synchronization is easy to control at the source, but tricky to maintain along the chain. If one device experiences a glitch, or an overload, it will cause one frame to get out of sync, and you'll have to chase down the bug. Experience shows that sounds tend to get out of sync faster than picture, especially with all the additional image-processing stages in a typical 3D setup from the camera to your TV. For example, the consumer industry standard HDMI 1.4 includes a sound delay flag to take care of the additional processing time for 3D images in the displays.

In most cases, time code (TC) sync is not that helpful, because image delay can be less than a frame. Sometimes just a few lines of drift will cause a frame drop later in the line. During transport, one can set a coherent TC in left and right feeds above the link, and retime it at the receiving station, but that may fail if someone on the line messes up the TCs. Even worse, if the synchronization was wrong to begin with, you'll propagate the imperfection along the line.

Evertz Microsystems has developed a 3D synchronization system that relies on correlation to correct 3D streams. Their system compares the left and right frames and searches for the higher correlation. Experience has shown that this method works for fixing 3D sync. There is always more correlation between left and right views than with the previous or following frames (with the exception of panning shots in the direction and speed equivalent to the inter-ocular, which is a well-known effect in 3D conversion).

Distributing 3D to the Home

The revolution brought by online content distribution will shape the deployment of 3D at home. Cable and satellite subscriptions; legal VoD and illegal P2P on coaxial, fiber, copper, or wireless links—altogether they will fight against optical disk and solid-state packaged media. The good news is: if you have some 3D content for sale and there's a 3D display looking for it, there should be more than one way to link them.

CABLE AND SATELLITE

Both cable and satellite technologies are managing large bandwidth resources with the freedom to assign it relatively freely, and both are decoded via a set-top box (STB) over which they have some control. The deployment of a new 3D service is mostly a marketing decision, with the affordable option of updating the STB software if the market share does not justify new hardware.

Operators see their 3D future in three phases:

- Phase 1: Keep the network, keep the STB, and use frame-compatible formats.
- Phase 2: Keep the network, change the STB, and distribute service-compatible payload.
- Phase 3: Change the network only when Phase 2 reaches its limit.

Phase 1 services are easy to understand: 3D channels are just 2D channels with two pictures stacked together. Even the DVR loves it. Your 3D TV takes care of decoding the image into stereoscopy. Recommended formats are SBS for 1080i and TAB for 720p. Basically, you take care of your 3D TV, and that's it for the cable company. Business is good and starts today.

Phase 2 services are much trickier for the cable company. The idea is to push the existing network to its limits in the black art of 3D distribution without changing anything in the infrastructure (aside from the STB in the living room). The objective is to push data payloads into the distribution tubes that will be decoded into 3D by an STB that is based on the same hardware as a Phase 1. The magic trick here is called *non-canonical (NC) frame size*: two NC frames together have the same number of macroblocs as one 2D image, in order to stay in the computational envelope of existing chips' hardware design. Here are the numbers:

- A 1080i is formatted in two 1344×768 frames, rather than two anamorphic 960×1080 frames.
- A 720p is formatted in two 960×544 frames rather than two anamorphic 1280×360 frames.

The decoded frames are then up-scaled to a canonical HD format, and sent to the 3D TV as full 3D.

PACKAGED MEDIA: BLU-RAY 3D

Blu-ray is expected to be the format of choice for 3D distribution, with strong proponents among the biggest and smallest content creators. Big studios can't wait to monetize their 3D movies on the home market; after all, 50% of 2D

revenues are from DVD sales. All of a sudden, the 2.5x revenue gain of 3D theater exhibition turns into a mere 25% increase. Small independent 3D filmmakers have realized that the battle for scarce 3D screens is a tough one, and
that there's a need for a direct-to-video channel in 3D too.

As of today, there are actually two 3D Blu-ray standards: official and informal.
The official 3D-BD (3D Blu-ray Disc) is a new format designed and promoted
by the Blu-ray Disc Association. It requires 3D encoders and 3D authoring,
and it delivers full-frame 3D. The informal 3D format is frame-compatible 3D,
obviously: side-by-side or top-and-bottom footage recorded on a regular 2D
disk. If you go that route, pay attention to designing the menus in 3D too, so
that the navigation does not requires switching on and off the 3D mode on
the TV. While you're at it, make both left and right occurrences of the buttons
active, so that the user doesn't have to guess which one should be clicked. Sony
Vegas Pro10 can export your 3D edits on SBS Blu-rays.

The following are full 3D-BD encoders and authoring suites:

- NetBlender Encoder: http://www.netblender.com/main/
- Sony Blu-print: http://www.sonycreativesoftware.com/bluprint
- Main Concept MVC Encoder: http://www.mainconcept.com/products/
  sdks/3d/blu-ray-3dmvc-sdk.html

In addition to these, Roxio is also working on a 3D version of its tools.

INTERNET DELIVERY

On the Internet, 3D video is spreading like wildfire. TubePlus has had a 3D
player since 2009; Netflix is offering 3D video on demand; Next3D is a dedicated service; and Sony PlayStation will also soon have a 3D channel. Samsung
has announced it will distribute 3D content, and Nvidia already does it, with
live events broadcasted on the Internet.

Underground distribution has already started, with FTP services in northern
Europe that host hundreds of gigabytes of 3D content of all levels of legality.

The 3D medium is the perfect content for IP delivery, with a low audience density that is highly technophile and connected. YouTube 3D is now part of the
Google video monetization service. (What will be the first viral 3D video to hit
a million views? Our bet is a 3D lolcat of Puss in Boots.)

Our point is: more than anywhere, the medium of 3D will not be fighting for
its spot on the Internet, because it is part of geek culture.

Both Roxio and Sony consumer 2D editing tools offer the option to upload
videos to YouTube directly from the timeline. How long before one can upload
full-resolution 3D trailers to Internet servers from an Avid?

Theatrical Distribution

DIGITAL

Digital 3D film distribution relies on the DCI specification. 3D DCPs are
frame-alternative 48fps Jpeg-2000 image streams. The encoding service is

The DCI spec
sheet: http://www
.dcimovies.com/specification/
Clyde's DCP recipe: http://
realvision.ae/blog/2010/09/
free-unencrypted-3d-movie-dcp-
mastering-for-digital-cinema-
servers/

usually provided by the digital intermediate (DI) house, where you will color-time your master. If you want to encode a short movie, trailer, or any content that does not need encryption and right managements, Clyde de Sousa published a recipe for homemade 3D DCPs on his blog, RealVision.

FILM-BASED

There may be thousands of digital 3D projectors in the United States, and tens of thousands on their way. There are hundreds of thousands of film projectors in the U.S., and a few million in the world. How will 3D content reach this audience? Some industry leaders are betting on innovative 3D-on-film distribution technologies to feed that market.

In 2010, Technicolor presented a film-based 3D projection system using an above/below image format on a 35mm support, with a periscope lens attachment that polarizes and realigns pictures on the screen. Such systems had already been used in the 1950s, the so-called golden age of 3D, but they had caused problems when, in the event of a film rupture, projectionists fixed the support by slicing out one frame. This inverted the left/right alternation of images, and subsequently presented *inverted stereo* to the audience. Addressing this headache-triggering hazard in 2010, 3D inventor Lenny Lipton introduced another system a few months after Technicolor. In this system, the images are recorded side by side on the filmstrip, and adequately rotated and realigned by a patented 3D lens attachment.

Occulus: http://
www.oculus3d.com

Technicolor: http://www
.technicolor.com/en/hi/3d/3d-in-the-
theatre

Panavision: http://3d
.panavision.com/

These two solutions are aimed at helping retrofit tens of thousands of existing 35mm projectors in the United States for a fraction of the cost of a complete digital replacement. They should help spread the 3D renaissance to worldwide locations where the money for a digital 3D projection system does not exist.

Formatting and printing your 3D movie with these processes should be discussed with your various vendors.

IMAX: http://www.imax.com/
impact/imax-3d/

For absolute completeness, we should mention the IMAX 3D process with dual-strip 70mm 15 perforations. IMAX employs a proprietary digital-to-print mastering system: the DMR (digital re-mastering).

CHAPTER 5
Stereoscopic Experience from the Front Lines

LOW-FX 3D FEATURE
Derrière les Murs

Céline Tricart, Binocle, France

Céline Tricart recently graduated from the ENS (École Nationale Supérieure) Louis Lumière film school in Paris. She is an independent filmmaker who is particularly interested in storytelling for stereoscopic cinema. She has already directed several shorts, two of which were shot in 2k 3D, and has received many awards around the world. At the present time she is preparing her own new narrative stereoscopic projects and shooting 3D for other filmmakers as a stereographer. She is working now as the stereographer for the first French 3D feature film, *Behind the Walls*, from directors Julien Lacombe and Pascal Sid (Sombrero Films).

FIGURE 5.1
Céline Tricart.

Can you briefly describe the 3D production you worked on?

Derrière les Murs is a feature with a budget of 4 million euros produced by Sombrero Films, a French production company specializing in genre movies. It's *Huis clos* [*No Exit,* 1954] set in the 1920s, about a female novel writer in the French back country. We shot it over eight weeks, in June and July of 2010, in the Auvergne and Poitou areas. One quarter of the shots were outside, and three quarters were inside, including houses, train stations, and underground caves.

How was the experience regarding the camera setup procedures?

In the morning, it took us about 30 to 45 minutes from when the truck arrived on location until we were ready to shoot. There were many inside shots where we were ready before the lights were set up and tuned. For the outside shots, that's another story. There's no light to set up;

FIGURE 5.2
Shooting *Derrière les Murs*. Two Genesis cameras on a Binocle Brigger III 3D rig.

the camera position is usually the last decision made, so the crew was basically waiting for us to be ready. That's the same experience as being the FX supervisor on a shoot. You are the last to set up before the shoot rolls on, and you feel like everybody wonders what you are doing.

We eventually timed ourselves, and we were able to change lenses in as little as 7 minutes; however, with long focal, it was much more complex, and our average time was closer to 20 minutes. The most complex rig manipulation was *low mode,* where the reflective camera looks down the mirror; we needed that configuration to get the camera very close to the ground, down to 5 cm rather that 30 cm. (You want to avoid this for normal shots, because the mirror catches more dust.) Turning the whole rig upside down and recalibrating the lenses took us 15 to 30 minutes, depending upon the focal length. Do that twice to get back to normal configuration, and it's an average of 40 minutes of lost time. However, we managed to get these shots first thing in the morning or last thing at night, so that the time waste was halved.

What was your camera unit composed of?

We shot with Panavision Genesis, Primo lenses, on a Binocle Brigger III. We recorded most shots on the Panavision Solid State Recorder, the SSR-1 flash disk. They are great for 3D. On the docking station, it can record 25 minutes of 4:2:2 3D before you send it to be copied onto tape or disk.

There were also a few green screen shots, which we recorded dual stream 4:4:4 on Codex. This piece is enormous: one cubic meter, noisy, and heavy. Still you need one to record hours of uncompressed full resolution at full color depth.

As for monitoring, we used Binocle's Disparity Tagger, which would warn us of any image symmetry issues. It was on a rolling table, with a 22-inch 3D display used by the stereographer and director to discuss the depth settings. We frequently used the "final corrected frame" onscreen display, which shows the eventual image area when it is shot (which needs to be stereo balanced in post). Additionally, the split-screen mode and the wiggle 3D preview modes were very useful in detecting specular lights, which are always troublesome in 3D.

FIGURE 5.3
The Binocle Tagger image processor on location.

How large was the 3D crew?

We were two stereographers, one supervisor, and one assistant. There were three assistant camera operators taking care of the two Genesis, and one additional ripper for the rig. This was needed for the total weight; with the rig slates and the mirror box, the two cameras, and the recorder, the whole thing was 46 Kg.

Can you describe the experience of a stereographer joining a movie crew?

It is a very interesting challenge to find your sweet spot in a movie crew. You have to make your way to your position at the heart of a complex hierarchy that has been patiently tuned over a century. The relationship between the director and his or her DP is a very subtle one—and then you show up one morning, interfering with both of them. You have to build a close relationship with the DP, and he usually wonders how much you are going to impede on his creativity tools, how much the 3D is going to dictate the cinematography, the lighting, etc. The truth is, the first week was a bit rough. However, then it started to go very well, because the 3D did not impede on anybody's job—just the opposite, actually. 3D forces everybody to go one step further, and pays back for the effort. I came to feel that the additional requirements of stereoscopy presented a challenge for the whole crew, who, in return, started to appreciate it.

One interesting example of this was the set dressing. Glossy and shiny surfaces are an issue with 3D. This started out being an annoyance to the prop staff—but very soon they get into it, and would never hesitate to come to us with new props they found that would do well in 3D, with nice textures and no brilliance. They seemed to enjoy it as a new treasure hunt.

And what about stereoscopic creativity?

On the one hand, there is nothing new under the sun, and we just confirmed that theory on an even larger scale. On the other hand, we gathered an incredible amount of experience in only two months.

To me, the 3D effect is composed of three feelings: immersion, realism, and the wow factor. Every movie has its very own blend of the three. *Derrière les Murs* has zero wow effect: it's only immersive and realistic 3D. That said, we still alternate rest sequences with more strong 3D, as in any stereoscopic movie.

Regarding focal length, we used a lot of 27 mm; in two-shots and over-the-shoulder shots, the 50 mm just doesn't do it. This is a paradigm shift for the DP. In 2D, the 50 mm is the golden number, the beauty shot, the perfect perspective that matches the human field of view. In 3D, that's somewhere in the 35 to 40 mm range. The problem is having enough leverage to convince everyone of this. This is difficult, because we would only have been able to see it to its full extent at the dailies, and we had no access to 3D projection. I took it upon myself to get one day back in Paris to check the footage on a DI suite, and that's how I confirmed that the specular would be an issue that we needed to address, no matter what. However, it was not easy to convey it to the crew back on location. For this reason, rehearsals and test shots with all the supervisors, light, and props managers are a must. Period.

What would you do differently?

3D dailies. This is crucial. We did not have the budget to move around a digital projector, or to rent a 3D theater, and we missed it a lot. I hope next time we'll have a solution that fits the production.

FIGURE 5.4
Shooting *Derrière les Murs*.

LIVE 3D TV SPORTS BROADCAST
RIP Curl World Cup of Surfing

Jordi Alonso, MediaPro, Spain

Jordi Alonso is a native of Barcelona, Spain; he has a bachelor of science in computer science, a master of arts in computer animation techniques, and is studying for a master of science in photonics. He is also an entrepreneur who started a business in computers in 1985. He has been a technical writer on computer graphics and 3D since the late 1990s for newspapers, magazines, and websites. He has participated in a variety of radio programs, and in 2009–2010 he hosted a weekly program talking about stereoscopy. He has worked as a cinema school teacher; a Softimage, Avid, and Brainstorm reseller; and a website developer, producer, freelance CG artist, VFX supervisor, and technical supervisor on feature film. In 2006 and 2007 he became CEO of cine.com, which he cofounded in 2002, to try to push a VoD service. In late 2007 he decided to dedicate himself full-time to live action stereoscopy, launching the website cine3D.com, and started to shoot HD-3D footage.

FIGURE 5.5
Jordi Alonso.

In late 2008 Jordi joined Mediapro, where he co-leads 3D initiatives with the research department, as a senior researcher. With his team he participates in the European research projects IP-Racine, 2020 3D Media, Apidis, Project FINE, and the Spanish projects i3media and Immersive TV, among others.

Since 2009, Jordi has also been involved as 3D technology consultant and producer in the 3D live productions of the MediaPro group, with technology partner Kronomav and Portugal-based company Medialuso. His main tasks are the development of live 3D tools, 3D workflow, 3D OB van design, and crew training.

FIGURE 5.6
Shooting RIP Curl World Cup of Surfing, in Peniche, Portugal.

Can you briefly describe the 3D production you worked on?

From September 11 through 14 of 2010, we produced the RIP Curl World Cup of Surfing, in Peniche, Portugal, for Medialuso. *RIP Curl Surf World Cup 2010—3D Experience* was shot and broadcast simultaneously in SD, HD, and 3D for up to 5 hours each day. The audience was made up of the cable subscribers of MEO, a cable provider in Portugal, as well as the people attending the event, through different 3D TV screens installed in booths near the beach. We shot for TV screen sizes; on the beach, our larger screen was a 52-inch 3D TV. The event was broadcasted live in 3D only to MEO subscribers, and it likely will be broadcasted as a recorded event later on, maybe even sold through electronic retailers or as a 3D Blu-ray disc.

What lead-up time did you have to set up for the event?

We had to improvise on a daily basis, due to weather changes affecting the wind and the waves. In less than 12 hours, we had to pack everything and move the OB vans and wires and deploy everything in another beach, a few kilometers away from the previous location. Our overall setup time was less than two hours.

What was your production infrastructure?

We had the main HD OB van, the 3D OB van, and the satellite link van. The 3D camera fleet included:

- Five positions with Grass Valley LDK 8000 Elite (ten cameras)
- One position with Toshiba's 3 CCD Mini (two cameras)
- One Panasonic 3D camera

As for rigs, we used five Kronomav fully motorized side-by-side rigs, and one fixed rig for the beauty shot. The LDKs were set up for very long distance shots, and thus fitted with powerful zooms and duplicators.

The 3D positions were up to 350 m away from the action. Regarding wires, we had one 3D position as far as 1 Km from the OB van, so we needed fiber optics for rig-to-OB van data communications. The Panasonic 3D camera was autonomous and connected through dual RF to the OB van. It was used for interviews with surfers and public reactions from the beach.

We mixed on a Grass Valley HD mixer and recorded on EVS XT[2]+ for replays and slow motions, plus Sony HD Cam for archiving. The monitoring was done on a Samsung active monitor with 3D glasses, and the satellite uplink was formatted in side-by-side frame-compatible and encoded on MPEG4 at 25 Mbps.

Can you describe the crew in charge of the stereoscopic production?

Our production staff was composed of the following:

- One stereographer (Ramon Dolz, Kronomav)
- One research engineer (Mediapro Research)
- Five convergence pullers (Medialuso and Kronomav)
- One director (Gustavo Fonseca, Medialuso)
- One EVS replay (Medialuso)
- Six camera operators
- All the support staff for engineering and communications were from Medialuso

What did you learn on the production?

About the equipment:

You'll understand I cannot comment extensively on this part. But I will mention that on the equipment, with so much zoom, plus the duplicator, any vibration is magnified, and even the minor ones are noticed in 3D. There are also some changes introduced in the cameramen's viewfinder positions.

As for procedures, we had to elaborate a detailed checklist, set up each position, and do the lens calibration. Some mistakes were made because we were not strict enough in following the checklist; as a result, new items had to be added to the list. For example, due to transportation and very bumpy, sandy roads, a computer card was detached from its slot, and we learned that it's important to double-check stereo processor cases, even if they were working fine the day before.

Regarding creative stereoscopy:

We learned three things with respect to creative stereoscopy:

- Slow-motion shots are the best shots.
- We expected cardboarding due to the use of long zooms, but the images were really great in 3D.
- We should have had a 3D cameraman in the water, for close shots of waves and surfers. Subjective shots were discarded; we were not allowed to install cameras on the surfboards or surfers.

What would you do differently?

I was not pleased with the quality of the Toshiba Mini cameras, and I don't think I would use them again. Additionally, it was not easy to deploy wires for such long distances in such a short time; next time, I hope we can leave the wires on location and move from one beach to the other depending on the wave conditions.

What was the feedback from the audience and your client?

Watch the video clip—they were extremely satisfied: (http://www.youtube.com/watch?v=zEckoGCYMkY).

Surfers were impressed after seeing their wave rides: (http://www.youtube.com/watch?v=zEckoGCYMkY).

FIGURE 5.7
Shooting RIP Curl World Cup of Surfing, in Peniche, Portugal.

All in all, the event gave us excellent press coverage.

LIVE 3D CONCERT RECORDING
Doc Walker Concert

Al Caudullo, 3DGuy.tv, Philippines

Al Caudullo utilized his thirty-plus years of video production experience as a foundation for stereoscope image capture. Sandy Climan, 3D industry icon and CEO of 3ality Digital, referred to Al as "a 3D evangelist."

After mastering 3D production techniques, Al created and taught Asia's first 3D production class at Mahidol University, Bangkok. In addition to training, he uses his vast 3D know-how to consult with major industry players on advancing their 3D hardware and software tools. His consulting clients include Panasonic Singapore Labs and Spatial View. He also works with Panasonic Japan on its worldwide 3D education initiative.

FIGURE 5.8
Al Caudullo.

As principal of Al Caudullo Productions, Al served as 3D stereographer and 3D editor on many projects, including film, TV, and corporate production. His clients include Panasonic, Hitachi, NVidia, Imagimax Studios, Spatial View, Toyota, and Wealth TV.

FIGURE 5.9
Side-by-Side Rig on Location. A pair of Sony EX3s shooting the Doc Walker concert in Kelowna, Canada.
Image courtesy of Al Caudullo.

Can you briefly describe the 3D production you worked on?

Charles Harring, with Wealth TV of San Diego, California, hired us to shoot a Doc Walker concert in Kelowna, Canada, on July 20, 2010. The 8:00 p.m. to 12:00 a.m. outdoor concert was a free attendance music event produced especially for DVD and BD shooting.

What lead-up time did you have to set up for the event?

We had only 18 days to get ready for the show. We arrived on site on the 19th day, and did the camera setup on the day of shooting.

What was your production infrastructure?

We had two Sony EX3s and two Panasonic AG-3Ds; no beam-splitter rig was used.

Position 1 was on the hilltop, our backdrop camera. There we set up the two EX3s, with a tri-level external sync generator, mounted side by side on a tripod, recording on 32 Gb SDHC cards. Monitoring was on a DIY 3D monitor made of two LCDs and one half-mirror turning polarization. I manned that position.

Position 2 was on stage. We placed one Panasonic AG-3D on a half circle dolly track. It was recording on 32 Gb SDHC cards, and the monitoring was on the camera's LCD, manned by Tim Dashwood.

Position 3 was our run-and-gun camera. It went backstage and on stage, getting audience and band shots. That was our second Panasonic AG-3D, recording on 32 Gb SDHC cards, and monitoring on the camera's LCD. It was manned by Mark Bone.

What did you learn on the production?

About the equipment:

The AG-3D has an impressive visual quality, despite its 1/4-inch sensors. This is a very capable camera. In terms of definition, it mixes very well with the EX3 pictures that originated on a 1/2-inch sensor. Still, we now have images that need to be matched, for they do come from cameras with a very different color behavior—but that's to be expected when you mix and match cameras from different vendors on a live shoot. That's something you never do in 2D; but in 3D, you have to use the available gear.

Tim has a few marvels in development, and we tried a couple of beta systems on this show. (I'll let him reveal these tools when and where he decides to; you can expect to see him at trade shows with amazing news.) Unfortunately, though, the power source over there, with all the lights and sound systems drawing on it, was not reliable enough, and we experienced a couple glitches during preshow tests. As a result, we could not use his tools for the real shot. It was a pity.

I won't give too many details, but one tool is an amazing white balance system for pairing 3D cameras. Two 2D cameras will never have the same color behavior—not even because of the mirror effect, but because their internal LCDs do not match. Getting them to color match is an endless battle, unless you use calibration tools designed for 3D like Tim's.

Regarding creative stereoscopy:

Tim pulled out great shots with moving backgrounds, even with the locked convergence. Because the dolly was on a semicircular track, the distance to the band was steady, and in most cases we didn't even have to reconverge in post. The free camera could get backstage and audience shots that would have been much harder to get with a 3D rig. This run-and-gun camera will be an amazing tool for 3D productions like documentaries and live TV.

Regarding camera positions:

Based on the metrics the production gave us, we originally planned to have an AG-3D at the top of the hill, but their distance estimation was so wrong that the IOD was eventually not adapted and the 3D was too shallow. We took apart the mirror rig that we planned would go on the dolly, and placed its two EX3s on a side-by-side mount. This created great 3D, where the miniaturization of the crowd and stage actually gave the feeling that the crowd was much larger than it really was.

What about the lighting conditions?

The show started at 8:00 p.m. and ended around midnight. We went through quite a wide set of light conditions, including the sunset at 9:10 p.m. We actually had a show break right after sunset to change stage lighting; we had huge blasters that shot light at the audience. We were afraid they'd mess up the images with flares and all sorts of direct light issues, but it eventually worked very well, with the flood of light helping to layer the 3D with all sorts of halo effects on the band and audience.

FIGURE 5.10
The AG3D-A1 on a Dolly. Shooting the Doc Walker concert in Kelowna, Canada. Operator: Tim Dashwood.
Image courtesy of Al Caudullo.

What would you do differently?

I would have brought a bigger JIB for the backdrop camera. The one we took could have handled the Panasonic AG-3D, but it was not strong enough to host the pair of EX3s. I wish I could have done sweeping shots from the audience onto the stage, and vice versa.

FIGURE 5.11
Doc Walker Wide Shot. Shooting the Doc Walker concert in Kelowna, Canada.
Image courtesy of Al Caudullo.

CHAPTER 6
Opinions on Creative Stereoscopy

RAY ZONE

Ray Zone is a 3D film producer, speaker, and award-winning 3D artist. Zone has produced or published over 130 3D comic books and is the author of *Stereoscopic Cinema and the Origins of 3D Film: 1838–1952* (University Press of Kentucky, 2007) and *3D Filmmakers: Conversations with Creators of Stereoscopic Motion Pictures* (Scarecrow Press, 2005). Zone's website is viewable in anaglyphic 3D at: www .ray3dzone.com.

FIGURE 6.1
Ray 3D Zone.

DEFECTIVE CINEMA: NOTES ON REPAIR

Ray Zone

In 1933, shortly after the invention and proliferation of sound motion pictures, philosopher and critic Rudolph Arnheim, in *Film as Art* (University of

California Press, 1957), wrote that "The temptation to increase the size of the screen goes with the desire for colored, stereoscopic, and sound film. It is the wish of the people who do not know that artistic effect is bound up with the limitations of the medium and who want quantity rather than quality. They want to keep on getting nearer to nature and do not realize that they thereby make it increasingly difficult for film to be art."

As an early theorist of cinematic art, Arnheim has isolated the fundamental artistic problem of the stereoscopic cinema. Very simply, it is this: technological advances leading to greater realism can create a corresponding loss of artistry. Raymond Spottiswoode, in *A Grammar of the Film* (University of California Press, 1950), shared similar concerns when writing in 1933 about the "unreality of the film image"; he was "exceedingly wary about the advantages of color (except in animated films) because [he] fears that it will prove yet another step on the road backward to a mere imitation of life" but noted that a few exceptional color films had "been able to move in the border world between abstraction and reality, and so share in the advantages of both."

Foreshadowing his later work with 3D movies, Spottiswoode also wrote:

> If the stereoscopic film were ever realized, it would seem that it too could enjoy these advantages. There is a world of solid shapes far removed from the luscious figures and glamorous interiors with which Hollywood will fill its stereoscopic movies. And beyond the third dimension looms the fourth. Even within the limits of present space, stereoptics can become a powerful instrument for transcending reality, not merely imitating it.

Both Arnheim and Spottiswoode had written these aesthetic commentaries about visual grammar in 1933 as sound film technology was driving a necessary reinvention of cinema narrative. A new narrative was then in a gradual process of replacing the universal pictorial language of the silent motion picture. The chief artistic glory of silent cinema, of primary usage, was montage. Spottiswoode defined montage as a "juxtaposition of shots, series, and sequences in such a way as to produce" a "concept or sensation through the mutual impact of other concepts or sensations." The bravura use of montage in silent cinema in the hands of filmmakers such as D.W. Griffith, Sergei Eisenstein, and others raised silent cinema to a level of filmic art.

Arnheim, however, was very clear about the advantage that the defect of flatness provided to the motion picture storyteller for the use of montage. "By the absence of colors, of three-dimensional depth, by being sharply limited by the margins on the screen, and so forth, film is most satisfactorily denuded of its realism," he wrote. "It is always at one and the same time a flat picture postcard and the scene of a living action. From this arises the artistic justification for what is called montage." It may have actually been the flatness of the motion picture screen, in fact, that made the use of montage necessary. "If film photographs gave a very strong spatial impression," observed Arnheim, "montage probably would be impossible. It is the partial unreality of the film picture that makes it possible."

A great struggle is now evident in the motion picture community, particularly with respect to professionals in the fields who write, direct, photograph, and edit the movies. These professionals have learned to speak a planar visual language. They have built their professional careers on, and become facile at working with, a fundamental defect of cinema. That deficiency is the flatness of the motion picture screen.

Now that digital technology has facilitated the repair of defective cinema, narrative artistry is at a loss. It no longer can readily resort to a familiar tool. A new language and new linguistics for z-axis storytelling are necessary. And, ironically, it is Sergei Eisenstein, one of the chief architects of the use of montage in cinema, who has perhaps most articulately suggested, even in vague outline, the importance of this new language. The "entire course of theatrical history," Eisenstein wrote, "through the centuries, at practically every step, unfailingly and consistently reveals the self-same tendency—distinct in its forms, yet single in purpose—to 'cover' the breach, to 'throw a bridge' across the gulf separating the spectator and the actor." In the last essay Eisenstein ever wrote, the master of montage characterized stereoscopic cinema as "a dream of unity between spectator and actor."

The stereoscopic realism now available to the motion picture storyteller can reinforce this dream of unity in the cinema. And it can drive equally well a narrative in the service of the abstract or the real. What is essential is the growth of a republic of dreamers equally adept at using the z-axis parameter for abstraction or realism in telling new stories on the stereoscopic screen.

The flatness of the motion picture screen is a defect of cinema. Photo by Ray Zone

FIGURE 6.2
The Cinema Screen.
Image courtesy of Ray 3D Zone.

YVES PUPULIN

Yves Pupulin is among the few movie professionals who had an early interest in the creative potential of stereoscopic 3D images. He started working on feature films in the 1980s as an AC, and then joined the French company Excalibur, where he supervised visual effects. As a true French stereoscopic cinema pioneer, Yves Pupulin spent twelve years developing new tools like dedicated camera motion control. He is one of the inventors of the first motion control 3D camera, and has worked on human brain and stereoscopy research. He is also one of the animators of the industry research ad-hoc group 3DLive. In 1998, he founded Binocle, a European leader in stereoscopic 3D movie and TV production.

Binocle was founded by cinematographers and engineers in order to create efficient stereoscopic production tools. This toolset includes 6-axis motorized camera rigs and software suites for real-time analysis and processing of 3D feeds. The Disparity Tagger is a GPU-based 3D monitoring and correction system dedicated to 3D TV and 3D cinema productions. The Disparity Killer is a software-only solution designed for 3D postproduction.

FIGURE 6.3
Yves Pupulin, Binocle Chairman.

TOWARDS A MISE-EN-SCÈNE FOR STEREOSCOPY

Yves Pupulin

The following are reflections on the status of stereoscopy today, with some specific focus on its *mise-en-scène*. These reflections emerged out of various meetings and conferences on the subject, and our intent is to clarify in which ways this technique is linked to others and to foresee its development from an aesthetic, historical, and economic standpoint. Can stereoscopy find a place within art history? Will it develop in parallel to cinema, or will it acquire its own mise-en-scène? Does it require a specific crew for its completion? Finally, we will consider stereoscopy in its current context, in order to envision its prospects.

Stereoscopy: A 3D Cinematography?

While the search for volumetric and spatial presentation punctuates art history, the conditions for the existence of a stereoscopic art form remain unclear. When we speak of stereoscopy today, we don't quite know whether it consists of an evolution of cinema, or of a cinema of its own kind. For this reason, we will begin by examining which distant or recent art forms can shed light on the relationship between stereoscopy and 2D.

Everyone knows cinema does not need volumetric presentation in order to exist. Fihman and Eyzikman, known for their work on holography, defined it as an industrial art, in the footsteps of Walter Benjamin. Let us consider the *industrial arts* simply as those requiring a technical device to enable their distribution on a great scale. This is the case for cinema, radio, and video. In order to define the specifics of stereoscopy, we ought to ask ourselves what particular status stereoscopy and holography can hold among them, as well as what relationship they have to one another and to technically more distant visual art forms such as painting and sculpture.

FIGURE 6.4A
Example of Bas-Relief. Lower half of the left pilaster, *The Gates of Hell,* Auguste Rodin.
Rodin Museum, Paris. Photography by Richard Kirsch.

FIGURE 6.4B
The Lovers. Example of bas-relief, detail from *The Gates of Hell,* Auguste Rodin.
Rodin Museum, Paris. Photography by Richard Kirsch.

FIGURE 6.4C
Example of Bas-Relief. Detail from *The Gates of Hell,* Auguste Rodin.
Rodin Museum, Paris. Photography by Richard Kirsch.

FIGURE 6.5A
The Thinker. Example of haut-relief sculpture, tympanum of *The Gates of Hell,* Auguste Rodin.
Rodin Museum, Paris. Photography by Richard Kirsch.

FIGURE 6.5B
Man Falling. Example of haut-relief sculpture, lower-left part of the tympanum, *The Gates of Hell,*
Auguste Rodin.
Rodin Museum, Paris. Photography by Richard Kirsch.

FIGURE 6.6
The Monument of the Burghers of Calais. Example of monumental sculpture, Auguste Rodin.
Rodin Museum, Paris. Photography by Richard Kirsch.

In stereoscopy, the technical devices and audience system are very close to those of cinema; this is because, in both cases, a screen in a dark room is being viewed. This is why stereoscopy is very often considered the natural evolution of 2D cinema; the new stage in cinematic techniques.

But does this perception, which seems to recognize the value of stereoscopy, give it a chance to exist viably and to become, like 2D cinema, an arena for a mise-en-scène constantly renewed, a practice reinvented each moment, on every set, in every editing room, in every auditorium, or on every color timing device?

A comparison with holography sheds light on this question. For when we speak of 3D, do we really speak of stereoscopy? Or is it rather, unconsciously, of holography, a truly volumetric presentation? It is clear that the definite rupture between cinema and 3D would be more on the side of holography.

The experience we have of holographic images does not enable us to know whether such images could be combined with the artistic practices of stereoscopy. However, while we are still unsure of the nature of the link between stereoscopy and holography from the point of view of a potential artistic continuity, there can be no doubt as to the discontinuity between 2D and holography or its stereoscopic attempt.

Table 6.1   Discontinuities in the Volumetric Visual Arts

Art		Dimensions		Continuity	
Classical Art	Industrial Art	Dimensions	View Point	Physiologic	Artistic
Painting	Photography	2D	Egocentric	Centered Perspectivism	Reference Space
Painting	Cinematography	2D	Egocentric	CP + Critical Frequency	Reference Space
Low Relief	Stereoscopy	2D½, or S3D	Egocentric	CP + CF + Stereoscopy Towards Discontinuity vs 2D	Continuity
High Relief	Stereoscopy in Negative Parallax	2D½, or S3D	Egocentric	Strong Discontinuity vs 2D	Towards Discontinuity vs 2D
Monumental Sculpture	Holography	Object 3D or Image 3D	Allocentric	Full Discontinuity vs 2D	Full Discontinuity vs 2D

It is interesting to raise this question because in the end we all dream of a truly 3D landscape. But to do stereoscopy while trying to create a holographic-type image comes down to creating in-your-face 3D, with too many invasive gimmicks. This practice, used on short films, could be damaging to the viewer's brain. It is impossible to strip stereoscopy away from the frame of the screen. The semblance of a holographic image by a stereoscopic image "off-the-screen" on a black background will long remain the limit of these practices.

Stereoscopy and 2D Cinema

The difference of operation between 2D cinema and holography is immediately obvious. But what is stereoscopy's place in relation to these two techniques? It gives an illusion of volume, but what sort of volume is it?

Painting, whether rupestrian, Renaissance, or modern, is unequivocal. It cannot be confused with sculpture, even if it presents a relief emerging from the canvas—such as Rainer's plane debris, or Rembrandt's rendering of the sleeve in *The Jewish Bride*—there can be no confusion with polychrome bas-relief.

Sculpture can be divided into two main categories: low and high relief on the one hand, and monumental sculpture on the other. If a parallel can be made between sculpture and 3D, we will suggest that low and high reliefs are more closely related to stereoscopy and monumental sculpture to holography.

Indeed, painting and low and high relief can only be observed from an angle inferior to 180 degrees, just as in cinema and stereoscopy. Moreover, certain conditions exist for their visibility (framing, architecture, projection screen) and part of the piece remains "invisible" to the viewers (related to the backside of its support).

In a sense, the stereoscopic image is similar to the $2\frac{1}{2}$D image (with depth) described by neurobiologist David Marr as an intermediate neuronal stage between the 2D retina and the 3D interpretation that reaches our conscience. Claude Baiblé, who teaches stereoscopy to aspiring cinematographers at the Louis Lumière National School in Paris, notices that images, whether in 2D or $2\frac{1}{2}$D, remain attached to their original point of view. The stereoscopic image does copy 3D reality but does not equate it: the viewer can move his head, stretch his neck, and the visual will remain the same, which is of course not the case in direct vision where each time the point of view is moved, a new appearance is created—a new glimpse—instantly convertible into O3D reality, allocentric, or centered on the object rather than the point of view.

The passage from $2D\frac{1}{2}$ to 3D (from "egocentric view field" to "reality before us") indeed implies that we access—by sliding or moving the eyes—a volumetric vision of objects (O3D) independent of the successive images: "what I am seeing is reality spatialized (I3D englobing O3D) and not a semitransparent hologram (I3D) or a stereoscopic image ($I2D\frac{1}{2}$) attached to my cyclopean eye." In cinema, moving the head has no effect on the image obtained; the image cannot, therefore, go beyond the stage of $2D\frac{1}{2}$ representation, and is besides fully dependent on a point of view previously imposed.

For more on this subject, readers fluent in French can refer to Claude Bailblé, "En relief, l'image et le son," *Cahier Louis-Lumière* 4 (June 2007): .

Stereoscopy: Disconnect or Continuity?

While common tools and techniques are sometimes shared, this criteria is not sufficient to differentiate art forms. We must also consider the use of these tools and techniques in relation to matter, to different dimensions, and to time. Photography cannot be reduced to a form of painting, no matter what practices they have in common. Photography is the result of a technical invention that allowed the emergence of a new art form.

The invention of cinema is one of combining techniques, adding to preexisting photography a chain of production where, in the end, an operation indistinguishable to the brain, but essential, takes place: an illusory movement brought on by the rapid projection of fixed images, the phi effect. For further exploration of the subject, readers fluent in French can look into Jacques Aumont and Michel Marie, *Dictionnaire théorique et critique du cinéma* (Paris: Nathan, 2002), page 65.

Moreover, it is the discovery of the critical frequency threshold, around 40 to 50 Hz, the threshold at which the brain no longer perceives the alternate lighting and shutting of the cinematic devices, that determines the frequency at which the images of a film are shot and projected. In the days of silent cinema, images were shot at 16 images per second and projected at 48 Hz. This was the result of adding two shutter blades to the intermittent sprocket, which made it possible to conceal the passage from one frame to the next in the image path, without perceiving image streaking on the screen (streaking being the vertical lines showing on the screen due to the sliding of nonocculted or improperly occulted images). The frequency of observation was thus of 48 Hz, or 3x16 images/second.

The transition to talkies brought shooting to 24 frames per second because of the reading speed of the sound reel in the projector. One of the two shutter blades disappeared and the frequency stayed at 48 Hz for the viewer's brain. The illusion of movement was thus maintained and cinema, as the art of moving images, maintained its conditions. Cinema includes photography, with its art of a fixed frame and light, 24 times per second, but cannot be reduced to it. Photography, the art of the fixed image, also does not disappear with cinema. The atemporal aspect of photography, linked to the contemplation of one sole image, is described by Roland Barthes in *La Chambre Claire* (*Camera Lucida*). In it, we see the photograph of a young American man waiting for his execution, over a century ago, for whom we "continue to fear." Photography had created a unique relationship to time, which was redefined with cinematography—for the latter adds to the dimension of time that of movement.

Certain techniques can also be practiced in different individual art forms, and be combined to allow for the emergence of new art forms (without particularly affecting the viewer's physiological functioning). The passage of cinema from silent to sound is indeed the adjunction of radiophonic art with cinematic art. Both radio and cinema survived, but cinema exclusively comes with sound from this integration on. The relationship between sound and image creates a new dimension inside of cinema, without changing the technical parameters of the image but enriching it. A play begins between image and sound. Indeed, cinema editing has contributed to developing the editing of radio shows, and vice versa. If a filmmaker such as Alain Resnais enjoys listening to the radio, it is most likely not just for pleasure and knowledge, but also for its endless invention of sound editing (temporal, amongst other things). The same goes for the passage from black and white to color, which, however, was not irreversible.

Cinema is sometimes described as the synthesis of all the arts. Today, it can be enriched with stereoscopy without disappearing in its 2D form. There is no reason why it should become an ancestor of stereoscopy if the latter adds an artificial reproduction of depth and volume to the illusion of movement and time.

However, we need to insist upon the fact that sound and color have transformed cinema without changing its relationship to the viewer's cerebral function. With stereoscopy, we have to reconsider the functioning of the brain and the conditions under which we must film and project the images. It is the first time since the invention of cinema that this problem has arisen. We have been able to make 3D films for a century, thanks to the anaglyphic projection of left and right images onto one sole support; however, anaglyphs are not satisfying for the brain, because of their drawbacks: loss of color, ghosting, and great visual strain. Starting in the 1950s, synchronized double projection and polarization to separate the eyes partially solved the issue; still, it was impossible to produce stereoscopic couples without disparities and with a lack of fixity for the brain. Stereoscopy had to wait for the advent of digital in order to develop, because of the ability to systematically correct images pixel by pixel and of the now perfect fixity of projection.

In this stage of stereoscopy's history, we notice its ambivalence. It falls on an aesthetic and technical plane in the continuity of cinema, but it is not yet an art on its own. There is no such thing as a purely stereoscopic aesthetic; indeed, we constantly use a glossary and notions borrowed from cinema to approach stereoscopy.

Nonetheless, it creates a physiological rupture, just as the differences between photography and cinema did. Here, the reproduction of depth of varying geometries reinvents an interpretation of space, imagined by the director.

Now, as far as the process of making a film, how must we think of this ambivalence? Does the physiological rupture also imply a rupture in the mise-en-scène practices? Is there continuity between the processes of shooting in 2D and in stereoscopy?

There are technical parameters specific to the stereoscopic mise-en-scène: convergence and interaxial. Today, we have tools at our disposal that enable us to manage and master these specifically stereoscopic parameters. Yet, only experience allows us to anticipate the limits of using 2D mise-en-scène elements inside a 3D production. This might constrain or restrain the possibilities of reusing your 2D mise-en-scène palette of tools.

The problem is the emergence of visual discomfort for the viewer—this is what will limit the combined use of parameters from 2D and 3D mise-en-scène. Digital techniques make it possible to avoid or to correct some of these disagreements. By working on the combination of these parameters, within the limits inherent to the physiological specificity of stereoscopy, an artistic expression specific to stereoscopy can emerge. However, for this to happen, it will be necessary to identify the given limits in order to determine, for each 2D and 3D technical parameter and their combined use, the possibilities offered to the stereoscopic mise-en-scène.

Parameters for 2D Cinema, 3D Stereoscopy, and 3D Holography

With regards to its image parameters, 2D cinema is mainly defined by the following:

- The point of view.
- The frame and its movement, integrating the subject's movement as a spatial decoupage.

- The lighting of the framed subject.
- The editing, taking its visual and rhythmical aspects into account.

In this discussion, we will leave aside the scenic parameters, such as the acting, the set and accessories, the costumes, the make-up, and so on, which are grouped under the category that qualifies the "subject" as "an object cast into light" as defined by Guinot and Pommard in their photometry class at the École Nationale Supérieure Louis Lumière.

How will these parameters of 2D cinematography coexist or be transformed in 3D visual arts, formed by stereoscopy on the one hand and holography on the other?

POINT OF VIEW

Cinema remains first and foremost a matter of *point of view:* the place from which we observe the object we are about to frame, light, and film. It is the point from which the director wishes the viewer to observe the world, and specifically the scene that is taking place before the camera. When a movement of the camera is involved, the evolution of the point of view makes sense, but also adds, by the variation of surfaces of lights and shadows, a graphic rhythm to the 2D image.

During the location scouting or preparation of a 3D film, it is necessary to have a viewfinder in order to locate the different axes and focal lengths, just as in 2D. To scope out the volumetric landscape itself is also important, and at this stage requires no other tool than visual observation. For this, we need to converge on the position of the subject, which occurs naturally, and at the same time on infinity, in order to scope out the succession of volumes in depth and their evolution in the simulation of the camera movement we wish to obtain. This scoping of volumes is crucial.

Volume can often be better appreciated during movement, when we are close to the subject, and with a rather short focal length. But it is difficult to make a film without close-ups; therefore, the scoping out of the set's volumes becomes decisive for the placement of the actors, and the point of view becomes decisive for the distribution of volumes in depth and along the edges of the frame.

In holography, we see an object reconstituted with light that can be observed from all sides. The viewer's place becomes indifferent, and the holographic filmmaker will no longer assign one single point of view. Therefore, because of this viewer's place, the audience system of cinema itself is questioned, or perhaps abandoned.

THE FRAME

The precision of the cinematic frame is one of the essential parameters of shooting. Its rules, whether they are bypassed or not, are very precise, and often come from painting. Throughout the centuries, painting evolved from a subject described in its entirety or a portrait as the identification of a character, to the cutting of the body into fragments evoking a suggestion—a play with the frame and the out-of-frame.

The frame is what the painter, and now the director, gives the audience to see. Its exactness in 2D cinema is one of the fundamental parameters of the image. It can escape no one, be they professionals or viewers; it cannot be crowded by elements that do not belong in it, and its value is always intentional.

In stereoscopy, the frame is imprecise.

Even though stereoscopy is projected onto a 2D screen, the precision of the frame is lost in comparison to 2D, because of the zones of disparity around its depth created by binocular shooting allowing stereoscopic vision. Anything entering the field on the edge of the frame is visible by one eye before the other. This is generally irrelevant if the volumetry is soft and the subject is in a zone with moderate contrast. This visual discrepancy is not easily quantifiable today and is the result of an accumulation of parameters that will make it acceptable or not. In all cases, just as in low and high relief, the edge of the frame becomes imprecise; for elements to pop out requires the use of floating windows. In bas-relief, objects on the edge of the frame—in this case, cast into the material, as seen on many historical buildings—present various details in depth that can even go outside of the sculpted frame. There is no way to solve this imprecision, for if the sculptor were to place a frame inside of the first frame, he or she would still face the indecision of the edges of this included frame.

The stereoscopic frame presents analogous imprecision. When the subject stands in the depth of the image and a rectilinear element stands on the edge of the projection window, the frame can give an illusion of perfection. However, this imprecision, rather than being detrimental, can become one of the elements of stereoscopic mise-en-scène; a high-angle zoom on a landscape of hills or on the bark of a tree can give an idea of the variations enclosed within the projection frame itself. Finally, the imprecision of the frame is different from the variation of the frame linked to image correction.

This imprecise value of the stereoscopic frame pushes some stereographers towards conceiving an evermore immersive experience for the viewer (for example, by enlarging the projection screen in order to push back the perceivable limits of the frame).

As for holographic technique, the frame from the screen has disappeared. We are seeing a subject created thanks to structured light, and, just as in monumental sculpture, we can therefore, in theory, walk around it. There is no longer a hidden side. We could imagine a decoupage in terms of frames, we could easily picture a bust placed in the middle of the audience—but can the out-of-frame still exist?

There might be two types of holography: one that could be observed from the outside, just as in theater or the circus, and the other from the inside, in an immersive space, just as if we were placed inside a snowball, which is done in certain installations.

LIGHT

In cinema, the subject, as a lit object, can receive any contrast and any of its temporal modulations, only limited by cinematographic support. It consists of, on the one hand, the source of white light, and on the other, the complete shutting off of this source, which the viewer can read as the contrast ratio of the screen. The emulsion, either as a support almost entirely transparent or as a black image, causing a near complete obturation, has been used in all eras of cinema—to suggest a storm, for example, or the repeated explosions of a battle or a fire. While there is a blinding effect that forbids the lengthy repetition of these successions of on and off, nothing on a physiological level will cause any damage as long as the norms for lighting and contrast on projection screens are respected. The blinding effect is part of the mise-en-scène, and its purpose is to provide emotion, not to damage the viewer's vision.

In 2D cinematography, light and contrast are only limited by projection norms and the power of the projector. However, the case is very different for stereoscopy. In 3D, high-contrast shots, particularly towards the edges, through foliage, via backlighting, or amongst the different components of the subject, can trigger a real cerebral discomfort for the viewer. This is also linked to stereoscopic occlusion, due to two separate points of view and to ghosting. This occlusion is the result of the contrast on the filmed subject, of the depth bracket, and of the projection device on the viewer's brain. To gauge them is even trickier, as other phenomena can further complicate this analysis, such as the polarizing effect of the beam-splitter mirror or the light interaction with different surfaces.

Lowering the contrast is therefore advised, though we cannot yet today quantify by how much. Our tools must evolve from shooting to projection. During shooting, the sensors must cover a greater dynamic in order to obtain images able to maintain volume in highlights and shadows. These sensors will enable a better adjustment of contrast during the color timing of stereoscopic movies. The material for perceiving 3D must also progress, the glasses in particular. Manufacturers are working on this.

In holography, structured light seems to emanate from the subject itself, and there is no longer a projection frame. The holographic reproduction of a subject might reach a realism of shapes and matter that we can hardly imagine today.

EDITING

In cinema, the shortest clip is only limited by the length of projection of one image; in television, it is limited by the display of the interlaced field. The longest clip, on the other hand, is limited by the duration of the program or of the film itself, such as in Hitchcock's *Rope* (1948), which was actually constructed of a few shots with quasi-indiscernible splicing, or in *Russian Ark* (2002), which Aleksandr Sokurov filmed in a single 96-minute sequence shot, at the State Hermitage Museum in St. Petersburg.

Editing in stereoscopy is naturally slower, since, in a new shot, it takes about one second for the brain to appreciate the new universe to be explored in its depth. Editing does exist, but, again, the limitation of the duration of short shots is directly linked to the cerebral strain resulting from it. There is a hypothesis that you can reduce the accommodation time at each change of shot, because a viewer becomes more accustomed to 3D during the course of viewing. This seems unlikely, but it is difficult to definitely dismiss at this point.

During postproduction, a dissolve enables a smoother transition from one shot to another for volumetric landscapes that are too different. Generalizing these practices can ease the cerebral discomfort and shorten the adaptation time between each shot, but can more difficultly eliminate it.

In practice, stereoscopic editing must be done from geometry-corrected images. However, this is not always possible, usually either for financial reasons or the availability of tools.

During a 2D editing process, the visual discomfort resulting from the lack of color continuity can interfere with the editor's decisions as to the choice of clip and cutting point, but its effects on strain and work are known and limited. In stereoscopy, the choice of a cutting point can be affected by different depth values between shots, and even more so by the uncorrected disparity between images. There are then four opportunities—depth and uncorrected rivalries added to action and unmatched colorimetry—for experiencing visual discomfort when reviewing a splicing point, while there are only two in 2D. For this reason, we must eliminate the one resulting from uncorrected disparities right from the start.

If a holographic mise-en-scène can be reduced to a continuity of a stage play or of a Roman circus show, it therefore adheres to the theatrical rules of unity of time and place; we have trouble imagining what a montage could be without experiencing the transition between the holograms. Thus we do not know whether a montage would remain possible in the sense of editing shot by shot, instead of a systematic succession of fade-to-blacks. Also, how would the entrance of a new character be managed?

An Example of Ambivalence and Shooting Decisions: Depth of Field

When Binocle built the first motion control camera in 1997 and 1998, which featured motorization of zooms, stereoscopic parameters, and real-time display, it shed light on a very interesting phenomenon. When the optical axis and the images were exactly the same, one saw a 2D image, with or without glasses. As soon as the optical axes were distanced from the cameras, however, the 3D appeared. It was detected more or less rapidly, depending on the observer, but became visible, in a prominent way, with only a few millimeters of interaxial. When 2D shots were inserted in a montage between 3D shots with a low interaxial, certain viewers perceived a continuity of volume rather than the discontinuity that was expected with going from stereoscopy to 2D then back to stereoscopy. This phenomenon is even more striking on shots with depth continuity.

During the capture of a Julien Clerc concert in 2009, a 2D camera framing an extreme wide shot of the audience and the stage revealed the skyline of Lyon, and the continuity effect made it evident that it was within the brain's capacity to create a 3D vision from a 2D shot, edited between stereoscopic images. This effect is not perceived by all individuals, independently of their status as professionals or audience members.

Similar observations had been made by viewers of Hitchcock's 3D film *Dial M for Murder* (1954), in response to the numerous 2D shots that were inserted inside of the 3D sequences, some of which remained invisible for some viewers. With the use of image-correction software, this phenomenon is even more pertinent because of the complete absence of accidental disparities between images, which creates a gentler progression of 2D towards 3D and between the different 3D shots. In such cases, the brain perceives continuity rather than the actual split between the two techniques.

To dwell further on these questions, we must ponder the stereoscopic shooting experience. Dealing with the depth of field, for example, is a very important component of a 2D image, since it enables a centering of the mise-en-scène on the subject. This is all the more convincing if the subject is a simple one. Limiting the depth of field on a filmed object, such as the face of an actress, is often desired for photogenic reasons or to soften the part of the face cut by the frame, but it is done mainly to enhance the intensity of the acting and of the eyes. Camera operators therefore add up neutral densities in front of the lenses in order to limit the depth of field.

The adverse effects of focus blur in stereoscopy have been documented. What is really the reason for this, other than the fact that it is not desirable to shoot all films with an 11 aperture? Experience makes certain observations evident: if the volumetry is soft, the contrast is reasonable in zones of high disparity, and the viewer's gaze is not attracted to the blurry zones, then it is perfectly acceptable. On the close-up of an actress, a sharp volumetry would, of course, not be photogenic.

Binocle did some tests on limiting the depth of field on feature-length trailers for such films as the forthcoming *The Krostons*, directed by Frederik Du Chau. The result proves satisfying up to a certain limit, at which point there is indeed a discontinuity or disconnect in what the brain can tolerate.

Limiting the depth of field in 2D is not only aesthetic, it is also narrative or meaningful. In the film *Husbands* (1970), directed by John Cassavetes, a man and a woman are sitting on the edge of a bed in a bedroom in London. We see them full-face. They lie down on the bed one after the other, and meet in a limited depth of field when they get back up. Naturally, this passage tells of the relation between the characters, and thus evokes the relationship between women and men. Limiting the depth of field is also used on exterior shoots, when one wants to center an action by the depth of field, as in the case of the face. It is also a matter of avoiding unimportant details that could crowd and interfere with the shot.

The importance of the use of the technical parameters of 2D as artistic parameters is fundamental in 3D. Consider that 2D has a depth bracket reduced to zero. As a consequence, everything that is valid in 2D can also be valid in stereoscopy, if we follow, step by step, a gentle evolution of the different variables of shooting. A graphic curve that would represent the viewer's disconnect or the end of his or her cerebral comfort will be more or less steep, depending on the viewer and the parameters that are varied.

The point of disconnect is easily identified when one parameter is studied at a time, but not so easily when they are put together. Tools for mise-en-scène and controls such as the Disparity Tagger are, in this respect, indispensable, because they make it possible to integrate geometrical or contrast limits on images corrected in real time according to an average audience comfort setting. This software also allows other limits to be included for each sequence according to the director's artistic sensibility.

From a practical point of view, it is essential to preserve a continuity between shooting practices in 2D and 3D, so that the same footage can be used for both cases. But different editing practices are required. If the opposite is done, discontinuity will be frequent and the viewer's comfort will be affected. This question is particularly delicate in the shooting of sporting events using a fast moving dolly or crane, where experience shows that the classical practices of 2D cannot be entirely transposed to stereoscopy.

Stereoscopy Jobs

We have just raised questions about the ambivalence of stereoscopy, which depends on cinema while also having to break from it and find its own means. If stereoscopy triggers a reevaluation of mise-en-scène and shooting practices and the necessity to create postproduction images beyond the editing process, which new skills will it require from the crew and the technicians involved in its making and, in the short-term, in its invention? There isn't a complete discontinuity between stereoscopy and 2D, but rather the need for a variation. We need to test and use all the variables of 2D while being aware of the limits of brain comfort and of the accumulation effect.

It is also impossible to strip the stereogram from the screen and to transform it into a hologram. Stereoscopy is included in the realm of cinema, but does not cover all of the possibilities offered and used by 2D without creating a disconnect in what the viewer's brain can tolerate, relative to stereoscopy's own parameters. So the use of technical shooting parameters in a stereoscopic mise-en-scène lies inside the play within these limits. Its conception is made by modulating the depth value throughout the process, sequence by sequence, shot by shot. And the one to give sense to this whole conception is not the stereographer, but the director. Only the director can think about the volume throughout the film, depending on the aesthetic, the emotions, and the meaning he or she wishes to convey to the viewer.

It is a commonly accepted concept that a 3D film must be written for stereoscopy. This point can be argued if the director is involved in the writing of the script and is already imagining the principles she will be using during her shoot; she will organize the succession of sequences according to the stereoscopic directing she has in mind.

There is no topic that cannot inspire a 2D movie if the director decides so. Why would it be any different for stereoscopy? The artistic rendering into stereoscopic form only exists in the director's mind, in its process of technical realization by his or her associates.

It is while creating the shooting script and/or the storyboard that indications relative to stereoscopy come into play. How should we answer the question, "What denotes whether a screenplay was written for 3D?" which was asked during a meeting of the CST (Commission Supérieure Technique du Centre National de la Cinématographie)? The only coherent answer is "because the director conceived of his movie in 3D."

The profession most closely resembling that of a stereographer is a special effects (SFX) supervisor. We can establish a parallel between the two because of the similarity of their interventions throughout all the stages of production. The stereographer must know the shooting conditions, the postproduction operations, and their follow-up in the digital lab, all the way to the projection of the movie.

Just as with the SFX supervisor, the stereographer is, first and foremost, the director's advisor. His role is to get the crews and tools to create the director's desired mood on the whole film, up to its finalization. He must therefore listen to the DP, who remains responsible for the image, and also works with the head set decorators, costume designers, and all the crew members contributing to the making of a film.

THE STEREOGRAPHER'S CREW ON A SHOOT

The stereographer has the assistance of technicians who ensure the practical tasks related to rigs, visualization devices, and lab follow-up. These people are added to the film crew and manage the tasks purely pertaining to stereoscopy.

The technician stereographer adjusts the rig and makes sure all the optical axes and volumetric parameters match the director's desires. Usually, she is a first assistant operator, but she does not replace the one for the film.

The 3D vision engineer manages the tools for stereoscopic vision in order to give alerts about the visible flaws or the changes needed to the shot being prepared. He makes sure left and right images present the least amount of faults and that the necessary correction, in live or in post, only relates to a tiny percentage of the image. Again, 3D correction aims to eliminate the imperfections that cannot be taken care of by the camera system rather than rectify poor shots while considering the risk of reducing the final image quality by reframing or introducing artifacts when correcting important disparities.

The assistant stereographer, in charge of following up on the rushes at the lab, has the responsibility for submitting a written report to the stereographer and to the entire image and postproduction crew after a viewing on a big screen. This report, quite the technical memoir, aims to foresee the postproduction operations, but also to warn the crew of defects that may have escaped their scrutiny.

THE STEREOGRAPHER'S PLACE IN THE CREW

During the first feature film on which Binocle was in charge of stereoscopy, we thought it was necessary for the image technicians to receive specific training, as it is truly essential that all technicians working on a 3D film be sensitized to stereography.

The first stereographer must be the director, but the entire crew must acquire skills in this unique cinematic field, so that every process will integrate the third dimension and take into account its consequences on the viewer's brain.

We systematically advise producers and directors to shoot a trailer or a short before shooting a feature film. The reason is very simple: If the director does not understand the use of technical parameters, reflections, and mise-en-scène applications that 3D allows, she will really be making a 2D film to which volume has been added. In other words, she will be a director that allows a "3D maker" to add a technical layer, as opposed to a filmmaker that combines the ensemble of technical parameters for the unity of a film. This is why the stereographer must, first and foremost, transmit his knowledge to the director and the entire crew.

Fortunately, these parameters can be learned very fast. Just as Orson Welles jokingly claimed to have learned the techniques of cinema within one morning, a contemporary director can seize these quickly. What Orson Welles really learned within one morning was how to reflect on the use of shooting parameters, not how to replace Greg Toland behind the camera. So the stereographer can help the director by working with him to consider the stereoscopy and its use for rendering emotion and meaning. The rules are simple, but the application and invention enabled by their combination is infinite, just as the parameters of 2D are.

All the technicians of a film reflect on their meaning when using these parameters for a specific sequence, but each will contribute according to his specialty. The DP will reflect on the structure of light in relation to volumetry and of the landscape's spatial arrangement in depth. He can no longer rely on effects—for example, by separating the backlit surface of a church window and the light beam coming through—without running the risk of revealing their real positions. For this reason, adding effects in post cannot be avoided. Inspecting the geometry-corrected images must help him to scope out the many traps of this double image, of its effects on the edge of the frame, of its contrast, and more.

Meanwhile, the camera operator and grip have to address the cerebral stress related to the speed of a movement subject to stroboscopy, or by an actor entering the frame and violating the stereoscopic window. They must also visualize the frame after volume correction, not before. The head decorator can no longer use trompe l'oeil, false perspective, or backdrops, without wondering about their stereoscopic value and the revealing of depth that will ensue. Make-up artists, hair stylists, and costume designers must be careful with the products they use. In other words: all the professions are involved in this rethinking; every technician must become a stereographer in his or her domain of expertise. Finally, when moving throughout the set's depth, the actors must comprehend the volume in which they move about, and be aware of where their gaze falls, taking into account both points of view.

Eventually, the stereographer will be less needed to train everyone on the set, but she will still remain the one who manages the stereographer's crew and ensures continuity of volumetry on the film in a relationship with the entire crew working on a production.

During postproduction, the stereographer supervises correction, the positioning of the window for sequences that will be shot in parallel (oftentimes shots with special effects), floating windows, and the homogenization of the entire film; for example, by creating dissolves not of shots, but of depth value.

A Turning Point in the History of Stereoscopy?

While the invention of stereoscopy dates back to the mid-1800s for photography (witness Nadar's erotic photographs produced in 1850) and to the early 1900s for cinema, the artistic practice was never mastered beyond short programs destined for amusement parks, and a few feature films made with inadequate tools. This does not mean the films made were bad, but simply that the techniques available were not yet able to produce a result always compatible with what the brain could accept.

The revivals of stereoscopy during the 20th century are linked with the need to face the dangers identified by American studios: in the 1950s, it was television; today, it is the lack of control on Internet circulation.

The difference between the previous attempt and contemporary attempts is essentially linked to the technical command of 3D: camera settings established by computer, and the operations made possible by digital images, from shooting to projection in an auditorium. At each stage, the quality of the 3D image, in combination with the viewer's cerebral comfort, truly allows us to confirm a mastery of the stereoscopic mise-en-scène. This hypothesis, presented in Table 6.2, has been proposed since the early 1990s by Roland Thepot and other stereographers with Binocle.

Table 6.2	Stereoscopy Is a New Cinematic Form Enabled by Two Innovations		
Digital image	+		motion control
= pixel-level accuracy	+		precision of settings
= cerebral comfort	+		artistic command

SHOOTING FOR CINEMA VS. TELEVISION

The prerequisites allowing for the emergence of 3D television included stereoscopic cinema's conditions of technical production, but also its economic value. It seemed obvious at the time that television, which implied the capacity to produce live shows—that is, in real time—would require the conception of revolutionary tools. These tools, once applied to cinema, would enable a stereoscopic film to be shot practically as fast as a 2D film. This is why Binocle had convinced Thomson, today Technicolor, and its R&D camera branch, today Grass Valley and Angénieux, to make the first digital, motion-control, stereoscopic camera. It already featured one single command for both the CCUs, a display system with real-time 3D playing, a visioning of disparities "by difference," anaglyptic, etc., and the management of axis, convergence, interaxial, zoom, focus point, and iris by motion control.

This camera, presented in the late 1990s at IBC in Amsterdam, allowed us to simulate today's live television streams by projecting to the audience concert captures on a large screen.

Final Thoughts

In the 1980s, there were predictions that a wide-scale colorization of cinematic works shot in black and white would take place, along with the invention of automatic systems of television colorization. Fortunately, this did not happen. But this concept of technical progress may be more easily realized with stereoscopic conversion—with the aid of a Zmap, for example—than its coloring counterpart. This could be useful for scientific applications, but by no means for cinema or television, where there is the desire to cater to an audience whom we expect to be demanding on an artistic level.

Today, the demands of new and competing markets are what is carrying the development of 3D cinema, accelerating a switch to digital screening rooms and ensuring new technology to television viewers as well as the users of new media. Of course, there is still the possibility that this momentum could be stopped by new perspectives or by the satisfaction of having reached a necessary and sufficient stage.

The deployment of Digital Cinema projectors in the theaters, justified by 3D, enabled the digitalization of movies and therefore eliminated transportation needs; it also enabled the protection of digital copies, thanks to watermarking. For television, the technological capacity to automatically turn a 2D image into 3D may seem satisfying, but it will have as a consequence the progressive destruction of 2D TV,

Table 6.3	Comparison of 2D and 3D Sports Event Direction: Shifting from 2D to 3D Affects Directing, from Camera Positions to Editing	
	HDTV, Monoscopic	**3D TV, Stereoscopic**
Points of view from current camera positions	Imposed by the event staging, yet made possible by zoom lenses with great focal length range.	Not adequate for creative stereoscopy. Would need to get closer to the field; difficulty to retain volume at the other end of the field.
Framing	Centered on the action, even if it creates motion blur and stroboscopic effect.	Same as cinema, with limited movement in range and speed.
Contrast	Strong contrast is acceptable.	Contrast must be limited to avoid ghosting.
Depth of field	Reduced to generate depth cues.	Increased to allow the audience's eyes to wander.
Zoom range	Full Zoom range is used.	Limited by technical and artistic constraints.
Motion blur and stroboscopic effect	Tolerated and even used on artistic purpose.	Limited by technical and artistic constraints.
Wide shot from high camera position	Used as bird's eye, covering most of the action.	Generates either miniaturization or shallow depth; solutions include: * Use a 2D shot in the 3D edit * Convert 2D into 3D * Shoot 3D with shallow depth.
Medium shots	Fine for the whole width of the field.	It's important to have cameras on both sides of the field, using reverse angle. The edit should move progressively to this positions, as in a circular motion. The movement of the players along the Z-axis reduces the motion blur.
Traveling speed and movements	* 10m/s is common and comfortable. * The movements precede the action. * Possibility to cover the entire field.	* 10m/s is too fast for foregrounds. * The movement should follow the action. * Impossible to follow the action at the other end of the field. Optional solution: use two travelings along the field.

and, in same the process the abandonment of a true reflection on the artistic possibilities of a creative stereoscopy. The stereoscopic revolution may then experience a sudden death both in television and in cinema, its two main sources of revenue.

For now, the recent success of stereoscopy is undeniable and increasing, even though 3D is often criticized as being too geared towards spectacle. We may hope, then, that the dream of stereographers and audiences alike also encompasses the tremendous possibility of a renewed art medium and refreshed narratives, capable, like other art forms, of triggering new ideas.

STEVE SCHKLAIR

Steve Schklair has been working at the front edge of new technologies for most of his career, and has left a mark in movies, special effects, and interactive media. Steve is currently focused on the development and production of new digital S3D motion picture technologies and the real-time broadcast of S3D programming. He is highly esteemed by an international client list as one of the world's leading experts in digital and live-action S3D and is one of the primary catalysts behind the recent resurgence of S3D in Hollywood films.

Steve served as 3D and digital image producer on 3ality Digital's U23D movie. In addition to supervising the production, Steve also oversaw the postproduction and completion at the 3ality Digital studio in Burbank. Other recent projects include the first live S3D broadcasts of a full NFL game delivered via satellite to theaters on both the east and west coasts, and the training and technology for the launch of the BSkyB S3D channel. Prior to 3ality, Steve was a senior executive at Digital Domain, the special effects studio responsible for films such as *Apollo 13, The Fifth Element, Titanic,* and *Terminator 2: 3D,* creative director for R/Greenberg Associates, and executive producer of The Columbus Project for computer graphics and interactive media pioneer Robert Abel.

Steve is a frequent speaker on S3D and new entertainment technologies at leading international digital and entertainment technology events. He is an award-winning member of the Visual Effects Society (VES), an associate member of the American Society of Cinematographers (ASC), and an alumnus of the University of Southern California (USC) School of Cinematic Arts master's program.

FIGURE 6.7
Steve Schklair, Founder and CEO, 3ality Digital Systems.

INVENTING THE TOOLS FOR A CREATIVE STEREOSCOPY

Steve Schklair

Inception of Modern 3D

I started thinking about 3D camera development in the middle of the 1990s, when the FCC mandated digital television. At the time, I foresaw that the best use of digital television was stereoscopic presentation, but that there had to be a path to create content on a realistic production schedule with realistic tools, and, to some extent, in real time (because television is a broadcast medium). There were no 3D televisions in the middle to late 1990s, and there really weren't any in the early 2000s; thus, even though I was building gear that would work for television, it also had to work for feature films. This was always the plan. Anything that works for television is capable of working in real time—which means it works even better for features because you don't have the editing timeline in a real-time broadcast.

GETTING OUT OF THE THEME PARK NICHE

I had done a number of 3D pictures prior to starting to develop 3D camera systems; as a director of photography, I would be called every couple of years to shoot a 3D project. However, they were all theme park or commercially based. I think the first project I ever did was Six Flags' *Sensoreum*. We shot with the Arri system, which was a lens adaptor you'd put on that would make two perfs left, two perfs right, and fixed interaxial with variable convergence. It was my first project, so I had no idea what worked and didn't work. But Arriflex published a depth of convergence chart (similar to a depth of field chart), that told you exactly what your settings should be, based on where the nearest and farthest objects were. I actually have one hanging in my office; it's an interesting piece of history, and it wasn't bad at suggesting settings. After we shot the *Sensoreum*, I got called to reshoot a Warner Brothers film for their new theme park in Australia, *Adventure in the Fourth Dimension*. And a couple of years later, I did another theme park piece. They were always theme park pieces.

Then, with Digital Domain, we did *Terminator 2: 3D* (though I wasn't directly involved in it, because I was in the middle of another project). After that, it became clear that, if 3D were to survive as a medium or to become mainstream, we had to address a lot of issues. One, we had to address the size and weight of the equipment, which was big and cumbersome. People doing theme park projects would use it, because they were used to all kinds of experimental equipment—but mainstream Hollywood would never use such equipment. Two, we needed a digital-based capture system, or it would never go mainstream; analog film and 3D just aren't very compatible when you take budgets and schedules into account.

Theme parks would sometimes take two or three weeks to prep a camera before the shooting, and then you might only get five shots in a day, because you have to realign the cameras between every shot and film. It was a difficult

ArriVision 3-D™

3-D convergence Chart
Single Lens System

"DEPTH" OF CONVERGENCE

18 mm			32 mm		
FEET	OBJECT DIST		FEET	OBJECT DIST	
CONV.	CLOSE	FAR	CONV.	CLOSE	FAR
3'	2'4"	3'10"	3'	2'6"	3'6"
4'	3'0"	5'5"	4'	3'3"	5'3"
5'	3'3"	7'10"	5'	3'8"	6'3"
6'	3'6"	10"	6'	4'4"	8'4"
7'	3'9"	16'0"	7'	5'2"	10'9"
8'	4'5"	26'0"	8'	5'4"	13'8"
9'	4'8"	30'0"	9'	5'17"	19'0"
10'	5'1"	36'0"	10'	5'11"	22'0"
12'	5'5"	130'0"	12'	6'7"	37'0"
13½'	5'7"	∞	14'	7'0"	80'0"
15'	5'11"	*∞-1/3	16'	7'4"	∞
25'	7'2"	*∞-2/3	21'	7'9"	*∞-1/3
			80'	12'0"	*∞-2/3

* For scenes without object in the close
convergence zone

ARRI
Arripleox corporation

500 Route 303,
Blauvelt, New York 10913
(914) 353-1400

ArriVision 3-D™

3-D Convergence Chart
Single Lens System

"DEPTH" OF CONVERGENCE

50 mm			85 mm		
FEET	OBJECT DIST.		FEET	OBJECT DIST.	
Conv.	Close	FAR	Conv.	Close	FAR
3'	2'8"	4'3"	7'	5'8"	8'0"
4'	3'0"	6'1"	8'	6'6"	10'0"
5'	4'6"	7'6"	9'	7'1"	11'4"
6'	4'8"	7'9"	10'	7'5"	12'6"
7'	5'4"	9'4"	11'	8'2"	15'2"
8'	5'8"	11'2"	12'	8'11"	16'5"
9'	6'1"	13'9"	13'	9'3"	17'6"
10'	6'8"	16'4"	14'	9'9"	19'9"
12'	6'10"	20'2"	16'	10'5"	24'0"
14'	7'8"	28'0"	18'	11'2"	31'0"
16'	8'5"	38'0"	22'	12'9"	46'0"
18'	9'4"	55'0"	36'	14'6"	75'0"
24'	10'3"	120'0"	40'	18'5"	∞
30'	11'6"	∞	52'	19'1"	*∞-1/5
48'	13'0"	*∞-1/3	68'	20'4"	*∞-1/3
90'	14'8"	*∞-2/3			

ARRI
Arripleox corporation

600 North Victory Boulevard,
Burbank, Callfornie 91502
(213) 841-7070

FIGURE 6.8
The Arri Depth Chart.

task, and, in those days, we didn't have tools (such as image overlays) that told us where we were. We'd line up one camera on a chart, and then we'd make sure the other camera also lined up. By today's standards, it was very crude—not even close in alignment.

CREATING A MODERN THEORY OF 3D

At the time, people theorized that theme park films were only 15 minutes because a longer time spent viewing 3D would cause headaches. Indeed, all the earlier 3D movies tended to do that. I had a number of theories about this, and one was that it wasn't the film duration but the image differences that caused headaches. It was misalignment, color differences, scratches on the left eye versus the right eye, sync differences, geometry differences. In other words, it was all the things that we now correct for—but in the late 1990s and early 2000s, these were all radical ideas.

THEORY 1: 3D EDITING IS THE CAUSE OF HEADACHES

In theme park projects, the editor cuts the film exactly as a cinematographer shot it. The cinematographer shoots knowing that there's going to be an edit point, so he makes sure that there are no jumps in depth around it. For theme park projects, this works fine, because you can spend two years story-boarding before you make it. On a feature movie, however, it's another story. Your director of photography is the director of photography for a reason, and the editor is an editor for a reason. Because of this, edit points started involving jumps in depth, which is what gave people headaches.

RIDING THE HD WAVE

So in building 3D filmmaking technologies, I knew we had to solve a lot of problems: we had to go digital; we had to make the tools light; we had to make it feel like real movie equipment; and it had to be deadly accurate. In other words, 3D would not succeed until we could shoot it on the same schedule as 2D, and for pretty much the same budget. That became the ultimate goal. In addition, 3D had to work for television, within the existing infrastructure. This was especially important because broadcasters had just gone through the transition from standard definition to high definition, which cost them millions of dollars (they had to throw away all their SD equipment and buy HD equipment) but didn't garner them any additional revenue. (The only people who made money on that transition were the equipment vendors: the Sonys, the Panasonics, and the Grass Valleys of the world.)

If we were to succeed with 3D in the high-definition world, we had to work with the existing infrastructure, because broadcasters would not be willing to invest a whole lot more money into something new and throw out what they just bought. That would've been a nonstarter for the business.

So, these were the parameters we discussed in the meetings with our team. We had to solve all of these problems, and we had to solve alignment differently than how we'd been doing it. No feature film or television show can take five days to set up a 3D rig to do a first alignment; it has to be done in a few hours at most. On 3D film cameras, everything was manual; everything took a huge amount of time. That wasn't going to be the business.

Inventing the Modern 3D Camera Unit

All of these issues were taken into consideration for the first big movie we got: U23D. This production is where we were able to put all these theories into practice. Our first focus was on alignment; we understood that if we couldn't align it on set, we would have to do it in post. Again, you can't let unaligned, unbalanced, unmatched images be shown—this is what gives viewers headaches. You can watch anything for five minutes. You can watch a lot of really bad stuff for ten minutes. You can watch stuff that is even borderline for fifteen minutes. But after fifteen minutes it gets pretty wearing. Your eyes get tired out. Once they are tired out, you can't make the rest of the movie good because it's too late. You've gone through people's eyes. Their eyes now need to rest.

So you have to make sure everything is good to start with. We worked on building a technology that ultimately let us do what we are doing now, which is remotely aligning the cameras and checking all the color balances.

IMAGE PROCESSING IS KEY TO MODERN 3D

Several years ago, I worked on a project for a company in Germany, Grundig, which was a consumer electronics company that had licensed an autostereo technology and was showing it at the big consumer electronics show IFA in Berlin. What they wanted to do was feed an eight-views monitor in real time. To do this, we built a 3D camera that would output some metadata, like the interaxial convergence figures.

We built the camera system in two months; meanwhile, the company in Germany built an image-processing system based on one of their current algorithms from using stereo vision to measure objects or buildings. They built a box that would take our two views and the metadata feeds, and then built a depth map from that. Then, from the depth map, they built very crude polygonal mesh, and combined the camera views on the mesh. Then they rendered the eight views from that. They were doing this in three-frame delay, maybe even less, which I thought was the most remarkable thing I had ever seen.

CREATING THE SIP

In the end, we acquired the company, even though I was just a startup myself. I saw that what they were doing was key to what I wanted to do, which was to start using advanced computing in image processing to speed up the process of shooting 3D. We used to go out there with calculators and measure distances and do math to figure out what the proper settings would be—but we needed to figure out a way around this, because it was just too time-consuming. This company could do imaging processing and image recognition so fast that image recognition became key to where we wanted to take stereo.

We bought them and hopefully developed the SIP (system in package), which is really using the same board and the box they had built for the IFA in Berlin three or four years ago. We redesigned the boards, but in the first steps the live boxes we had used all those boards.

> ## THEORY 2: THE MORE AUTOMATION, THE BETTER
>
> The second theory of 3D is that the more automation you can put into it, the more acceptable it will be to the business. We had to automate all the functions that weren't creative. There is no creativity in setting the math—but there is creativity in varying from the math. So if we could come up with computers and image recognition that would do all of the noncreative aspects of 3D, we could save our time for the creative aspects. The byproduct would be to speed up the process immensely.

FAST TRACKING THE CAMERA SETUP

U23D required three days of preparation, because we used the older camera systems. Subsequent projects could be reduced to two days of preparation. Now that we use motorized systems and image processors, we can roll onto a location and be ready to shoot in one hour or less, usually a half hour, which is conducive to being part of a mainstream business. We can now set up 3D cameras in just about the same time, or in just a few minutes more, than a 2D camera. The way to get it there was to automate all the things that took us so long to do manually in the past—especially alignment, which just took forever.

The fact that the cameras self-align so that we can get through our broadcast is great for a movie production schedule. They can shoot 40 or 50 setups a day, we don't care; the gear is just as fast as 2D gear.

TAMING ZOOM LENSES

In making 3D a viable medium, we also had to consider zoom lenses, which are required for real-time television. Live television broadcasts use zoom lenses, and you can't suddenly decide you're going to change the whole paradigm of how an event is shot because you're shooting in 3D. And you certainly can't march into the middle of a playing field with a camera to get those close-ups. So zoom lenses were our next task; after all, if our primary job is to not hurt people, our secondary job is to enable creativity. And to do this, we have to give directors a full range of tools.

Once we had the basic image processing settled, making zoom lenses work was the first really critical task. Physically, we did it by adjusting the rig to counter the zoom, as opposed to electronically shifting the images in a box. I'm still a believer in this method; when I shoot data for a motion picture screen, the last thing I want is to have an electronic box rescaling my data to put it into alignment. In those days, we were shooting 1920 by 1080 and then blowing it up to 4000 for film release. That's a huge jump, and it would be terrible for visual effects, for the blowup or for the up-res.

For these reasons, we decided not to do it electronically, even though we had the image processing capability. Instead, we decided it had to be done physically at the rig, so that we could record an image that was as high quality as possible. That's how we came up with the function of tracking zoom lenses, which was critical.

BALANCING COLOR

We performed color balancing via a nine-by-nine color matrix that was incredibly sophisticated, as opposed to three primaries. Because of this, we were able to remove all the aberrations that a beam-splitter puts in—keeping in mind that you can't take everything out, because then you lose some of your depth clues. It's important to keep some of the aberrations, because they're critical to depth perception; depth isn't judged just on the basis of convergence and interaxial, but on everything else as well: color, shape, receding sizes, occlusion, and more (there are around 20 or 30 depth clues in 2D). We didn't want to lose any of the key depth clues, so we focused on removing geometric aberrations, pretty much everything.

Another problem we wanted to address was the possibility of someone jumping in front of one camera and not the other. To avoid this, we built a system that would constantly look at the stereo images. If the image was the kind of thing that would hurt to look at, like someone blocking one eye and not the other, the image processor would detect it within the space of one frame, and would switch to a 2D version from the good eye until the blockage was over. Then it would switch back to 3D. In most cases, you can't even detect the switch, because it took the good eye and did a little bit of an offset to it and put that straight up in the screen. And it's all happening in real time.

ADDRESSING THE NEED FOR MULTIPLE CAMERAS

On a ten-camera broadcast, you have ten convergence pullers. This means that you need ten places for these convergence pullers to sit, ten hotel rooms for them to stay in, ten round-trip airline tickets . . . in other words, it's a big expense. So the next piece of software that was developed aimed to allow multiple cameras to shoot matching depths. This is only in beta, but it's still helpful. Now if you're doing a shot with five or six cameras on a set because of the stunt shoot or two or three because you have to get to your dialog scenes quickly, they can be matched automatically.

3D OB VANS

There's not a lot of difference between a 2D OB truck and a 3D OB truck. Both have facilities for laying graphics, audio, engineering, and recording, and a production area where your director, graphics people, and producers sit. There's some difference in terms of equipment and monitoring, but there are more similarities than differences—and when you really get down to the basics, the only difference is 3D monitors. (We'll get to that in a moment.)

To make a truck 3D, all we had to do was add image processors so that we could have a stereo view of the cameras, and additional image-processing channels so that we could do graphics offsets. With controllable offsets, we can steal a shot from 2D cameras. With more image controllers, the instant replay guys can all get a quick preview of what they are looking at in 3D. Because they're cutting, you never know what they're cutting together, and you don't want a lot of depth jumps in the material. At the end of the day, though, it's not that different—except for the monitoring.

The monitoring is significant to a few specific people. First, the convergence pullers who look at the technical monitors. In our broadcasts, they are all looking at a subtractive view, also known as a difference view. Above that is a 3D monitor showing the line cut, which is more of a confidence monitor to check how the shots actually look in stereo.

Second, technicians in charge of replays need to have monitors so they can watch replay packages. In football, for example, a replay will often have a package built and ready within seconds of the play ending; that's how fast the equipment builds these quick edits. Naturally, it's better if the replay technicians can look at it once in 3D, to avoid airing anything that has problems.

Third, the director needs to see the program and the preview in 3D. (He doesn't need to look at all the small camera monitors in 3D; he can figure out what those look like.)

Experimenting with the Medium

After learning how to make sure 3D didn't hurt anyone's eyes, we started doing a lot of experimentation, asking questions like, "How much is too much divergence?" and "How much is too much negative parallax?" In the early days, we shot a lot of tests and would look at a lot of material. We'd also pay attention to studies done by other people. Ultimately, we came up with our own personal formulas for what makes good 3D; specifically, we established a comfortable depth budget and determined where to place that depth budget in terms of negative and positive parallax. This became our key for shooting.

> **THEORY 3: THE 4% DEPTH BUDGET**
>
> We came up with a general principle of no more than 2% negative parallax and no more than 2% positive parallax. There are always exceptions to this rule, of course, depending on the shot. But, for the most part, we work with a 4% depth budget, and we try to keep things a little more positive than negative.

We have moved on to the next technology which is doing a multicamera production. Here we bounce back and forth between features and broadcast, but again features benefit from every function we build for broadcast.

GETTING RID OF NON-CREATIVE CREW

The stereographer has a creative job, but the convergence puller does not; the work of a convergence puller is very mechanical, like pulling focus—you either hit your marks or you don't. There's creativity in the director of photography deciding where the focus should be, but that's separate from the actual act of turning the knob to keep things in focus.

If you know the rules (for example, each shot is 2% of background parallax at the farthest object, and 2% of negative parallax at the nearest object, with no edge violation), you don't need to know anything about stereo at all to sit there with an interaxial and convergence control. You can get anybody, even people who have never picked up a controller; they can set up an interaxial convergence. They just read the words, pick up the dial, and go straight to that knob, that setting. They will have to play a little until they find it. So they would be balancing the interaxial convergence settings until they have that measurable setting.

There's no reason why image-recognition technology can't do these camera adjustments when all you're doing is trying to match the measured settings. The same is true, to some extent, for the job of the stereographer; there's no reason why the stereographer can't define the depth of the space and let the software adjust the cameras to meet her needs.

Eventually, I believe machines and image processing can take over all non-creative work. But machines are not capable of anything creative; only people can do that. And 3D should remain a creative medium.

THE END OF THE STEREOGRAPHER

Although the job of a stereographer is quite essential and important right now, this will probably become less true as time passes. This is because stereography is part of visual storytelling, and it's really the director of photography's job to do the visual storytelling. In other words, as soon as DPs are up to speed on stereography, they will want to be their own stereographers.

Depth starts to get used creatively when you put the decisions in the hands of the people that make all the other visual creative decisions, and it seems inevitable that the stereographer's role will change at some point.

MONITORING 3D

Shooting stereo used to be considered to be voodoo and black magic, because you were never able to see anything until one or two days after shooting, when you could see the dailies. Establishing camera settings was almost a black art, involving magic calculations that were known only to a very few. Now, however, almost anyone can make a good stereo shot if he or she knows how to use the tools, whether it be a 50/50 mix, a flicker view, a checkerboard, or a subtractive.

To be clear, I'm not saying that you should be wearing 3D glasses; your 3D monitor is only for confidence. In my opinion, the best way to get a 3D shot is not to wear glasses and instead to look at my negative and positive image parallax. This data is independent of whether someone's eyes are tired or not, so you can completely eliminate the fatigue variable. If a 3D shot is hurting people, the first thing I do is take off my glasses and look at the elements of the shot. You can't see these things with your glasses on.

Indeed, I'd love to debunk the myth that you have to be wearing glasses to shoot stereo. In fact, I think the opposite is true.

That being said, when we shoot wide broadcast, everybody is wearing glasses. But in this case, we are actually looking at 2D monitors, and we wear them so that we can easily switch between the confidence monitor showing 3D, and the regular 2D monitors. You could lose that confidence 3D monitoring and still do the 3D shot, but you can't lose the picture coming from the image processors. To reiterate: Glasses are just for confidence. The best way to shoot 3D is not to wear glasses, look at the two images you're capturing, and adjust them so they're consistent, comfortable, and don't hurt people.

Most people miss a lot of details when looking at a 3D image, because the novelty of seeing any depth at all sometimes blinds viewers to any problems with the picture. If you point them out, though, they become obvious; and, either way, the viewer would be able to *feel* the effects after fifteen minutes. For this reason, I'm in favor of training your clients, just a little, so that people know what to look for. I do that in speeches where I show a slide with all things wrong with 3D. It takes five minutes. It's not complex to see what's wrong with an image as soon as you know how to measure an image, how to look at it.

SHOOTING CONVERGED OR PARALLEL

I've always shot converged because it allowed me to see my background. There is, of course, a risk of diverging the backgrounds, but you can avoid this as long as you're careful to shoot looking at exactly what your background and foreground parallax is. In my opinion, shooting converged gives you a better depth budget than the alternative.

On a recent feature, I had a long discussion with Rob Engle of Sony Pictures about *Pirates of the Caribbean 4* being shot parallel, and I hear the footage looks fantastic. The process of shooting parallel is really almost the same as shooting converged; you are just adjusting that infinity point in post. However, I don't think it gets you quite the same results. Since Rob and I disagree, we're going to shoot a series of test shots that I think would only work with the converged method, and then he's going to add some that he thinks only work in parallel—and we're going to see which theory actually works out.

I don't really know the answer, but I do know this: when you see a movie in a theater, you are looking at converged images, even if they were converged in post. So why wouldn't you want to converge on set, and take one time-consuming thing away from post? Well, a lot of that depends on whether it's a live action movie or a special effects movie. If you are going to have that reshot in a computer for weeks anyway, you might as well do the convergence in post. But in straight live action, you could take days out of post if you were to converge on set.

You don't have to blow up your picture, you don't have to compromise your data, and you don't have to waste a lot of time. You might want to spend some time adjusting your 3D in postproduction, and you'll certainly need to do depth balancing at the edit, but at least you're done shooting with 80% to 85% of your work done.

But, again, in an effects movie, you're opening up every shot anyway, so shooting parallel provides a consistency that simplifies the effects process. Ultimately, you end up with a converged movie, but at least you are giving the effects people a little more room to work.

With the new tools that are now available, we can actually see 3D on a set. In some cases, this may compromise the depth when you shoot parallel. In practice everyone is staring at the 3D monitor, and when you are shooting parallel everything is negative. You've got a director and clients all staring at that monitor asking, "Why isn't this shot comfortable?" So the stereographer is going to make a few adjustments to make it a little more comfortable. All he's doing, because you shoot parallel, is closing up the interaxial, which is going to pressure depth. You are going to end up compromising your depth when everybody says the shot is not comfortable or doesn't look good.

DEPTH TRANSITIONS

When working on the U23D show, the director wanted both a lot of cuts and also a lot of multiple elements layering. However, multiple element layering using the material as we shot it would have been visual chaos—so we built a tool that let us very quickly reconverge shots. Nowadays, most tools do that. But it let us do it fast enough so that it became part of our production tool.

What we would do was reconverge shots so that wide shots had more positive parallax, while close-ups were more negative; in other words, we wanted the images in wide shots to be farther away, and close-ups to be closer. This was a general rebalance that we did on this film, especially in terms of layers. But in terms of every set, the most important thing this new tool offered was the opportunity to do this adjustment in the edit.

The technique we used was to put the monitors into a flicker mode, and then overlay the two shots. We'd adjust them over the space of 24 frames to 36 frames, depending on how large the move was, so that a shot that was playing with the last second or second and a half would start a depth adjustment. This would meet the incoming shot at some halfway point, and then the incoming shot would continue the adjustment until it was back to where the filmmaker had intended. We were basically doing soft transitions of depth in about two seconds; and wOr whatever you edit maybe, one second in front or one second behind the cut, if there wasn't a lot of jump. When there wasn't a wide shot to wide shot issue, the transitions could be much faster.

The fast cutting worked. Without jumping at depth, fast cuts work. You just can't jump at depth. It's so easy that there's not much to say about it. This stuff is incredibly easy to do.

Creative Stereoscopy: The Art of Cinematographic Depth

PUT DEPTH ON YOUR CINEMATOGRAPHER PALETTE

As a director of photography, I use a lot of tools to help tell stories—shape, color, texture, etc.—and 3D is just another example. The design of a film can have a huge impact on the story. If you want an audience to be afraid that something is going to happen, there are visual cues you can use to do exactly this—this is part of the filmmaker's art. For example, say you have associated certain characters with certain background shapes; one character always has square objects in his scene, while the other only has rounded objects. When you want the audience to feel that something frightening is about to happen to one of those characters, switch the background objects so that the rounded objects are associated with the wrong character, and vice versa. The audience won't realize what, specifically, is different, but they *will* get the sense that something is wrong. You can use the same technique for camera shots. For example, if you always use a fairly wide shot (30 mm) to shoot one character from head to waist, and then change to 60 or 80 to 90 mm, the audience is going to know something is wrong—even if you're still shooting the character head to waist. Finally, one last example: color. If you change the color palette associated with a character, the audience will feel it.

Now, imagine the even more powerful element that 3D adds: depth. What happens if you always associate a very shallow depth with one character, until this character has a sudden realization—and then all of a sudden the whole world opens up behind him? What if we only see a character in positive parallax? No matter whenever we see this character, even if it's a single shot, she's not fitting in a plane of convergence. She's sitting two to three feet behind the screen, and is always in positive parallax. And then all of a sudden this character warms up. She has an understanding. She realizes something. There's a change in the character, and now all of a sudden this character is always a little bit in negative parallax. The audience absolutely feels this.

We can start using depth in a couple of ways. Say, for example, that you've got two characters who are at odds: to symbolize this, you can create a vast gulf of depth between them. You could take one character and push him all the way to 2%, and have another at 2% forward, negative parallax. Then, when they achieve reconciliation, you can close up the giant gulf of 4% of depth, putting both characters almost on the screen plane, together in the same space. Just let the backgrounds go negative and positive, and the foreground objects go negative; you're still maintaining a consistent depth, but your characters are now occupying a similar space, whereas before they were in a radically different spatial relationship with the audience.

You might choose to shoot everything on an 18 mm lens and then suddenly go to a 60 mm lens. What does that do to the depth setting? We know what that does to the depth setting, but can you use it to tell a story? I think so. You've got the whole world of depth on that 18 mm, whereas you've got very compressed depths at 60—but the image size of your characters doesn't change. So as you're mixing image size and field of view, narrowing it up without confining the character, the space is closing up as well. That's kind of cool.

There are so many ways you can use depth to help analyze and tell a story or to help an audience feel, to foreshadow, and we used all these things for foreshadowing. You can foreshadow things about to happen by adding depth to the tools you're already using.

COLLABORATIVE DEPTH CREATIVITY

Using depth creatively is part of visual design. And though visual design isn't exactly a luxury, there aren't a lot of projects that go to that level of thinking. It requires working in deep cooperation with your set designer, your art director, and your director; everybody has to be on the same page. The set designer has to give you sets that let you achieve these depths settings, going all the way back to the storyboard phase of the movie that needs to be carefully thought out, carefully mapped. Everybody needs to be on the same page so that you get these depth settings in. Even the wardrobe and art department have to cooperate so that the color palettes are controlled. The production designer should give you a set that has close walls so you can avoid too much positive parallax in the background, while also giving you other areas with very deep space, so that you have both near and far to use as framing elements depending on where you are on the storytelling.

If you have a set that doesn't have anything that's deep, it's very hard to use depth to tell your story because there's not a lot of leeway to move there. But there's still some.

Meet with production and have a whole discussion about color palette and wardrobe changing over time. Meet and discuss depth and depth over time, and make sure your various craftspeople and designers are all understanding what you're trying to convey through the use of depth, so that they can make their elements be conducive to do those depth changes and balances.

GOING FURTHER

The language of 3D is one that is not yet developed—everything we discuss here is still in the theory phase. I've done some experimentation with 3D symbolism, but it takes an extraordinary amount of preparation time, which most projects can't afford. Still, we get a little more of it on every project that comes up. And as directors of photography start to learn this language, then you'll see more and more of it because it will become second nature. That's the most exciting thing about previews: it's a whole other tool in the box and lets us redefine what the language of film is.

Creative Stereoscopy in Live 3D TV

The real wow shots in 3D are the ones that look through multiple layers of depth: the playing field, the players, and the fans behind them. The less impactful shots are those taken with high overhead cameras; in other words, the high 50 cameras. They see a flat field, essentially.

MIXING WOW-ING AND STORYTELLING SHOTS

One of the first things we learned was you have to go to those shots that aren't big wow shots, because you need those to tell the story of your game. It's very hard for fans to follow the action if every shot is shot at field level. It soon became clear that the wow factor of 3D has to be secondary to actually telling the story of the game.

Creatively, we use fewer cameras with 3D. At the George Lucas Editing and Film School, I was taught that you hold a shot until it's imparted all its information. When it is done giving you information, you cut to the next shot— until that one is done giving all its information. In other words, you only hold shots long enough for the information contained within the shot to be imparted to the audience. If that's true—and the theory does seem to hold up—you have to consider that 3D has more information in every shot, so you have to hold the shots longer. This explains why slower cuts work better; if there's more information in the shots, people want a chance to look at it and explore that information.

Because there are fewer cuts in 3D, you don't need as many cameras. It is not for budget reasons that we are showing up for these big sporting events with half as many cameras as are usually used. It's just not necessary. In 2D, the excitement of a game is sometimes artificially inserted through a lot of fast cutting; in 3D, the excitement is inherent within the shot, so we don't need to do fast cutting to get across the same exciting message. The editorial pace is slower, so we need fewer cameras.

Remember: It's more important to tell the story of the game than to get big wow shots. It's a combination of both wow shots and regular shots that tells the story of a game in 3D.

WORK IN A CONSISTENT DEPTH WINDOW

When shooting live 3D, you don't have a chance to fix anything in post, so you absolutely have to work in a consistent depth window, and you want to balance the depth window between all the cameras. The object within the picture should be about the same depth on a cut-to-cut basis.

In U.S. football, when a quarterback takes his hike and fades back, and you prepare to cut to another camera, it's really important that he does not jump position. People's eyes are already converged on that spot, so you have to cut to that exact depth position for a comfortable transition. Every transition in television needs to be comfortable. It may or may not be the wowest use of 3D to make every shot comfortable and balanced to the next. But the alternative is worse. It's going to hurt your audience.

Those are the basics of live 3D television. The next question is: How do we use it creatively? How do we tell a story, get great slow-motion replays, and show enough of the ground cameras so that viewers really feel the 3D experience? These questions are still being explored, and the answers are still being learned.

VINCE PACE

As an acclaimed cinematographer and co-inventor of the world's most advanced stereoscopic 3D system, known as *Fusion 3D*, Vince Pace is leading the effort to reinvent the entertainment experience. He has been instrumental in capturing some of the world's most captivating productions of our time. His career marks many significant achievements within the industry, from supporting the camera challenge of BBC's award-winning series *Blue Planet* to designing innovative lighting technology for *The Abyss* and being nominated for an Emmy in Cinematography for bringing back images from the deck of the Bismarck, three miles under the ocean. His contribution to entertainment has been in the areas of natural history, features, sports, and concerts.

Almost a decade ago, Academy Award-winning director James Cameron, president of PACE Patrick Campbell, and PACE founder Vince Pace shared a desire to revolutionize the entertainment experience. Together, they embarked on a world's first, to develop innovative technology for the most advanced stereoscopic acquisition system ever created, known today as Fusion 3D.

Today, PACE/Cameron's Fusion 3D system is trusted by many of the top directors and entertainment companies in the industry. The use of PACE's innovative technology has resulted in over $4 billion of box office receipts and major 3D benchmarks recognized within the industry, including *Avatar; TRON: Legacy; Resident Evil: Afterlife; U23D; ESPN Masters, NBA Finals, and All-Star Games; Journey to the Center of the Earth; Hannah Montana/Miley Cyrus: Best of Both Worlds Concert Film;* and *The Final Destination.*

Based in Burbank, California, Vince Pace's company PACE houses a full creative and technical team that infuses "Imagination through Innovation" into major motion pictures, live sports and entertainment experiences, concerts, music videos, and more.

FIGURE 6.9
Vince Pace, Founder, CEO, PaceHD.

THE OLD AND NEW LANGUAGE OF 2D AND 3D

Vince Pace

Many people make the mistake of assuming that we previously didn't interpret depth and dimension when looking at 2D images, and that 3D changed that. In fact, however, cinematographers have long been dealing with perspective and techniques that enhance the view of depth dimension in the 2D frame. This new venture into 3D shows the growth of professional individuals who have been doing successful work in 2D—whether it's storytelling, composition, lighting, or cinematography—and who are now learning about the additional benefit of working in the 3D medium.

As opposed to an almost entirely new language that we need to learn, I feel that 3D is just a better methodology for conveying an artist's work to the viewer. For me, it's been exciting to work with some of the best in the 2D business, and to see them embrace what 3D is adding to their ability to convey a message and apply their own creative talents. Again, though, it's important to realize that we did not invent depth and dimension overnight; it has always been a part of the cinematographer's toolset. It's just that now we are emphasizing it more in the way we present it to the viewer.

Live production presents the same challenges as feature productions. In major feature productions, they spend so much money that you don't have a second chance to shoot anything twice. In live production, the ability for the equipment to perform correctly the first time is even more critical; all the money in the world won't buy that shoot again.

Unfortunately, most productions realize the hard way that there's a lot more to the production system than simply a camera. The creative professionals involved are also a part of it: the cinematographer, the AC, the editorial department, the mobile unit companies, and many others. For this reason, the strength and growth of 3D will come on the back of 2D: those who did 2D well are the prime candidates to do 3D well. There's no reason to start over with a whole new set of rules or a whole new set of people. Similarly, companies like Discovery or ESPN are the perfect ones to create this new channel or stream of content, as opposed to adding new or different players to the game.

Obviously, there are many differences between 2D and 3D. What would be a simple lens change in 2D is a whole configuration change in 3D, with mirror rigs, side-by-side rigs, inter-ocular control, and so on. The complexity and variety of configurations is much greater in 3D, and in the future we'll see more of a variety of configurations that service a particular need in production. Our concentration will be on introducing as many different configurations and variety as the cinematographer needs. It all started with a beam-splitter and a side-by-side rig—but soon we'll have aerials, cable cams, handhelds on a football field, sky cams over the field, slow-motion cameras, 500 mm long lenses, and robotics-based cameras.

What has been successful in 2D will be successful in 3D. Image quality still matters—3D does not mean we no longer have to worry about it. After all, if we're going to ask the public to pay more, we have to make sure we deliver. Some of these solutions work very well in the B-roll environment, when you need to pick a shot or to send someone out to the locker room. But most of our concentration is on the real heart of production, on the production cameras that capture the images on the field, and where the audience expects the quality to be the best that it can be.

Editing Live 3D TV

The key in 3D is balance. That is, you must balance the cameras so that when you cut from one camera to the other, it's pleasing to the audience. People need to refrain from just looking at one particular image or one isolated event; the real trick to successful 3D is when they all work together. This is similar to an orchestra, where all the instruments have to complement each other. When they are taken out of context, it can be disruptive.

The key for anyone in a live production is to look at it as a complete whole. Too often people get excited about one camera, or the 3D effect of 3D, but you don't want the experience of the viewer to be a highlight reel. Some of the young guys in the business get too excited about that one camera that gives a strong 3D effect, when, in order to convey the event, you need the cameras to complement each other.

We need to get beyond the effect of 3D and into the fact that it's a better viewing experience than 2D. The question is "Did you enjoy that more than a 2D presentation?" If the answer to that is "Yes," you won. If the answer is "It was really cool when this and that happened, but I was missing the score, I did not get the action on the field," then you kinda lost what the production was about.

Camera Positions in 3D

There's a misconception that all 3D can do is get the camera closer to the action, but this is incorrect. A 3D experience still has to tell the story. But to do this, you need premium camera positions—that is, where 2D cameras would be. You can't put 3D cameras in a corner. We are working very hard at getting to the premium positions and delivering a 2D feed as well as a 3D feed. That's the key, to get to where the 2D is really told. Sometimes it's helpful to have lower camera positions to enhance 3D, but that's not where the whole 3D production value is. I'd rather win the battle of having a key camera position, a court camera, or a slash camera on a basketball game, rather than being somewhere else on the court and that's all I have. I want to deliver everything the viewer wants to see in 2D—but in 3D.

We are certainly learning. The definitions of 3D filming and broadcast are in their inception. The filmmakers and production people are getting over the poke-it-in-your-face effect and are starting to realize that a little 3D goes a long way. The power of 3D is so much greater than people realize that they don't have to use it as much. In the future, it's going to be a more pleasing way to watch entertainment. In fact, the goal should be to make you forget it's 3D in the first five minutes—what I want you to do is to get into the project. If you're only thinking about the 3D, then you have left everything else behind. High-level creatives in this business, they get it. They understand that this is a medium that can help them do their business. It does not have to be all about the 3D.

Monitoring 3D

It's not a requirement for a director to have a 3D monitor—it's more important that the cinematographer has the 3D monitor. That said, all the directors I have seen working with 3D monitors have used them to their advantage to better set the performance and the actors. It helps gets everybody on board and excited. Now, how much time did the directors spend concentrating on that monitor? Maybe only 3%, because they quickly realize that there's so much more for them to get done. The 3D is an end result, not a creative result.

For the same reason, there's no need to run dailies on a large screen. Good 3D is scalable. I had firsthand experience with this on *Avatar*; if it looks good on my 45-inch monitor, I can guarantee it will look good on my 30-foot screen. When people say, "I have to see it on a 30-foot monitor to make my decision," in my opinion it's an excuse.

And it's also not a question of experience with stereoscopy; you judge 3D by the visual cues that are necessary. 3D a DP he can't judge lighting on a small monitor. The visual cues for 3D, just as for correct lighting, are visible on a small monitor as well as on a big screen. To reiterate: good 3D, if you know the visual cues, is very scalable.

THE 3D CREATIVITY CHALLENGES

Bernard Mendiburu

The Triple Challenge of Stereographic Arts

The conversion, or evolution, or maturation of cinematographic art into a stereoscopic form is an extremely engaging intellectual challenge. If 3D has been my dream job for the last 15 years, it is not because I am a 3D maniac. Truth is, I am not. It's not because it brought me great Hollywood jobs and payrolls, as I only contributed to two animated features in all these years. For me, 3D has been a wonderful place to work because it is a perfect blend of three intellectual challenges: technical, artistic, and scientific. It involves quite a lot of diplomatic skills too, as any disruptive waves do, but that's not the subject of this book.

TECHNICAL

Properly producing and displaying 3D used to be a technical nightmare, but recently turned into a mere digital challenge. Any geek with a sweet tooth for cable mazes and overheating power supplies had a blast in the early years of digital stereoscopy. If you are into motion controls, optics, data wrangling, or in any technical or engineering job in the entertainment industry, you are most likely experiencing that 3D challenge in your everyday activity.

Most of this challenge will soon—in, say, a couple years—be behind us, with the deployment of standardized tools and procedures, intelligent rigs, and top-notch image analyzers. There will always be a new frontier where new image acquisition and processing systems are invented. Still, we have a road map of what the 3D path will eventually look like.

ARTISTIC

The second challenge we face is to learn how to create 3D effects with a purpose. An introductory lecture on stereoscopic 3D production usually ends with the concept that we are about to reinvent the visual art. I sometimes phrase it like this: "We are a generation of artists, who have an incredible chance to rewrite the rules of our art." Art forms have always been extended by radical artists who refuse to follow the rules and instead invent new paths. Some of them revolutionized their art, like the cubist painters or the *nouvelle vague* directors. Stereoscopic 3D has the potential to put all entertainment professionals in such a position. There's an open debate on the most important rule of 3D: Is it "Do no harm" or "Break all the rules"? The former is an obvious statement in the entertainment industry, but the latter is a cornerstone of artistic creativity. Constraints are the number one source for creativity. If Spielberg had had a shark, we never would have had *Jaws*.

SCIENTIFIC

The third challenge is more difficult to describe—even to define or name. It relates to the way we process the stereoscopic 3D imagery, from our eyes to our feelings, in their biological incarnation somewhere in the wetware we host between our ears. The challenge is to understand what happens with the eyes in the brain's visual cortex when we see natural 3D and when we watch artificial stereoscopic 3D. There's consensus that this understanding should be called "the human factor in 3D." It covers medical science, neurology, optometry, cognition, evolution, psychology, and numerous other hard and soft science domains. It is quite a new research area, not widely addressed until now, as it is not a public health subject; only highly selected and trained professionals, like medical researchers or car designers, use 3D displays in their everyday life. In the general population, only specialized optometrists were concerned with the binocular vision of their patients. And because seeing in 3D isn't critical to life, stereo-blindness was not considered a disease that deserved a cure. To our knowledge, the first and only stereopsis therapy documented so far is "Stereo Sue" in 2007 (see http://www.fixingmygaze.com/ for more information).

We are not implying that the wide release of stereoscopic 3D imagery is a public health hazard that should be legislated by the U.S. Surgeon General or the

U.N. World Health Organization. Far from it, as preliminary research points to the opposite; S3D seems actually to help in detecting and curing potential strabismus. What we have to address is merely the issue of visual fatigue. What we want to understand is the interactions between visual comfort and visual activity, between spatial placements and inner feelings, between motions and reflexes.

The Technical Challenge: Producing Coordinated Pairs of Pictures

The stereoscopic technical requirement is simply put: Produce and reproduce pairs of images that present exclusively comfortable disparities. This is achieved by controlling all the shooting parameters, inside and outside the cameras. Identically, the postproduction and exhibition processes should follow that requirement all the way to the audience's eyes. This is the subject of this whole book, and of the many lectures on 3D you can attend.

What is interesting to observe is the current relationship between this requirement and the creativity of the 3D TV producing crews. So far, the 500-pound gorilla is the technical challenge, and the creative opportunities are more like a chimp waiting for a chance to voice his concern. Whatever tune a stereographer will sing you about the importance of creativity in 3D TV, his very presence on set or in the OB van is justified by his role in achieving that technical challenge. He might have been selected among others because of his attention to stereoscopic creativity; still, his presence on the credit roll is justified by the mere canonical quality of 3D TV.

THE IMPACT OF THE TECHNOLOGICAL CONSTRAINT ON CREATIVITY

At this stage of the adoption of 3D, from a MediaPro Research/Medialuso perspective, we are focusing on an academically correct 3D at a cost and setup time that becomes possible for weekly, or even daily, productions. Until now, most 3D productions have needed an infrastructure and preparation more similar to shooting a commercial or making a movie.

Due to all the training needed, the novelty of the art for many of the people involved, and the immaturity of most of the tools used, many issues can pop up in a 3D live production. Thus, at this first stage of live 3D TV, our focus is on getting a comfortable 3D on screen, with the right settings for the screen size, right transitions, and right titles.

When the fact of recording 3D live events become as usual as the HD events are for our group, we will think of making creative advances in audiovisual language adapted to 3D. The main change we have already adopted is to have two separate productions, one for 2D and one for 3D, with different directors, different staff, different OB vans, different camera positions, and different operations in camera framing and motion.

Jordi Alonso, MediaPro

You may have heard 3D specialists discard this opinion. To our understanding, unless you are speaking with one of the top five stereographers in the world, disregarding such reality is either infatuated ego or unfair marketing. The truth is, we are still creating the tools and learning how to use them.

TECHNICAL TOOLS FOR CREATIVITY

The designs of stereoscopic rigs and image analyzers are now quite established, but engineers are not yet done with the research and development of 3D production tools. The next big step forward in 3D production is in the field of depth acquisition technologies. This will be to 3D what the Eastman Kodak's mono-pack was to color film. There's no clear picture as to what will be the leading technology—panoptic, LIDAR, miniaturized rigs etc.—but what is a definite is the need for single-camera 3D filming.

In addition, we could use better tools for depth reconstruction. Depth reconstruction based on visual analysis seems to hit a limit at a quarter of the source image resolution. Using super-high resolution cameras, like the 33 megapixel prototypes created for the Japanese U-HDTV project, would be interesting to try. We are seeing the first prototypes of virtual camera systems that can replay action from a complete reconstruction of the field, with virtual cameras that can be placed in the middle of the action. It'll soon be possible to replay an action from the player's view, or from the goalie's position.

However, all these existing and expected production tools are only toys until we use them to tell a story to the audience in a way that has never been done before—and yet, does not disturb the experience. Story is the key, and storytelling is the art.

An Artistic Challenge: A Renewed Cinematographic Language

What do we know about 3D storytelling? Nothing. But only the most advanced experts will dare to admit this. (Actually, they may think they know a very tiny little bit, but, as gentlemen, they will stand along with all of us, and acknowledge we all know nothing.) Once again, you'll hear different stories, and, as a producer, you'll enjoy hearing someone showing some experience in the field. Listen to him or her for one hour, and you'll learn a lot. Unfortunately, whatever you'll be told about stereoscopic storytelling in the second half of that hour will be obsolete within the year, two years at best.

> All stereographers are right in their respective approaches—up to the point that they start to claim the others are wrong.

There's only one thing I'll stand by to the end of my stereoscopic life: there's no such thing as "stereoscopic truth."

Obviously, there are as many stereographies as stereographers. Would anyone listen to a cinematographer who claimed to be the only guy on earth who knows how to take a picture? In my experience, when someone states he has the 3D truth, it's a red flag in a genuine 3D chat.

AREAS FOR CREATIVITY IN 3D

Stereoscopic creativity will make use of two main sets of tools: first, the existing 2D movie-making elements that are deeply affected by the 3D evolution, mainly the screen and continuity. Second, all the new constraints in 3D filming that have not yet been brought to their interesting boundaries. Cinematography isn't just about reproducing reality. Actually it's as far away from that as possible. The same is true for stereo-cinematography. So many more emotions are conveyed by tweaking the world as you reproduce it. Eventually, even the technical rules of stereoscopy and stereopsis should be challenged in the search for new effects.

Geometrically Realistic Depth

By selecting your camera placement, focal length, inter-ocular distance, and convergence point, you create your own 3D interpretation of the world. This basic world translation is explained at length in the good 3D lectures and books. These settings will affect the roundness of your characters, the objective sizes of your universes, the subjective sizes of your audiences, and the distances or distanciations towards the action. All these parameters may be imposed upon you by the metrics of your set and by the limitations of your 3D equipment. They can be a creative freedom area too, if you have a chance to preview them, to influence the camera positions and lens selections. Your monitoring tools are key assets in this artistic progress.

Still, we are only talking here of scaling decisions: the audience, the subject, its roundness or flatness. All these parameters are linked together. For example, if you reconverge a shot, you affect the distance to the action and the volume of the objects.

Until now, only CGI animation had the versatility required to really play with these factors for a decent cost. For this reason, animated 3D was on the leading edge of stereoscopic creativity and brought to us new tools: nonrealistic depth (NRD) and the floating stereoscopic window (FSW).

Nonrealistic Depth

How great would it be to be able to change one stereoscopic characteristic without affecting the others? In other words, to be able to inflate or deflate a character, make him rounder or flatter, farther away . . . and yet not bigger? Some of this will never be feasible, but a surprising number of visual cheats are now possible in CGI stereoscopy, and soon in heavy VFXed real images.

The basic effect is the dual-rig rendering, with one interaxial for the background and another for the foreground. This creates nonrealistic 3D universes where volumes, positions, and sizes are not related. It's a form of per-depth-layer stereoscopic setting that can be achieved with real imagery shot on green screen. The *Coraline* (2009) team did a great adaptation of this by building miniature sets that were compressed along the z-axis. They performed their magical puppetry and shot what is, to our knowledge, the only stereoscopic that is both 100% practical effects and compressed depth.

The Screen, the Stereoscopic Window, and the Audience Space

Actually, there's no screen in 3D. There's a window, and if you see the screen, it's because that window needs to be cleaned. The screen presence in the stereoscopic cinematography is reduced to form the boundary of the viewing frustum. The two pyramids defined by the four corners of the screen and the audience's eyes are our building blocks. We'll add the space enclosed in the continuation of these pyramids behind the screen, and paint the non-overlapping volumes on the sides in orange. This is the volume where you'll place your action that tells your story.

Why is there no screen? Because in a properly set up stereoscopic projection room, you'll be unable to see where the screen is, in distance. What you see is the position in space of its four corners, and, from them, you infer where the screen is likely to be. But you are unable to "see" it; all you see is a window defined by its borders, or corners. And you see through this window.

If you move this corner in the 2D space of the screen, it moves in 2D. Moving it in 3D is much more complex, however; it requires moving the screen. If you move it in stereoscopy, on the other hand, it's quite easy: just move the left-eye points along the horizontal axis, and you'll move the perceived window along the z-axis. This is a well-known issue of dual-projector installations. IMAX 3D uses this to reset the 3D space at the exhibition stage; hence the legend of 70 mm projectors that are separated by a 65 mm distance. It is their projection areas, on screen, that are reset by one human interocular distance.

Among many other brilliant ideas, stereographer and 3D consultant Brian Gardner brought to Disney's *Meet the Robinsons* (2007) the concept that stereoscopic windows (SW) could be tweaked in many more aspects than mere replacement. First, in a pixel-accurate digital production and exhibition, it was possible to include the SW in the postproduction process. Black masking a few pixels on the sides of the left or right pictures would replace the window in the theater room. That was the concept of the floating stereoscopic window (FSW). This effect was pushed farther by asymmetrically moving the eight corners (four left and four right), which allows the tweaking of the window in all directions: backwards, sideways, twisted, leaning up or down. The next step was to animate the window positions within a shot, and to set it along a cut. Actually, there's no limit to what you can do to an FSW, sometimes renamed *dynamic stereoscopic window* (DSW).

How does that affect our storytelling? It totally redefines the use of the audience space and screen space in 3D. You, as the director, decide where that boundary is, what its shape is, and how it evolves within a shot or along a sequence. Think of the screen as a window that has motion controls. You can move the 3D TV inside the living room.

Depth (Dis)continuity

Continuities are all over the cinematographic art. Light, color, frame, action, movement . . . we constantly take care not to disturb the viewer's mind beyond that thin threshold bordering the suspension of disbelief. The same care should be given to our story's depth settings; depth continuity is as important as any other continuity. This means that we want to respect it as much as possible, for the sake of our stories.

Depth continuity lies both within and across shots, and the amount of depth discontinuity you impose on images creates a *depth velocity.* That depth velocity has to be followed by the viewers' eyes and brains. This is not like color; it's more like sound or light, which can exhaust the audience into discomfort, or even wake them up from their cinematographic second state.

You'll manage to keep the stereoscopic velocity under control up to the point that you *have* to edit a cut that does not match; these types of cuts are known as *depth jump cuts.* The worst example of this kind of cut is going from a far away landscape to a close-up talking head. Steve Schklair explains his cut-cushioning technique in his section of this chapter.

Whatever stress you impose on the audience's visual systems, remember to provide them with depth rest areas, where their ocular-muscular system is not called to action. It's important to remember that 3D visual fatigue is muscular fatigue caused more by the duration of the effort than its intensity.

Stereo Stress as a Storytelling Tool

Stereo stress as a storytelling tool: what a strange concept! Aggressive art is not really the cup of tea of mainstream media and movies, but an audience enjoys listening to loud soundtracks, looking at gory pictures, and identifying with suffering heroes. Why would it be different in stereoscopy? If there's no flying saucer or dragon head invading the theater, most of the audience will feel cheated on the additional bucks they spent on 3D. However, if you provide them with "flying-at-ya" 3D, you get scorned as a gimmicky movie maker. James Cameron famously created a 3D effect with a drop of water floating above the audience in the first seconds of *Avatar* "to be done and get rid of it," according to apocryphal accounts. "Then people know I can do it if I want—and as a matter of fact, I don't; therefore we are done with it for the next two hours."

Is there another way to stress the audience's stereopsis that will generate the same reaction that a reaching pole or sword does? Is there a way to feed the audience's craving for 3D feeling without poking your story in the eye? If the audience has a sweet tooth for 3D effects, is there an adrenaline provider other than negative parallax?

We would like to see that road explored. What about some *Alien*-like stereo clutter? So many depth layers, so many volumes, objects, tracks, and trajectories, that your brain cries for help. Creating such visual experience is not a simple task, as experience has shown that the brain seems to falls back to 2D vision in visually complex situations. We used to set the depth to its maximum during climactic action scenes, but this is actually counterproductive; the trend is now to balance between action and depth, between 2D and 3D velocity, between edit speed and interaxial distance.

LINES OF DEBATE

Good stereographers make use of all existing 3D storytelling tools. That being said, you will see various emphasis on this or that, depending upon the relationship between the tool and the stereographer's overall 3D style or current interpretation of a story. When used as a key creative element, a tool will define a style. In other cases, it will be used as a mere technical solution to smooth an edit locally or straighten the discourse.

Is There a Screen?

As we have seen, the screen disappears from the viewer's sight and mind when 3D imagery is adequately performed. Yet the wall at the end of the theater room, where the sound comes from, still exists. The cinema space has a boundary—and the screen, where the image we are looking at is located, is the medium our eyes are locked on while we follow the story unfolding in space.

So, is there a screen or not? Yes and no. That's up to the cinematographer. On the one hand, there's a screen, an optical object, that you can't control and that has a secondary role; on the other hand, there's a stereoscopic window, a strong storytelling object, that you can place and move at will.

Depending upon your willingness to move away from 2D cinematography, and your confidence in new 3D visual effects tools, you'll stay in the "screen" paradigm or jump into the "window" one. No need to rush here.

Soft or Strong Stereoscopic Effects

Stereoscopic creativity will lead to your developing your own stereoscopic style. You may even use and balance it in a way that you invented, that catches on and eventually becomes a genre bearing your name. Tempting, isn't it? So far, the parameters describing a stereoscopic style are quite rudimentary—they basically consist of strength and placement; or, in other words, interaxial and convergence.

James Cameron, definitely the most famous modern stereo-cinematographer, is among the most conservative in terms of staying away from tearing eyes apart. His masterpiece, *Avatar*, shows a very subtle use of the interaxial distance and stereoscopic effects. He keeps the action close to the screen level, and mostly behind it. If you remove your 3D glasses during the projection, you'll barely distinguish the stereoscopic parallax fringes from the out-of-focus blur. Watching a 3D copy of *Avatar* in 2D, without glasses, is a surprisingly comfortable experience, and it would be possible to actually dive into the story without feeling any visual weirdness.

Ben Stassen, on the other end of the spectrum, is well known for the strong 3D stamina of his stereoscopic features. He uses very strong parallax values, and creates huge places and volumes where his characters evolve far away from the screen plane. If you remove your 3D glasses, you will definitely see two movies at once and want to put your glasses on as soon as possible to get back into the stereoscopic storytelling.

Depth Placement of Action and Characters

The overall depth size of the scenes is not the only artistic factor describing a stereographer's interpretation of a story in 3D; where that universe is placed relative to the screen plane is also important. In Ben Stassen's feature 3D movie *Fly Me to the Moon* (2008)—a staple stereo-strong movie—the director makes constant use of the fly-by nature of its winged main characters to fill the theater room. His vision of 3D seems to be that the action has to occur between the screen and the shoulders of the two viewers seated right in front of you. This style comes from Stassen's early years of IMAX 3D shorts and theme park rides.

In 2010, Zack Snyder's *Legend of the Guardians: The Owls of Ga'Hoole* received the closest thing to a standing ovation on the specialized mailing list of 3D cinematographers, in large part for its stereoscopic treatment, which consists of putting almost all the action behind the screen, up to a sustained parallax of 3%, or 34 pixels—an unheard-of number until then.

Another approach is not to consider where your action is relative to the screen plane, but to concentrate on the size and volume of the characters. Depending upon the value on the shot, from close-up to large, this will place the characters anywhere from -1% (-25 pixels at 2 K) to $+\frac{1}{2}\%$ ($+15$ pixels). You'll then make extensive use of the floating window and cut cushioning to accommodate the framing and smooth the cuts. This approach was developed by "Captain 3D," Phil McNally of DreamWorks. It requires implementing two postproduction 3D effects directly into the CGI production tool. The DreamWorks 3D Camera in Maya has both effects implemented and animated at the 3D layout level, offering live 3D preview in the 3D viewport of the proposed final edit.

In *Avatar*, the object of attention is always in the screen plane. This is especially obvious during dialogue shots, when two characters talk alternately. The convergence point is shifted continuously to keep our eyes converged on the screen. If you remove your 3D glasses when two protagonists talk, you'll see the speaker's image clear and sharp, and the listener's fuzzy and duplicated. As soon as the role shifts, the visual presence does the same.

Replicate the World or the Vision

All these stereoscopic characteristics form a dichotomy. There are two options: replicate the human 3D vision, or replicate a 3D world. As James Cameron claims, his approach is to "grab the eyeballs of the audience and use them for two hours." He replicates the human vision, and lets us walk in his footsteps along a visual 3D journey.

The other approach is to replicate a 3D universe with the intention of making it a perfect visual illusion, not a scripted experience. The viewer will be allowed to freely scan the vistas and select his or her own point of attention. A typical shot will be a fixed camera on a gorgeous landscape, or inside a room filled with details of the story. You'll notice that such fixed camera positions never occur in *Avatar*. Even if the main protagonist is the planet Pandora, we almost never see her by herself, but beside or over shoulders, traveling with a character, or through a spaceship window. Cameron is leading our vision, not offering vistas to wander around.

A Scientific Challenge: The Human Factor

The third 3D challenge is to understand how our body processes the stereoscopic experience. Seeing the world in 3D and watching a 3D movie are two different things. There are orders of magnitude more information on the set than what is recorded by the cameras. When color TV or digital movie standards were designed, the objective was to identify the minimum amount of visual information that makes the medium enjoyable. The result is to analyze only the three wavelengths (red, green, blue) that our eyes need to recreate the full color spectrum. Interlaced scanning was designed to cope with fast movements, while staying at the bare minimum frame rate of 25 or 30 fps. Theoretically, we should process more color depth, at a higher frame rate; yet we settle for the required minimum. Later digital and high-definition enhancements will only increase image stability and resolution. The current approach to 3D follows the same philosophy: if two viewpoints are enough, why bother recording more of them?

The point with 3D is that we not only under-feed our visual system, giving it the bare minimum, but we also make it perform physical actions that are not natural. This has always been present in 3D creators' minds; however, it gained new recognition with the mass production of 3D displays for home and personal use. Because of the fear of public health issues, consumer electronics goods manufacturers are looking into serious scientific research to back up the safety of 3D. Naturally, they don't want a whole generation to turn blind because of a visual effects trick.

So far, there is only one documented case, in Japan in 1986, of a child whose visual system was affected by a stereoscopic 3D experience. This is fairly insignificant, considering that millions of people are seeing 3D in theaters all around the world. We do see recurrent warnings in the press, but there is no epidemiological data that supports the theory that stereoscopic 3D can harm the human visual system. We even know that professional users of 3D—people working in the military, virtual reality, medical research, or geological research—have had no issues after working in 3D for years.

Still, there are good reasons to investigate how our body reacts to stereoscopic 3D. If watching stereoscopic images is not the natural binocular vision of a 3D universe, what are the differences and their impact?

3D FATIGUE

There are two main sources for 3D fatigue: muscular-ocular and cerebral effort. The causes of muscular fatigue are the non-canonical use of the visual muscles: the eye lens and the extra-ocular muscles used to control our sight direction. The causes of cerebral fatigue are all the discrepancies in the image domain that impair the surface matching and other factors involved in the stereoscopic fusion.

The Focus/Accommodation Reflex

If you are an entertainment industry professional interested in 3D, there's a good chance you've been told about the issue of the *convergence accommodation reflex*. Indeed, I mentioned this in my first book, *3D Movie Making,* and in the many talks I have given on 3D. Three years later, this seems like less of an important factor. To start with, personal experience with going against a reflex is that it isn't easy. Try to hold your breath; try not to duck to avoid flying objects; try not to pull your hand when someone pinches you. You'll agree: it's somewhere between difficult and impossible. It requires practicing, and it's an obvious intellectual task that involves having your conscious mind fight your body's automated behaviors. That's not quite my experience when I'm watching a 3D movie.

If you want to know how it feels to work against your focus/accommodation reflex, free-view a 3D picture, or look at a "magic eye" autostereogram. I can tell when my brain and eyes are working against each other, and I can see how blurry the picture is until my eyes give up and accept to accommodate out of the convergence point. Once again, that's not quite the experience I have in a 3D theater.

This all became clear while listening to 3D expert John Merrit's presentation at the July 2010 SMPTE 3D conference in New York. We look at (i.e., converge) and focus on the virtual objects, yet we watch the screen—and that screen happens to be within the depth of field of our eyes. In other words, we don't have to force our focus on the screen, because the screen is sharp enough when we look and converge on the virtual 3D objects floating in the room.

This is possible because we are far enough from the screen and the depth of field increases with the viewing distance, up to the *infinite focus* point, where everything is in focus from that point to infinity. That point is clearly shown at the far end of the focus ring on any photographic lens.

This explains why 3D shots have to be very conservative on a small screen; we look at small screens from a shorter distance, so the focus range is smaller, and therefore the virtual objects should remain closer to the screen.

To form your own opinion on this point, get to your regular 3D computer with a version of Peter Wimmer's Stereoscopic Player, load a 3D movie, and play it with the horizontal parallax correction. Bring the virtual image all the way inside and outside the screen and observe. Do the same experiment in a windowed player, and in full screen, on a 3D TV and in a projection room, close to the screen and far away. Playing with the display brightness may affect the results, with your eyes' depth of field affected by the size of your pupils.

Vertical Parallaxes and Other Factors

While you are at your 3D station, let's do another experiment. But first, let's make one thing clear: when playing with your vision system, you must be very careful. Isaac Newton explored human vision by pressing on his own ocular globes and drawing pictures of the deformed images of geometrical figures he saw. We will obviously not advise such extreme behaviors. Again, be careful: make sure you are okay with a possible bad headache, and don't do it while crossing a street in downtown Manhattan. In extreme cases, stop the treatment and consult a doctor.

Now, go back to your 3D station playing a 3D movie. Bring one eye up or down and listen to your pain neurons firing up in alarm. You are obviously making your body do something it's not built for. Search for the setting at which the discomfort feels tolerable, remove your 3D glasses, and observe how much vertical parallax your visual system accepts to compensate for. It's quite a lot; in my case, on the order of magnitude of the artistically accepted horizontal parallax, 1% to 2%. What part of the compensation comes from your eyes and your visual cortex? One thing is sure: if we were chameleons, we would be able to aim our eyes independently all the way up and down. We are not. On the other hand, chameleons do not enjoy 3D movies.

In a correctly produced 3D movie or program, there should be no vertical disparities. There's a debate about the acceptability, or even necessity, of keystone-induced subtle vertical disparities. Other production errors in image geometry will generate various combinations of inadequate vertical and horizontal parallaxes in complex patterns, as with rotations. However, if we're used to aiming our sight up and down, there's no muscle to put in action to rotate our eyeballs or change our field of view or focal length.

Other retinal rivalries will come from purely photographic impairments, like unbalanced colors, luminance, or focus. After all, a cross-fade is a double exposure, a technical mistake that impairs 2D vision, and editing was invented by Georges Méliès via an accident while filming. Somewhere, there is a non-canonical use of imperfect stereoscopic imagery that will be discovered and eventually be a staple effect that even the general audience knows by name.

The Duration Effect

The stereoscopic discomfort threshold is a complex blend of image defaults and time duration. Stereoscopic defaults will have various reactions with time.

Some image defaults will bring you into the pain zone almost instantly, like vertical disparities. Some will be bearable for a while, then get more and more painful, like excessive parallaxes, or depth discontinuity with no "rest areas" between bad 3D sequences. On the other hand, your brain *can* cope with some defaults, and will get more and more used to them. Left/right inversion is an interesting example of this; if you don't detect it and decide to cope with it, you'll eventually forget about it. But you will still get serious brain shear.

The actual subject and content of the 3D images will affect the time factor. Let's consider the synchronization default, when left and right images are not displayed in the appropriate synchrony. The amount of stereoscopic disparity is a direct result of the time disparity: no action, no default. However, any horizontal movement generates depth artifacts, and vertical ones generate unpleasant rivalry. Consider someone walking, for example; his torso will be in a constant false depth position. His arms and legs will oscillate from the false depth of the torso at the shoulders and hips, to a back-and-forth exaggerated depth position at the hands and feet. The standing foot will be in the correct depth, while the moving one will either pass through the other leg or dig into the ground.

Even if we could rule out technical mistakes, we still have to deal with geometrically correct stereoscopy that still produces potentially disturbing 3D effects, for example, strong negative parallax, on-your-lap 3D, and other eye-popping moments. When is 3D too much? There may not be an academic answer beyond, say, two degrees of divergence—which will eventually be acknowledged as the stereoscopic sibling of the 100 dB sound pressure pain level. Badly mixed soundtracks insult the audience long before reaching that legal threshold. When is 3D too much?

Stereographers invariably answer such questions evasively. Game and 3D artist Peter Anderson's catchphrase is said to be "the situation dictates." My own experience giving 3D lectures has been that the best answer is that the solution depends on what you are framing and on how you'll edit it. After a while, I'll also say that it has to do with the music score; if there's a silence or a loud explosion, you can and can't do certain things. Eventually, the attendees will understand they are asking an artistic question, not a technical one. There's no theoretical answer to an artistic question.

We could get away with this if we were only a bunch of creatives involved in 3D. We all know the extent of the magic tricks a good movie editor, color timer, or talented soundtrack artist can do to save the day when the material we are working with is not blending. Still, that's not a valid answer in overseeing the deployment of a new mass media visual form.

SCREEN SIZE AND THE HUMAN BRAIN

The *human inter-pupillary distance* (IPD) is the key value in 3D image geometry, along with on-screen parallax. All the virtual images will be either behind the screen or in front of the screen, in proportion to the distance from the viewer to the screen. If this rule is true, it is an oversimplification. The art of stereographic movie making has reached the point of revisiting and deepening our understanding of this geometric relationship. Obviously this rule is still the basis of 3D; however, there are many areas where it has to be tweaked.

This simplification has been so powerful that we still hear that the cameras and projectors should be placed 65 mm apart. All these distances are called inter-ocular distances, even though we actually have an inter-pupillary and an inter-optical distance. This shows us that the art of 3D started as an art of replicating human vision, not as entertainment—similar to what it would have been like if painting had been invented by naturalists. As long as most 3D movies were science movies in IMAX theaters, or illusionist entertainment in special venues, this made sense.

Screen Size and Maximum Parallax

The first consequence of this realistic approach is the maximum parallax per screen size rule, which dictates that one should not show virtual objects beyond an inter-pupillary distance of 65 mm, and that one should not generate divergence. On the other side of the screen, any off-screen effect in negative parallax follows the same size increase as the screen itself, which is what inspired the rule that you should always create a movie on the same screen size on which it will be shown.

This rule made total sense for movies shot for a single dedicated screen in a theme park; for a dedicated format like IMAX, with known metrics; or even for a single format like a 35 mm. Modern 3D, however, sees a very different use of 3D content. Films are shown on giant screens, regular cinemas, home theaters, TVs, computers, and, soon, hand-held devices. In theory, this should be plain impossible—and yet it works, at least for screens in the same size class. Why?

How the 3D Experience Changes with Screen Size

As a visual engineer who landed in 3D via programming interactive and multimedia games, my approach was all about counting pixels. When I came out of my geek cave to receive the digital light from movie makers, counting pixels happened to be the de-facto lingo. We were all about pixels in the files and inches on the screens. The limit of this approach, though, is that our visual system doesn't care about pixels. When you're looking at the world around you, what you experience is light rays bouncing and refracting. In other words, it's all about trigonometry. Indeed, stereoscopic math is almost all trigonometry. Parallax on screen, with inter-pupillary and viewing distance, generates angles that our visual cortex turns into 3D.

The first consequence is the impact of viewing distance, which happens to be quite closely related to screen size: the smaller the screen, the shorter the distance. The SD resolution was designed for viewing at three to four times the diagonal of the screen. Many countries and studios regulate the ratio screen size versus seating distance in theaters. In France, the ratio is 0.6 to 2.9.

Creating 3D only for screen size is like putting your cell phone, laptop, and TV set in a cinema, and then walking to the middle row and comparing the images. This makes no sense at all, of course. Instead, put all these devices at the distance you would normally use them, and then compare the field of view

(FOV) they offer. My cell phone is five times smaller than my laptop, yet offers 50% of its FOV. The TV set in this hotel room is 2.5 times wider than my laptop, yet offers 50% of its FOV. That said, this TV is too far away. When I watch movies on my computer, I push it farther away than when I'm typing, where it will occupy the same FOV as this TV.

Creating 3D only for specific screen sizes would be comparable to designing all of our electronic displays, including theaters, for an FOV, not a surface. And this is actually the case. Still, the field of view tends to increase with screen size, as we do not want our cell phones to block our view, yet we want the cinema to be an immersing experience.

Now, remember that the 3D screen is a window. Let's consider three typical screen sizes: cinema, TV, and cell phone. Where would you have a 10 m window, which is basically a glass wall? In a sky resort, a beach house, or any other gorgeous vista—in other words, somewhere it makes sense. Extra-large windows are for exceptional views. Where would you have a 1 m wide window? Anywhere you need daylight. A nice view would be great, but not compulsory. Finally, where would you have a 3-inch window? On a prison cell door to watch inmates, or on a fortified wall to shoot at enemies; to see without being seen, to control, to harm. These three windows describe the whole spectrum of feelings of freedom, from gorgeous vacation resorts to life and death behind bars. How can you pretend to tell the same story through such different mediums?

It happens to be the same in 3D trigonometry. We have seen how the viewing distance and screen size interact, but what about the IPD? In a theater, there's a point where it becomes negligible, because we have the ability to diverge our vision to a certain degree—say, one degree—and remember, it's all about the music. At some point, that one degree of divergence becomes more important than the increasingly positive parallax on screen. It all depends on your ability to diverge, but there's one ratio (distance-to-the-screen versus screen-size, or size/distance) where you'll always be comfortable.

Regarding the two other classes of screens, hand-helds and TVs, we have either the IPD metrics superseding the screen, or the IPD and screen size in a balance of power. Just as IPD jumps in at this size/distance, so does the focus/convergence. Our depth of field (DOF) is proportional to our focusing distance: the farther away we look at something, the deeper our in-focus box is. On the other hand, the closer we look at something, the smaller our DOF is. One can hold a laptop close enough to emulate a theater screen FOV, but it will not recreate the comfort of a large faraway screen. The same is true in 3D. One cannot fuse images at stereoscopic infinity (65 mm parallax) on a desktop screen; they have to be scaled down. Negative parallaxes require the same treatment. To some extent, the reduction of the FOV that comes with the reduction of the screen size and viewing distance follows the same curve as the reduction of the *dioptric box* presented by John Merritt. This has been our great chance as stereographers: to be able to work on various screen sizes and still be able to judge the quality of a picture.

3D A to Z

Richard W. Kroon

# #

2D compatibility   The extent to which stereoscopic content can be processed by standard 2D equipment without a negative impact on the content.

2D for 3D;—capture   Applying stereoscopic best practices when shooting and editing a 2D work to support a possible later 2D to 3D conversion. Otherwise, the finished work may be difficult to convert to 3D or may deliver disappointing 3D results.

2D to 3D conversion   The process of producing a 3D image from a 2D source. This is a computationally complex process. Low-quality, inexpensive conversions have a cardboard cutout feel, with a series of flat objects set at different distances within the scene. Higher quality and considerably more expensive conversions can approach the appearance of works originally recorded with full stereoscopic views.

3D-compatible   An electronic device that can detect and pass stereoscopic content on to another device without altering or acting upon the stereoscopic content in any way.

3D display   An image delivery system that presents separate views to the left and right eye, creating a three-dimensional representation. Commercially available 3D displays can be categorized generally as stereoscopic (requiring special eyewear) and autostereoscopic (viewable without eyewear).

3D metadata   Additional information recorded along with stereograms to assist in their decoding or presentation.

3D signal processing   The analysis and manipulation of electronic data unique to stereoscopic images. Processing equipment must be aware of the type of signal it is processing (2D or 3D) so that it can take appropriate steps to produce the desired result.

3D source master   The original material from which a stereoscopic program is produced. Before being released for digital cinema, the 3D source master is first assembled into a collection of uncompressed picture, sound, and data elements (the digital cinema digital master, or DCDM) and then compressed and encrypted to form the digital cinema package (DCP) for delivery to the theater. Alternatively, before being released to the home entertainment market, the 3D source master is first assembled into an uncompressed and unencrypted 3D home master and then into compressed and possibly encrypted 3D distribution data.

4D   A 3D work presented with live, in-theater special effects to enhance the viewing experience. The live effects are synchronized with the 3D presentation, such as the smoke and laser light effects that accompanied *Captain EO* (1986) at the Disney theme parks, to the water, air, and rat-tail effects that accompany *R.L. Stine's Haunted Lighthouse* (2003) at Sea World in San Diego, California. (The rat tail is a thin rubber tube that extends from under each chair, whipping back and forth against the back of each audience member's legs to simulate the feel of a rat's tail during a segment when a hoard of rats appears on screen.)

A

accommodation   Changes in the shape of the eye's lens that allow one to focus on objects at different distances, such as when following a close moving object. Similar to adjusting the focus on a camera's lens.

accommodation/vergence; accommodation/convergence;—link;—relationship The neural association between accommodation (focal adjustments to the eyes) and vergence (turning the eyes in equal but opposite amounts to line up on the same point in space). Useful in the estimation of depth for objects up to 200 meters away (stereo infinity). Matching accommodation and vergence signals for objects closer than stereo infinity reduces eyestrain, improves depth perception, and decreases the time required to perceive a three-dimensional image.

accommodation/vergence reflex; accommodation/convergence reflex The automatic focal adjustments made as the eyes converge or diverge. This reflexive response must be overcome when viewing a stereogram, since the focal distance to the screen is constant even though the amount of vergence changes when viewing different objects at different apparent distances.

accommodation/vergence rivalry; accommodation/convergence rivalry A mismatch between the amount of accommodation (actual focal distance) and vergence (based on apparent object distance) required to clearly view a three-dimensional presentation. Common when viewing stereoscopic images; because everything is at the same distance from the viewer (on the surface of the screen), even different objects appear to be at different distances (thanks to positive or negative parallax).

active stereo   A stereoscopic device that requires the viewer wear active eyewear that switches the right and left lenses on and off in time to the presentation of left- and right-eye images on the display. Autostereoscopic devices and technologies based on passive eyewear are excluded.

anaglyph; anaglyphic process A frame-compatible stereogram where the left- and right-eye images are color-coded and combined into a single image. When the combined image is viewed through glasses with lenses of the corresponding colors, a three-dimensional image is perceived. Different complementary color combinations have been used over the years, but the most common are red and cyan, a shade of blue-green. Anaglyphs may be projected, displayed on a monitor, or produced in print.

audience space   The perceived area in front of the plane of the screen in display/viewer space. When objects in a stereogram appear to extend off of the screen or float in front of the screen, they are said to occupy the audience space. Such objects must lie within the flat-sided pyramid that extends from the center of the viewer's gaze through the edges of the screen (the stereo window). *Also* **personal space; theater space.**

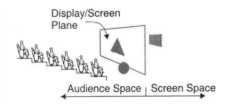

B

barrel distortion   A lens aberration where straight lines bow outward away from the center of the image and rectangles take on the shape of a barrel. Resulting from a decrease in focal length moving outward from the center of the lens. Most common in short focal length (wide angle) lenses. The effect becomes more pronounced as the image aspect ratio increases. The amount of barrel distortion is generally expressed as a percentage of the undistorted picture height. *Also* **fisheye effect.**

beam-splitter; beam splitter   An optical device that divides incoming light into two parts using prisms or mirrors, such as a 50/50 two-way mirror; a device that is both reflective and transmissive, though not necessarily in equal measures.

binocular   Relating to having two eyes or coordinating the use of both eyes.

binocular cue; binocular depth cue   Depth information that can only be interpreted by calculating the differences between two simultaneous views of the same scene taken from different perspectives, generally those of the two eyes separated by the width of the nose.

binocular depth perception   The ability to perceive three-dimensional space and judge distances based on the differences in the images recorded by the left and right eyes (disparity) and the angle of the eyes (vergence).

binocular disparity; disparity   The differences between the images perceived by the left and right eyes due to the physical separation of the eyes. Those same differences are simulated in stereoscopic systems to create the illusion of three-dimensional depth from otherwise flat images.

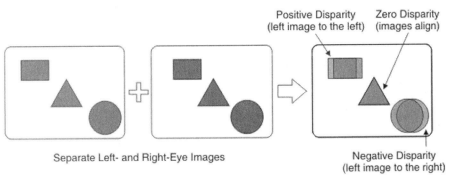

Separate Left- and Right-Eye Images

binocular rivalry When the differences between left- and right-eye images are so large that binocular fusion is not possible, resulting in a confused visual state. The brain may alternate between the two eye images, may select portions of each eye image and blend them into a sort of variable mosaic, may interpret the overlaid eye images as static, etc.

binocular suppression When the brain ignores some portion of the image from one eye and only registers the overlapping image from the other eye. Occurs in response to diplopia (double vision), since the suppression of one eye image eliminates the double vision that would otherwise have resulted.

binocular vision Visual perception based on two eyes working together. Binocular vision provides a number of evolutionary advantages, hence its popularity within the animal kingdom. The most important feature of binocular vision for 3D systems is depth perception.

binocular vision disability A defect in the vision system that prevents proper interpretation of binocular depth information. Approximately 5–10% of the population suffers from a binocular vision disability sufficient to interfere with the perception of depth in a stereoscopic presentation.

brain shear The brain's inability to properly and comfortably fuse poorly-constructed stereographic imagery into a three-dimensional representation. Causes eye fatigue, double vision, and, in extreme cases, pain or nausea. Coined by American film director James Cameron in 2009.

C

camera coordinate system A three-axis (x, y, and z) system of Cartesian coordinates (oriented so x, y, and z represent width, height, and depth, respectively, and grow in a positive direction to the right, up, and away, respectively) oriented to a camera's imaging plane so that the origin is aligned with the principal point (the point where the optical axis of the lens intersects the image plane).

cardboarding; cardboard cutout; cardboard effect The lack of a true 3D effect in a stereogram, giving the appearance that the image is made up of a set of flat cardboard cutouts as in a child's pop-up book. Generally caused by inadequate depth resolution in the image due to a mismatch between the focal length of the recording lens (or virtual CGI camera) and the interaxial distance between the cameras. Also a common side effect of poor-quality 2D to 3D conversion.

checkerboard; CK;—3D A time-sequential stereoscopic display system where the left- and right-eye images are alternated one pixel at a time to create a combined image with a checkerboard pattern of left- and right-eye image pixels. The checkerboard image is then presented using a digital micro-mirror display (DMD) projection system and matching active eyewear.

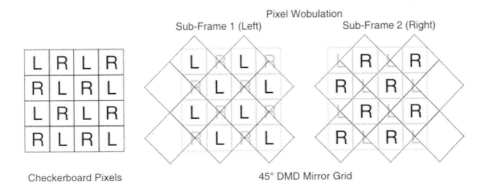

Pixel Wobulation

Sub-Frame 1 (Left)   Sub-Frame 2 (Right)

Checkerboard Pixels   45° DMD Mirror Grid

circle of isolation   The area of sharp focus surrounding the subject of a stereogram when set against a completely defocused background. Coined in 2010 by Indian stereographer Clyde DeSouza after *circle of confusion,* the concept describing the area of sufficiently sharp focus that defines a lens' depth of field.

circular polarization; CP   An electromagnetic wave, such as visible light, where the wave's electric vector travels through space in a corkscrew pattern, rotating either clockwise (right-hand) or counterclockwise (left-hand) over time.

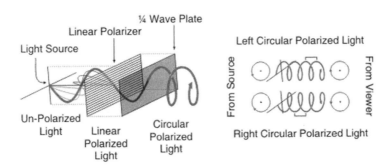

color rivalry; color mismatch   When the colors of conjugate points in a stereogram are contrary to what the brain expects given their parallax difference or other available depth cues, leading to contradictory depth information in the fused image.

column-interleaved;—3D   A 3D raster image format where left- and right-eye stereoscopic image information is presented in alternating columns within the image. By convention, one starts with the left eye in the leftmost column of the image and moves to the right. May be used with interlaced or progressive scan images. Generally viewed on a lenticular display.

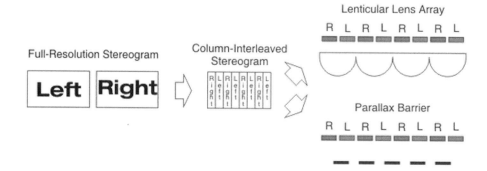

conjugate points The pair of points in the left- and right-eye images that represent the same point in three-dimensional space. When each image is viewed by the corresponding eye, the positional difference between the conjugate points in the two images is interpreted by the brain as being caused by visual parallax (disparity) and is converted into depth information. *Also* **corresponding points; homologous points.**

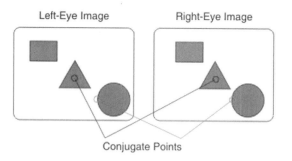

convergence 1. The coordinated inward turning of the eyes when focusing on a close object, such as when reading; visual convergence. The inability to maintain proper convergence (convergence insufficiency) commonly leads to double vision (diplopia). The amount of convergence necessary to achieve image fusion can be used as a depth cue for objects up to six meters from the observer. **2.** The amount of symmetrical inward turning (toe-in) away from parallel of left and right stereoscopic cameras; angulation; stereoangle. **3.** When the two separate images registered by each eye in binocular stereoscopic vision combine in the perception of the viewer to form a single image with apparent three-dimensional depth; fusion. **4.** When the two separate images in an over/under, split-lens 3D projection system (such as Technicolor 3D) are brought together on the screen, eliminating vertical image disparity. **5.** When parallel lines do not appear parallel in an image but instead seem to approach each other.

convergence angle   The amount that the optical axes of a pair of lenses are rotated inward from parallel, measured in degrees. May apply to eyes in binocular vision or cameras in a toed-in configuration. An important factor in stereoscopic calculations.

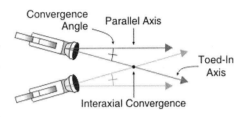

convergence animation   Subtle image disparity adjustments made at the tail of the outgoing shot and/or the head of the incoming shot in an edited sequence to help smooth the cut between the two shots. This helps avoid abrupt depth changes between shots, which can be quite jarring for the viewer.

The depth characteristics on either side of a cut can be adjusted in three different ways:

- The outgoing (or hand-off) shot and incoming (or receiving) shot are both adjusted so that the cut comes at a mid-point between the two.
- Only the outgoing shot is adjusted.
- Only the incoming shot is adjusted.

The duration of the adjustment can also vary:

- Adjust: change the convergence of an entire shot.
- Blend: adjust the convergence over the course of X frames during the head or tail of a shot.
- Drift: adjust the convergence over the course of an entire shot.

Experiments conducted during the production of *Legend of the Guardians: The Owls of Ga'Hoole* (2010) found that the smoothest transition occurs when only the incoming (or receiving) shot is adjusted, since there is a natural period of visual adjustment at each cut that tends to hide the convergence animation taking place. Most of the convergence animation sequences in *Legend* were only 8 frames (⅓ second) long—the longest approximately 40 (1⅔ seconds). Rather than match the depth characteristics exactly at the cut point, most of the convergence animation sequences eliminated only 50% of the depth difference, leaving a slight jump at the cut.

convergence distance   The length between the midpoint between a pair of stereoscopic cameras (measured from the point used to calculate the interaxial distance) and the point where the optical axes cross. An important factor in stereoscopic calculations.

cue conflict   When two or more depth cues provide contradictory depth information for an image. For example, when monocular depth cues (blur gradient, interposition, relative size, etc.) do not agree with each other or conflict with binocular depth cues, especially image parallax. *Also* **depth cue confusion.**

D

depth budget 1. Disparity limit or fusible range; the total range of depth that may be comfortably represented by a stereoscopic display system, from maximum negative parallax (distance in front of the screen) to maximum positive parallax (distance behind the screen). **2.** The cumulative amount of depth information that may be depicted throughout a stereoscopic work. To avoid overexerting the audience, a limit may be placed on how much depth will be presented in a work so that one scene with a great deal of depicted depth is balanced by another scene elsewhere in the work with relatively little depicted depth.

depth change stress   Discomfort caused by repeated changes in image depth that are too abrupt, too great, or too fast. Generally caused by cutting between shots with significantly different depth characteristics or by the intemperate use of subtitles with variable *z*-depths.

depth cue—perceptual Information that helps the visual system determine depth and distance.

depth discontinuity   An abrupt and unnatural change in perceived depth between neighboring or overlapping objects.

depth jump cut   An abrupt, unexpected change in image depth between shots in a stereoscopic work. The audience will require additional time to adjust to the new shot. *Also* **3D jump cut.**

depth map   A graphical depiction of the distance between the observer (usually, a camera) and each visible point in a scene. May be used when generating stereo views for 2D to 3D conversion or autostereoscopic displays. In many cases, storage space and transmission bandwidth can be saved by representing a stereogram as a single-eye image and a depth map (2D+ depth) rather than two full-eye images.

depth nonlinearity   A stereoscopic distortion where linear distances in the recorded scene are not perceived as linear in a stereogram: physical depth is recoded accurately at the screen plane (the point of zero parallax or image convergence), but increasingly stretched towards the viewer and increasingly compressed away from the viewer. This distorts motion as well as depth. For example, an object moving towards the camera will seem to accelerate even though it is moving at a constant speed.

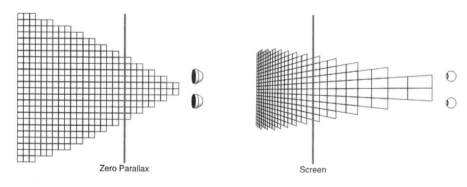

Zero Parallax   Screen

depth perception The ability to register depth in a three-dimensional image or judge distance between objects thanks to a combination of binocular depth cues (made possible by disparity and vergence) and monocular depth cues, such as the relative size of different objects, occlusion, geometric perspective, motion parallax, etc.

depth plane curvature A stereoscopic distortion characteristic of toed-in cameras where points off the central axis of the display appear to be farther from the viewer than on-axis points recorded from the same physical distance. A side effect of keystone distortion.

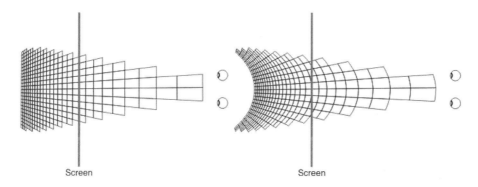

Screen   Screen

depth plot A document detailing the stereoscopic decisions in a work from one shot or scene to the next. Used when planning and producing a stereoscopic work. *Also* **depth script.**

depth range The distance from the physical or virtual stereoscopic cameras to the nearest and farthest points within the cameras' views or between points representing the maximum negative parallax and maximum positive parallax.

depth/size distortion; depth/size magnification 1. The altered perceptions of object size that result from hyperstereo and hypostereo. **2.** A stereoscopic malformation that results when presenting a stereogram in other than its intended viewing environment, causing image depth to be stretched or compressed. This effect is exaggerated when there is a nonlinear relationship between object depth (as recorded in the natural world) and image depth (as represented in a stereogram).

difference map A set of data that describes the visual differences between the left- and right-eye images in a stereogram. Since both eye images share more similarities than differences, a difference map can be much smaller than a full-eye image and a stereogram may be more economically stored and transmitted as a single-eye image and a difference map (2D+ delta).

diplopia Double vision; when the separate images recorded by each eye fail to fuse into a single image and separate images are perceived. Often a side effect of convergence insufficiency, where one is unable to maintain proper visual convergence when looking at a near object or when the left- and right-eye images contain too much disparity.

disocclusion The recreation of hidden parts of an object based on visual information in the neighboring areas. Often necessary in 2D to 3D conversion or when selectively adjusting depth information in a stereogram.

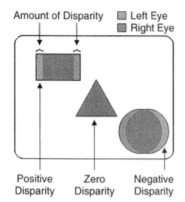

disparity—binocular 1. The distance between conjugate points in a left- and right-eye image pair that makes up a stereogram. Only disparity in the same plane as the viewer's eyes (generally, horizontal disparity) contributes to depth perception. **2.** The apparent distance between an object and the plane of the screen, either closer to or farther from the viewer. **3.** A difference between left- and right-eye images that is not caused by parallax. Such differences conflict with the depth cues in the image pair. Minor disparities interfere with the 3D effect, while significant ones can cause physical discomfort in the viewer.

disparity map A graphical depiction of the positional differences between conjugate points in the two images of a stereogram. Used to help identify camera misalignment, judge the relative distance separating different objects, highlight areas of positive or negative parallax, etc.

display plane The set of conjugate points within a stereogram that have zero parallax (they are in the same position in the left- and right-eye images) and describe a two-dimensional plane that appears to lie upon the surface of the screen. This plane lies between the audience space and the screen space. All 2D images appear to lie upon the display plane. Stereograms may depict objects on the screen surface (zero parallax), in the audience space in front of the screen (negative parallax), or in the screen space behind the screen (positive parallax).

duration of comfort The amount of time during which one can view a stereoscopic work without experiencing discomfort.

dZ/dt Parallax change; the amount of change in the parallax of conjugate points in a stereogram over time, calculated by dividing the amount of change in image depth (dZ) by the elapsed time (dt).

E

edge violation 1. When an object with negative parallax (seeming to extend out of the screen) is cut off by the edge of the screen. The brain does not know how to interpret this visual paradox. One expects far objects to be cut off by the edge of a window, but objects closer than the window should not also be cut off. This paradox leads to a visual/brain conflict and impairs the illusion of depth in the image. **2.** When an object lies within one of the monocular areas along the edge of a stereoscopic view. (It will be depicted in one eye view but not the other.) *Also* **breaking the frame; window violation.**

extrinsic camera parameters The parameters that define the position (location and orientation) of a camera in relation to a world coordinate system: *T*, the translation (in *x*, *y*, and *z* space) necessary to align the world coordinate system's origin with the camera's principal point (the point where the optical axis of the lens intersects the image plane), and *R*, the rotation necessary to align the *x*, *y*, and *z* axes of the world coordinates with those of the camera coordinates. The extrinsic camera parameters change when the camera moves. Often used in computer vision applications or when reconstructing three-dimensional objects from a series of two-dimensional images. *Also* **exterior orientation.**

F

far point 1. The conjugate points in a stereogram that appear to be farthest from the viewer. The far point can change from frame to frame, but should not exceed the maximum allowable distance defined by the depth budget. **2.** The farthest distance that can be seen clearly.

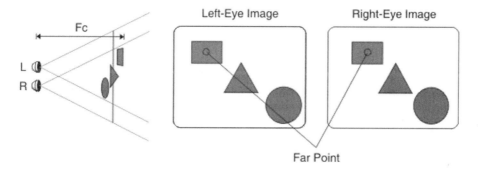

Far Point

field of depth; FOD   The range of depth that a stereoscopic display can physically produce given a particular voxel size and the angular resolution of the anticipated viewer.

field of view; FOV   The largest solid angle that can fit within one's vision or can be captured by a camera lens, generally measured as a certain number of degrees from side to side (less often from top to bottom). An important factor in stereoscopic calculations.

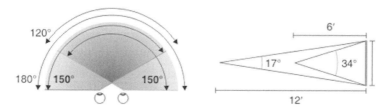

floating window   Dynamic adjustments to the stereo window, generally asymmetrical expansions and contractions to the right and left edges of a stereogram used to reduce depth cue confusion or avoid edge violations. May be prerecorded (made a permanent part of the image) or generated dynamically (by providing suitable metadata to the display system). Generally attributed to British stereographers Nigel and Raymond Spottiswoode. *Also* **dynamic window.**

focal length mismatch   Differing amounts of magnification in the left- and right-eye images of a stereogram. May be static (the same throughout a shot) or dynamic (a zoom mismatch, where the focal length is not synchronized during a zoom in or zoom out, or the result of unintended focal length drift during a shot). If both lenses do not have exactly the same focal length at all times, or if there is an optical mismatch between the lenses to begin with, the two images recorded for a stereogram will not align properly, interfering with image fusion and the 3D effect.

focal volume   The area within a scene that is in focus. When recorded by a camera, this is taken to be a truncated pyramid with the sides established by the image aspect ratio and depth equal to the depth of field.

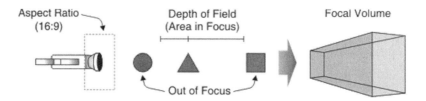

focus mismatch   Differing levels of image sharpness (focus) in the left- and right-eye images of a stereogram, either because the camera lenses were not focused properly before recording the images, or because the focus was adjusted during a shot and both lenses were not adjusted in perfect synchronization. This can interfere with image fusion and the 3D effect.

frame-compatible;—3D;—encoding   A stereogram recording format that allows both the left- and right-eye images to be presented in a single standard image frame.

free-viewing; free vision—binocular   A method for perceiving depth in a flat stereogram without special eyewear by adjusting the vergence of one's eyes.

front-silvered mirror   A mirror with the reflective material applied to the side from which it is viewed, rather than on the back side as is the case with traditional household mirrors. This produces an optically precise mirror and avoids the slight double images that are common with rear-silvered mirrors (caused when light is reflected off both the top glass surface and the lower reflective surface). Front-silvered mirrors are particularly susceptible to damage and difficult to clean. To maintain optimal performance, such mirrors may have to be resurfaced periodically. *Also* **first-surface mirror.**

frustum   A three-dimensional slice between two parallel planes taken from a cone or pyramid. *See* **perspective frustum.**

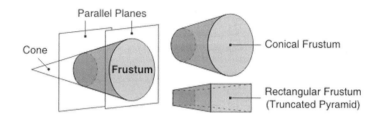

full HD;—3D;—encoding Full-frame stereo where each eye image is recorded in high-definition video.

full-frame stereo; full-resolution;—3D;—encoding A stereoscopic system that records and presents separate high-definition images for each eye—generally progressively scanned video images with 1,080 lines of resolution per eye image (2 × 1080p), or 35 mm motion picture film where each stereoscopic image pair spans eight perforations rather than the standard four.

fusion—binocular The process performed by the brain that combines separate but overlapping two-dimensional left- and right-eye images into a single three-dimensional representation. Binocular fusion can be divided into *sensoric* fusion, the neural process performed on images registered near the center of the retina, and *motoric* fusion, the physical movement of the eyes (vergence) to align images of interest with the center of the retina.

G

geometric distortion Unequal magnification or reduction across an image, including barrel, keystone, mustache, and pincushion distortion.

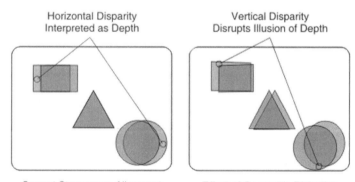

ghost busting The process of adjusting a stereoscopic recording during post-production or presentation to eliminate ghosting.

ghosting When one eye inadvertently sees some part of the image intended for the other eye, resulting in an apparent double exposure; a subjective measure of crosstalk. May be caused by incomplete channel separation during stereoscopic encoding, presentation (a problem with projection or display), or reception (a defect in the selection device, such as an active eyewear lens that remains open too long during each cycle). Most noticeable around areas of sharp contrast, such as the bright highlights caused by streetlamps at night or sunlight reflecting off metal.

giantism; gigantism A stereoscopic effect where an object appears unnaturally large. Caused by recording an image with too narrow an interaxial distance (the separation between the cameras' lens axes) given the lens focal length. Tools exist to help calculate the optimal interaxial distance for the recording cameras given a set of image and display characteristics, such as those at www.binocularity.org and www.stereotec.com.

H

half-resolution;—3D;—encoding An image that only uses half of the available horizontal or vertical frame; stereoscopic encoding where the left- and right-eye images are both included in a single frame with each eye image taking up only half of the available space. This allows both left- and right-eye information to be encoded in a format that can be processed, recorded, and transmitted using standard 2D systems and techniques, though a specialized display is required for final stereogram presentation. *Also* **split-resolution.**

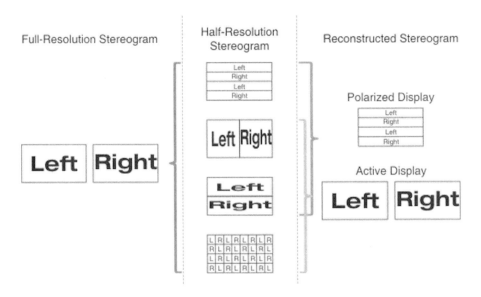

horizontal disparity; horizontal parallax The horizontal distance between conjugate points in the left- and right-eye image pair that makes up a stereogram. Only disparity in the same plane as the viewer's eyes (generally assumed to be horizontal) contributes to depth perception. Too much horizontal disparity can interfere with three-dimensional image fusion, leading to viewer discomfort and double vision.

horizontal image translation; HIT   A change in the relative horizontal position of the left- and right-eye images that make up a stereogram, performed to change the distance between conjugate points and thereby adjust the perceived depth in the images. Affects all conjugate points in the image by an equal amount.

hyper-convergence   When an object in a stereogram is too close to the viewer (too much negative parallax) for proper image fusion, requiring the eyes to converge excessively (cross-eyed) and resulting in visual discomfort or double vision—generally anything closer than half the distance from the viewer to the screen. Most often caused by recording objects set too close to the camera or by using too sharp an angle of convergence with toed-in cameras.

hyper-divergence   When an object in a stereogram is too far from the viewer (too much positive parallax) for proper image fusion, requiring the eyes to diverge more than 1° beyond parallel (wall-eyed) and resulting in visual discomfort or double vision—generally anything farther than twice the distance from the viewer to the screen. Most often caused by using too much divergence with toed-in cameras or by using a very long focal length lens.

hyperfocal distance   The length from the imaging plane to the nearest object in acceptably sharp focus when the lens' focal distance is set to infinity. All objects at or beyond the hyperfocal distance will be in focus at the same time. An important factor when establishing image depth of field.

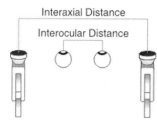

hyperstereo; hyper   Using an interaxial distance that is larger than the inter-ocular distance of the nominal viewer when recording a stereogram. This enhances stereo depth while reducing apparent image scale, causing objects to appear as if they are unusually small. May be used when recording landscapes or to draw attention to depth details in architectural applications.

hypostereo; hypo   Using an interaxial distance that is smaller than the inter-ocular distance of the nominal viewer when recording a stereogram. This increases apparent image scale, causing objects to appear as if they are unusually large. May be used when filming miniatures to make them appear full scale. *Also* **macro stereo.**

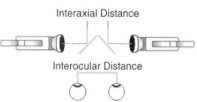

I

interaxial; IA   Literally, between axes. A comparison of some characteristic between two lenses, usually the interaxial distance in a stereoscopic camera system (the distance separating the optical axes of the two lenses).

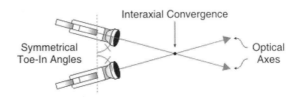

interaxial distance; IAD; IA; interaxial separation The horizontal space between the left and right images in a stereogram. An important factor in stereoscopic calculations. Measured between the optical axes of the cameras' lenses for parallel cameras. If the cameras' optical axes are not parallel, then the IAD is more accurately measured between the centers of the lenses' entrance pupils or rear focal points. *Also* **inter-lens separation; stereo base.**

interlaced A video image scanning pattern where half the image detail is captured at a time, generally the odd numbered lines (the odd field) followed by the even numbered lines (the even field), such as NTSC and PAL. This results in two fields per image frame and allows for field-level movement.

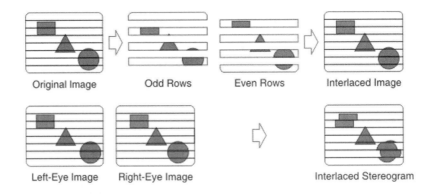

inter-ocular; IO Literally, between the eyes. Generally taken to be a comparison of some characteristic between the eyes of an animal with binocular vision or between the two optical elements in a binocular viewing device, such as a stereoscope. *Also* **interpupillary.**

inter-ocular distance; IOD; IO; inter-ocular separation The physical space between the optical centers of the eyes in an animal with binocular vision or between the optical axes of a binocular viewing device, such as a stereoscope. An important factor in stereoscopic calculations. Generally measured with the optical axes set parallel, such as when the eyes are focused on infinity. The average adult inter-ocular distance ranges between 50–70 mm, while children old enough to wear eyeglasses tend to range between 40–55 mm. The average IOD is about 63 mm (or about 2½ inches). *Also* **inter-ocular separation; pupillary distance.**

intrinsic camera parameters   The factors that determine how a particular camera and lens combination maps a three-dimensional image onto the camera's two-dimensional image plane, including focal length, the principal point (the point where the optical axis of the lens intersects the image plane), the vertical and horizontal scale factors (the height and width of an image pixel, or the distance between each row and column), and the geometric distortion introduced by the lens. Often used in computer vision applications or when reconstructing three-dimensional objects from a series of two-dimensional images. *Also* **interior orientation; inner orientation.**

K

keystone distortion   An image malformation caused when the optical axis of the camera or projector lens is not perpendicular to the surface of the subject or screen, respectively. When these elements are out of alignment in a camera, the portion of the image that is closest to the lens will be abnormally large while the portion of the image farthest from the lens will be abnormally small, causing the shape of the image to resemble the keystone of an arch. In a projector, the effect is reversed (close is small, far is large). May rarely be caused by a misalignment between the imaging plane and the lens.

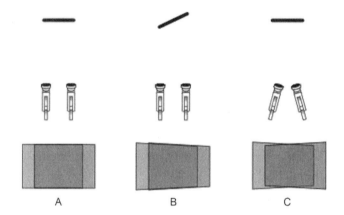

L

left eye   The left half of a stereo image pair; the image intended to be viewed by the left eye.

left eye dominance   Using the left as the starting eye for a sequential 3D application.

left field   Information from a stereogram intended for the left eye only.

left homologue   A point in a left-eye image that corresponds to a point in the matching right-eye image.

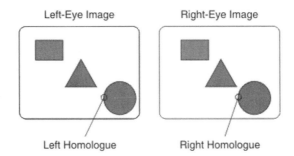

Left-Eye Image   Right-Eye Image

Left Homologue   Right Homologue

Lilliputism   A stereoscopic effect where objects appear unnaturally small. Generally caused by recording an image with too wide an interaxial distance (the separation between the cameras' lenses) given the lens focal length. May also be simulated by adjusting the depth of field to mimic miniature photography on a much larger scale, using a tilt lens or digital postproduction image manipulation. Tools exist to help calculate the optimal interaxial distance for a set of image and display characteristics, such as those at www.binocularity .org and www.stereotec.com. The term was coined in reference to the land of Lilliput, a parody of English politics that appears in Jonathan Swift's *Gulliver's Travels* (1726). *Also* **dwarfism; miniaturization; puppet effect.**

luminance differences   A measure of the reflected light off of a surface, usually in foot-lamberts, as the value changes from the center of the screen to the edges of the screen:

- **drop off:** The absolute value of the luminance change across the surface of a screen.
- **flatness of field:** A relative measure of the drop-off value for screen luminance—the lower the drop off, the flatter the field. Digital cinema systems have a naturally flatter field than traditional 35 mm film projectors.
- **hot spot:** The maximum brightness point of the entire screen, based on screen and projector geometry.
  - On low-gain screens, there is a single hot spot.
  - On high-gain screens, every observer experiences a slightly different hot spot depending on their angle of view.
- **vignetting:** Illumination drop-off moving out from the center of a lens. Digital cameras may employ lens shading to correct for this.

luminance rivalry   When there is a significant difference in brightness between conjugate points in a stereogram that is not explained by the available depth cues, leading to contradictory depth information in the fused image. Common to anaglyphs and film-based polarized 3D systems. The two separate film images that combine to form a polarized stereogram may not be equally bright if the projector is misconfigured or unbalanced light is passed through the two chambers of an over/under or side-by-side lens. *Also* **luma mismatch.**

M

micropolarizer; micro-polarizer; μPol   A very small polarizer, typically a circular polarizer one pixel tall running the width of a display. Polarized 3D displays have an alternating array of orthogonal micropolarizers covering their surface, generally in an alternating left circular/right circular pattern to match the polarized glasses worn by the viewer. The two eye images are row-interleaved (spatially multiplexed) and presented simultaneously with one eye image on the odd rows and the other eye image on the even rows. This technique was originally developed by Sadeg Faris, founder of Reveo, Inc., in 1994.

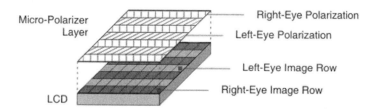

monocular cue; monocular depth cue   Depth information that can be interpreted from a single image or sequence of images, such as when looking through one eye or viewing traditional 2D film images. Monocular cues include static depth cues (atmospheric perspective, blur gradient, linear perspective, geometric perspective, relative height, relative size, shadows and lighting cues, static interposition, and texture gradient) and motion depth cues (kinetic interposition and motion parallax). For example, if two similar objects appear to be different sizes, the smaller one is assumed to be farther away; as the observer moves, nearer objects will appear to move faster than more distant objects; a near object may block part of a far object, etc. *Also* **extrastereoscopic cue.**

monocular vision   Visual perception based on individual eyes working independently of one another. Monocular vision with two eyes provides a much wider visual field than binocular vision (since the two eyes do not have sufficient overlap to support stereopsis) but reduced depth perception (since only monocular depth cues are available). This tradeoff is most advantageous to prey animals, which tend to have their eyes on opposite sides of their heads to help them spot and avoid predators.

motion-control rig; moco rig   A mechanical framework with computer-controlled electric motors. Designed to support and precisely control the movement and operation of a camera. Stereoscopic motion-control rigs may hold two or more cameras. For stop-motion stereography, a single still image camera is often employed with the motion-control rig shifting the camera left and right (and possibly adjusting convergence with each shot) to record the two halves of a stereogram.·

N

negative parallax   When a point in the left-eye image is to the right of the conjugate point in the right-eye image (and vice versa) in a stereogram. Conjugate points with negative parallax will appear to extend out from the screen, occupying the audience space. The viewer's eyes must converge on conjugate points with negative parallax to fuse them into a single image.

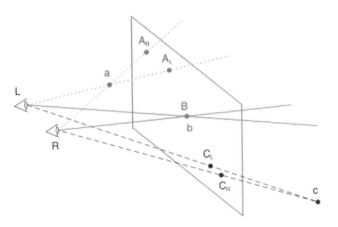

nodal points   The two points along the optical axis of a lens where the angle of a ray of light upon entry is equal to the angle upon exit with respect to the front and rear nodal points, respectively. The nodal points may not lie within the physical lens, but if the front and back surfaces of the lens are in contact with the same medium (usually air), then the nodal points will lie upon the principal planes. The principal planes lie perpendicular to the optical axis in a lens. When viewed from the front of a lens, an entering light ray will appear to cross the front principal plane the same distance from the optical axis as it appears to cross the rear principal plane. Depending on the configuration of a compound lens, the principal planes may not lie within the physical lens.

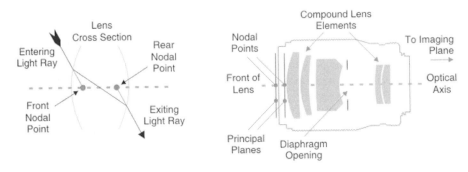

nodal shift   The changes to a varifocal lens' nodal points as the focal length is changed. A natural characteristic of physical lenses that must be simulated for the virtual lenses used in computer graphics.

O

occlusion   A blockage or obstruction; when an object that is closer to the observer blocks from view some portion of an object farther from the observer. Commonly used as a monocular depth cue. Can cause a visual conflict if an object that is supposed to be in the audience space is cut off by the edge of the screen. (It seems as if the edge of the window surrounding the more distant screen has occluded the nearer object—a situation that cannot occur in the natural world.) *Also* **overlap.**

occlusion information   Stereographic metadata that describes the objects within a scene, indicating whether specific points on each surface are visible or occluded from each viewpoint from which images were recorded. These data allow for adjustments to the binocular disparity for each depicted object, selectively increasing or decreasing the apparent depth in a stereogram.

occlusion resolution   The precision with which occlusion information is recorded.

optic axis; optical axis 1. An imaginary line that extends through the physical center of the lens, and on into the distance. This represents the optical center of the image created by the lens. **2.** The imaginary line that passes through the center of the eye and represents the direction of one's gaze. *Also* **principle axis.**

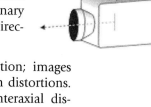

ortho stereo; orthostereoscopic   Perfect stereoscopic reproduction; images that appear as did the original recorded scene without any depth distortions. With theoretically ideal stereoscopic viewing conditions, the interaxial distance used to record the stereogram matches the inter-ocular distance of the observer; the images are presented using lenses of the same focal length as those used when the images were recorded, and the stereogram is viewed from a distance that ensures the image has the same visual angle for the observer as was recorded by the camera.

P

page flipping   Quickly switching between left- and right-eye images in a stereoscopic display system. Viewed with active shutter glasses synchronized to switch in time with the images.

Panum's fusion area; Panum's fusional area   The region surrounding the horopter where image disparity is small enough that the left- and right-eye images can be fused into a single image. Beyond Panum's fusion area the disparity is too great to fuse the two eye images, resulting in double vision, or diplopia. First described by Danish physician Peter Panum.

Within the fovea (at the center of the retina), retinal disparity is limited to about 0.1°—if the conjugate points in the images recorded by the retinas are any farther apart, they cannot be fused. Moving outward from the fovea by 6° increases the acceptable retinal disparity to about 0.33°; at 12° from center, acceptable disparity increases to about 0.66°. Extended viewing times and vergence can extend the range of fusible disparities to 1.57° for uncrossed disparity and 4.93° for crossed disparity.

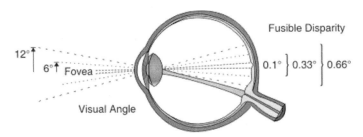

The physical position and size of the fusion area in three-dimensional space depends on the vergence of the observer's eyes. When the eyes are directed at a near object, disparity increases greatly as an object moves away from the horopter, narrowing the fusion area. When the eyes are directed at a distant object, disparity increases slowly as an object moves away from the horopter, extending the fusion area.

parallax   The apparent displacement of a fixed object when seen from two different positions or points of view at the same time; the distance between conjugate points in the left- and right-eye images of a stereogram. Typically measured in pixels (image resolution dependent), as a linear distance between conjugate points (taking into account display size), or as an angle of so many degrees (taking into account both display size and viewing distance).

Human binocular vision uses parallax to give depth perception. (Each eye records a slightly different image of the same object because the eyes are separated on either side of the nose. The brain interprets these differences to calculate the distance to the object.) Non-reflex cameras suffer from parallax error between the taking and viewing lenses. When the subject is at a significant distance from the camera, this is not enough to notice. As the camera moves closer to its subject, allowances may have to be made for the fact that the two lenses see a slightly different image.

Stereoscopic imaging systems rely on the parallax between left and right eyes to create their 3D images. In such systems, two images are separated by the average distance between a pair of adult human eyes—approximately 50–70 mm (the exact distance is adjusted based on the composition of the subject being filmed and its distance from the camera). When these two images are presented to the viewer, one to each eye, the brain interprets these slightly different images to create the impression of three-dimensional depth.

In stereoscopic systems, parallax is characterized with respect to an object's apparent position with respect to the screen:

- **positive parallax:** The left-eye image is to the left of the right-eye image and the object appears to be behind the screen (in the screen space).

- **negative parallax:** The left-eye image is to the right of the right-eye image and the object appears to be in front of the screen (in the audience space).
- **zero parallax:** The left-eye image is aligned with the right-eye image and the object appears to be on the surface of the screen (equivalent to a traditional 2D presentation).

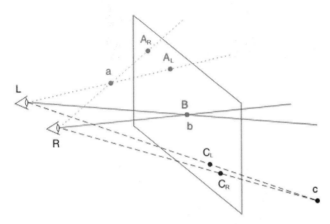

parallax budget   The total range of parallax from largest negative (in front of the screen) to largest positive (behind the screen) that may be comfortably presented by a stereoscopic display system. Essentially the same as the depth budget, but represented by amount of parallax rather than by apparent depth. The total parallax budget is largely dependent on the average viewing distance (increases with the size of the screen) and the average viewer's inter-ocular distance (larger for adults than children).

parallel cameras   A stereoscopic camera configuration where the cameras are positioned so the lens axes are parallel, resulting in a fixed interaxial distance to infinity. Parallel images must either be cropped or recorded with imaging grids that are off-center from the optical axis, since they do not completely overlap. This avoids the geometric errors common to toed-in cameras.

parallel rig   A mechanical framework designed to support two identical cameras set side by side. The optical axes may be set parallel to one another or, if the rig supports convergence adjustments, toed-in by equal amounts.

Percival's zone;—of comfort   The area within the visual field where binocular images can be fused into a single three-dimensional view without particular strain or discomfort, defined as the middle third of the distance between the nearest and farthest fusion points when the eyes are focused at a particular distance. First proposed

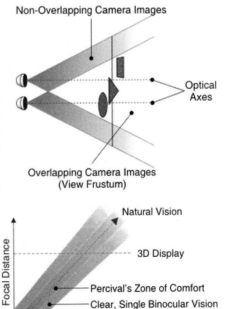

by British ophthalmologist Archibald Stanley Percival in *The Prescribing of Spectacles* (1920). *Also* **zone of comfort.**

perspective frustum   The pyramid that results from the intersection of the left- and right-camera view frustums when recording a stereogram. *See* **frustum.**

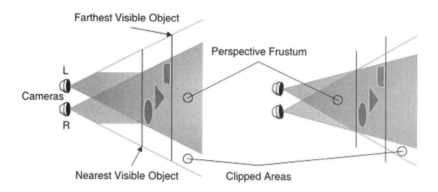

pincushion distortion; pincushion effect   A lens aberration where straight lines bow inward toward the center of the image. Resulting from an increase in focal length moving outward from the center of the lens. Most common in long focal length (telephoto) lenses. The effect becomes more pronounced as the image aspect ratio increases. The amount of pincushion distortion is generally expressed as a percentage of the undistorted picture height. *Also* **pillow effect.**

positive parallax   When a point in the left-eye image is to the left of the conjugate point in the right-eye image (and vice versa) in a stereogram. Conjugate points with positive parallax will appear to extend into the screen, occupying the screen space. The viewer's eyes must diverge to focus on conjugate points with positive parallax and fuse them into a single image.

posterization   A visual artifact that results from representing an image with far fewer tones than were in the original. Smooth gradations of color are replaced by bands of solid color with an abrupt shift in color between each band. This can be an intentional effect added to an image or the side effect of color aliasing, re-compression artifacts, or the use of too little color depth in a digital image. *Also* **banding; color banding.**

pseudostereo; pseudo stereo; pseudoscopic; pseudo-stereoscopic; pseudo-3D   When the left- and right-eye images in a stereoscopic system are reversed (the left eye sees the right-eye image and vice versa). This has the effect of turning things inside out—what should be near appears to be far, and what should be far appears to be near. With twin-film 3D systems, such as the polarized process often used during the 1950s, it was possible to invert the film reels and accidentally project in pseudostereo. Pseudostereo also results if one uses the cross-eyed method to free-view a stereogram prepared for parallel-viewing (or vice versa), though turning the image upside down will correct for this. *Also* **inversion; reverse stereo.**

Pulfrich;—effect;—method;—stereo   A stereogram presentation technique where depth is perceived in a moving two-dimensional image by placing a neutral density (gray) filter over one eye. The darkened image perceived by the covered eye takes longer to process and so is matched by the brain to a later image coming from the other eye. Since the two eye images that are fused into a single 3D image come from slightly different points in time, an object moving horizontally will exhibit stereo disparity, which is interpreted as depth. Named for German physicist Carl Pulfrich, who first documented the phenomenon in 1922.

Q

quincunx 1. An X-shaped geometric pattern of five points—four at the corners of a rectangle and the fifth at the rectangle's center—common to the five-spot on dice or dominoes. **2.** An anti-aliasing pattern where the value of each pixel is based on an average of five different samples taken in the shape of a quincunx. The pixel itself is aligned with the center of the quincunx. The corner samples are shared by adjacent pixels, so only twice as many samples as pixels are required, rather than five times as many. **3.** The pattern of left- and right-eye pixels in a checkerboard stereogram, which can be taken to be a series of interlocking X-shaped pixel groups.

R

reconverge   To adjust the apparent depth in a stereoscopic image.

retinal rivalry   The reception of images by the eyes that contain differences between the left- and right-eye image that are not due to horizontal disparity and interfere with stereoscopic fusion. This can lead to distraction, eyestrain, headache, or nausea. Often caused by vertical parallax. Also caused by color rivalry (different colors perceived by each eye) and luminance rivalry (different levels of brightness perceived by each eye). Some rivalries occur naturally and are not stereoscopic defects, such as iridescence, sparkle, and occlusion.

right eye   The right half of a stereo image pair; the image intended to be viewed by the right eye.

right eye dominance   Using the right as the starting eye for a sequential 3D application.

right field   Information from a stereogram intended for the right eye only.

right homologue   A point in a right-eye image that corresponds to a point in the matching left-eye image.

row-interleaved;—3D   A 3D raster image format where left- and right-eye image information is presented in alternating rows within the image. By convention, one starts with the left eye in the top row of the image and moves down. May be used with an interlaced or progressive scan system. Generally viewed on a polarized display. *Also* **IL; interleaved; line-interlaced 3D.**

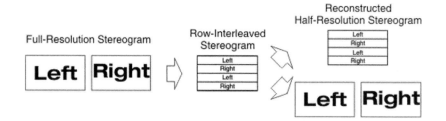

S

saccade The rapid eye movement necessary to take in a large or complex image. The human eye only senses image detail at the center of the visual field. Therefore, it is necessary to move the eye over a large object in order to take in its entirety. On average, the eye moves once every $1/20$ of a second—approximately the time span of persistence of vision. This is a subconscious action, but it means that one cannot comprehend a large or complex image all at once. These eye movements are not random and tend to follow visual patterns, but different people will scan the same image differently, and therefore have a different subjective experience. Sounds, unlike images, are taken in all at once. There is no aural saccadic equivalent.

screen parallax 1. The physical distance between conjugate points when a stereogram is presented on a particular size screen. **2.** The plane of zero parallax aligned with the surface of a display screen.

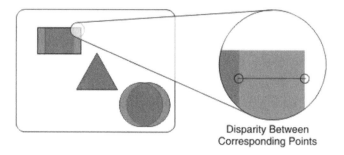

Disparity Between
Corresponding Points

screen space The perceived area behind the plane of the screen in display/viewer space. When objects in a stereogram appear behind the screen, they are said to occupy the screen space.

screen width The horizontal dimension of a display screen. An important factor in stereoscopic calculations.

segmentation The separation of overlapping objects at different depths in a scene when extracting z-depth data or converting 2D to 3D. Outside edges, where one object overlaps another, are most common, but inside edges, where an object overlaps itself, can be particularly challenging. For example, when an actor's arm extends towards the camera, it should be closer to the camera than the torso, but it can be difficult to segment the arm from the torso when they are both the color of the actor's costume.

selection device The physical component that separates and directs the left- and right-eye images of a stereogram to the corresponding eye. Auto-stereoscopic devices include an integrated selection device (generally lenticular or parallax barrier). Other technologies use some form of eyewear, either passive (anaglyph or polarized) or active (mechanical or liquid crystal shutters). ChromaDepth and the Pulfrich effect use special types of selection device eyewear to create a 3D effect from a single flat image. *Also* **analyzer.**

separation 1. The degree of isolation between signals flowing in two paths; a lack of crosstalk. **2. interaxial**—The distance that separates the left and right cameras in a stereoscopic process, measured along the optical axes of the cameras' lenses; interaxial distance. **3.** The distance between the conjugate points in a stereogram.

sequential stereogram A stereoscopic image where the left- and right-eye images are recorded one at a time by the same camera, shifting the camera horizontally by the desired interaxial distance between exposures. If a toed-in configuration is desired, then the camera must also be rotated the correct amount between exposures. This works best when the subject is not in motion (since the two images are not recorded at the same instant in time) and when camera movement can be carefully controlled.

Stop-motion stereography often employs a motion-control camera rig to achieve precise horizontal separation of the left- and right-eye views, such as for the movie *Coraline* (2009). For hand-held photography, the horizontal offset may be achieved by simply shifting one's weight from one foot to the other (the *shifty* or *cha-cha method*). This latter technique is not generally employed by professional stereographers.

shading Slight variations in an object's color or brightness that offer visual clues to the object's shape and size.

shear distortion A stereoscopic malformation that occurs when the viewer's gaze is not perpendicular to a stereoscopic display. As the viewer moves progressively off-axis horizontally, objects nearer than the screen (with negative parallax) will shift in the viewer's direction while objects farther than the screen (with positive parallax) will shift away from the viewer. In addition to geometric shear, any movement in the stereogram along the z-axis will take on unintended movement along the x-axis.

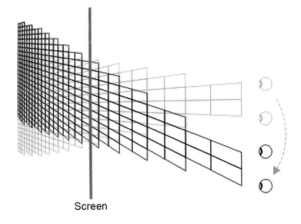

Screen

After a short time, most viewers who are significantly off-axis get used to the shear distortion.

In presentations where the viewer is free to move about, shear distortion may be used as a creative effect, causing still images to appear to move as the viewer changes position. Anamorphosis can be used to correct for shear distortion by recording the natural perspective of the depicted scene from the viewer's off-axis position. However, this only works from the one defined off-axis viewing position and exhibits shear distortion from all others.

side-by-side; SBS;—3D   A technique for recording stereograms where the left- and right-eye images are compressed horizontally and presented next to each other in the same frame.

For line-interlaced displays, every other line is discarded when the images are expanded to their full width to fill one frame, resulting in individual eye images that are ¼ the resolution of the original. Even so, in video applications side-by-side 3D remains more popular than over/under 3D (which produces ½ resolution images), because side-by-side does not requires a frame buffer to store the first eye image while the second is received, and it performs better with MPEG encoding. Since side-by-side configurations preserve the vertical resolution but reduce the horizontal resolution by half (and all stereoscopic depth information is recorded in the horizontal direction), they generally do not deliver the same depth representation as over/under configurations, which preserve the horizontal resolution but reduce the vertical resolution by half.

side-by-side rig   A mechanical framework designed to support two identical cameras set next to each other. The two cameras may be fixed in a single position, or the rig may allow them to be moved horizontally to adjust the interaxial distance or to be turned symmetrically inward from parallel (toed-in) to converge at the desired plane of zero parallax. When toed-in, the recorded images may contain geometric distortions that have to be corrected in postproduction to ensure proper registration when presented as part of a stereogram.

The characteristics to consider when selecting a side-by-side rig include:

- The ability to align the cameras (to ensure equal angles on the subject)
- The ability to toe-in the cameras (for converged, rather than parallel, stereograms)

- Rigidity of the rig (so the cameras remain properly aligned)
- Physical size (side-by-side rigs are smaller and lighter than comparable mirror rigs)

single-lens camera A camera that records two or more views of the same scene through a single lens from sufficiently different vantage points that they can be used to construct a stereogram. Single-lens 3D cameras avoid the bulk and inconvenience of multiple cameras and the image fusion problems that can result from multiple camera misalignment, zoom or focus mismatch, etc., though they are generally limited to a fixed interaxial distance.

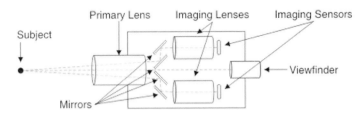

single-projector;—3D;—system A stereogram presentation system where the left- and right-eye images are presented using a single film or video projector. This generally avoids stereogram misalignment and pseudostereo, which tend to plague dual-projector systems, and is less complex to install and operate. All common 3D presentation systems are supported, including both passive (anaglyph and polarized) and active (eclipse method).

slide bar A simple camera rig for recording sequential stereograms with a single camera by providing a means for controlled horizontal movement between exposures. The camera is mounted to the slide bar, the first image is recorded, the camera is slid to the left or right by a controlled distance, and the second image is recorded. This provides more accurate interaxial distances and greater control over vertical parallax and rotation than similar hand-held methods.

spatial capture Recording scene depth information (each object's size, shape, position, etc.). This may be combined with visual images of the same scene to provide z-depth for stereoscopic representation or used to create a three-dimensional computer model of the recorded space. Spatial capture is also used in virtual reality and gaming systems to capture the user's body position and hand gestures. *Also* **depth acquisition; depth-sensing.**

static depth cue A monocular cue that can be represented in a still image. For example, if two similar objects appear to be different sizes, the smaller one is assumed to be farther away; a near object may block part of a far object, etc. Static depth cues include: aerial perspective, linear perspective, relative height, relative size, retinal image size, shadows and lighting cues, static interposition, and texture gradient. *Also* **pictorial depth cue.**

static interposition A monocular depth cue where a nearer object partially obscures or casts a shadow upon a farther object, allowing the observer to interpret the relative depths of the objects.

stereo Solid or three-dimensional. Generally used as a prefix, as in stereographic (literally, writing with solids) or stereophonic (literally, three-dimensional sound).

stereo acuity 1. The ability to perceive depth or distance based on stereoscopic visual cues. **2.** The accuracy with which depth or distance can be perceived. Measured as the smallest angle of parallax that can be resolved through binocular vision.

stereo blind; stereoblind Unable to perform stereopsis and fuse separate left- and right-eye images into a single, three-dimensional image. One who is stereo blind may still be able to perceive depth to a certain degree using vergence and monocular depth cues, but will not be able to appreciate the 3D effect in a stereogram. Approximately 5–10% of the population is stereo blind to a measurable degree.

stereo extinction ratio The degree to which the left- and right-eye images in a stereoscopic display can be seen by the opposite eye; a measure of crosstalk, perceived as ghosting.

Stereo Image Processor; SIP The trade name for an electronic device produced by 3ality Digital, designed to perform a number of stereogram adjustments in real time, including image synchronization, geometric and color correction, image alignment, and output to anaglyph, frame-compatible, and frame-sequential display formats.

stereo imaging device A complete apparatus used to record a stereogram, such as a single-lens 3D camera or a side-by-side rig with cameras attached.

stereo infinity The maximum distance at which binocular vergence (the inward turning of the eyes) can be used to judge depth. Beyond this point, generally 200 meters, the eyes are parallel and do not continue to diverge when viewing more distant objects.

stereo+2Z The images and depth data obtained from two separate cameras recording the same scene.

stereo+depth; stereo+Z A left- and right-eye image pair with depth data that describe the three-dimensional nature of the objects depicted.

stereo window 1. The plane of convergence; the point within a stereogram where the left- and right-eye images meet, generally set so that it appears to be at or slightly behind the position of the screen. **2.** The frame through which a stereogram is viewed. Regardless of whether an object is perceived as being in front of, on, or behind the screen, it cannot extend outside the stereo window bounded by the flat-sided pyramid that extends from the center of the viewer's gaze through the edges of the screen.

stereographer   One who specializes in the technical and aesthetic aspects of recording stereoscopic images. The roles of stereographer and cinematographer may be combined or the stereographer may act as a technical advisor (stereoscopic supervisor) working with the cinematographer. According to American stereoscopic supervisor Phil McNally, "One can teach the whole theory of stereoscopy in two hours. You can learn all about 3D moviemaking in two months. That will never give you the 10 years of experience needed to master it. Good movies are made with experience, not with knowledge." The mathematical calculations necessary to establish the optimal interaxial distance, toe-in angle, focal length, etc. may be performed using a spreadsheet or a special purpose stereoscopic calculator such as those available from www.binocularity .org and www.stereotec.com.

stereography   The art and technique of recording three-dimensional images, which requires expertise in cameras, film stock or video characteristics, lighting, aesthetic image composition, and the mathematics of stereo image recording. *Also* **stereoscopy.**

stereopsis   The ability to register depth in a three-dimensional image or judge distance between objects based on the disparity (parallax) between left- and right-eye images. Depth perception involves both binocular depth cues (stereopsis and vergence) and monocular depth cues (relative size, occlusion, geometric perspective, motion parallax, etc.). *Also* **stereo vision.**

The function of stereopsis can be demonstrated by observing a Necker Cube (named for Swiss scientist Louis Albert Necker, who first published this optical illusion in 1832 based on his observations of line drawings of crystals). Is the dot at the top right or the bottom left of the front face of the cube? With only two-dimensional (monocular) depth cues, the brain will alternate between the two states since there is insufficient information to be sure. If the cube existed in three-dimensional space, then stereopsis (binocular depth cues) would come into play and resolve the controversy.

stereoscopic;—3D;—S3D   Appearing to have three-dimensional depth, often applied to the creation of three-dimensional perception from a pair of two-dimensional images.

stereoscopic calculator   An electronic tool that helps calculate the optimal interaxial distance and convergence given a variety of factors, including the types of lenses used, the lenses' focal lengths, and the target viewing angle (a function of screen size and viewing distance). Such tools range from basic spreadsheets, such as the one available at www.binocularity.org, to special purpose programs, such as the one available at www.stereotec.com.

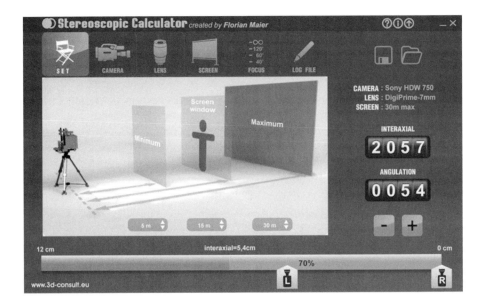

stereoscopic multiplexing   Combining the data necessary to reconstitute left- and right-eye stereoscopic images into a single data stream no larger than for a standard 2D image, including half-resolution video formats and anaglyphs. *Also* **stereoplexing.**

stereoscopic rendition   A high-quality, analytical process for 2D to 3D conversion that first generates a three-dimensional mathematical representation of a two-dimensional scene, and then uses virtual cameras to produce computer-generated stereo views of the scene.

sync error; synchronization error   A timing mismatch between the left and right images in a motion stereogram where the left and right eyes are one or more frames out of registration. Generally introduced during postproduction or playback. *Also* **temporal mismatch.**

T

temporal multiplexing; temporal separation   Separating the individual views in a stereogram or multiview 3D image in time and presenting them in sequence.

time-sequential;—3D   A stereoscopic display system where left- and right-eye images are presented one at a time in a high-speed alternating pattern. Only one eye is receiving an image at any given time, but the switching is so fast that this is imperceptible to the viewer. Active or passive eyewear ensures that each eye sees only the correct images. Polarized time-sequential systems alternate the polarization direction as each image is presented, while active systems turn the lenses in the eyewear on and off in time with the left/right image sequence.

By convention, one presents the left-eye image first, followed by the right-eye image.

- For interlaced video display systems, the eye images are in alternate fields of the same frame (field-sequential).
- For checkerboard systems, the eye images are combined into a single frame, alternating the presented eye with each pixel.
- For all other time-sequential display systems, the eye images alternate with each frame (frame-sequential).

toe-in   The degree to which the lens axes of a pair of stereoscopic cameras are turned inwards from parallel so that they converge at a distant point. *Also* **angulation; stereoangle.**

toed-in cameras   A stereoscopic camera configuration where the cameras are rotated so the lens axes verge at a point. This also causes the right and left edges of the recorded images to align. Objects at the same depth as this point will appear to be on the screen in the final stereoscopic presentation, while other objects will appear to be in front of or behind the screen corresponding to their relationship to the point of convergence.

Toed-in cameras are most often used for natural imaging (photography with a physical camera) when the cameras are too large to fit next to each other at the desired interaxial distance, but this introduces geometric errors that reduce image quality and must be corrected in postproduction.

The amount of image disparity (perceived 3D depth) primarily depends on the interaxial distance (the distance between the camera lens axes), but is also directly affected by the lens focal length, the vergence distance (the distance from the film plane to the point where the lens axes converge), the size of each object, and how far each object is from the point of convergence.

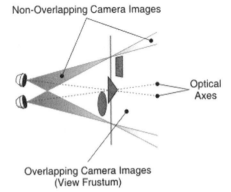

Non-Overlapping Camera Images

Optical Axes

Overlapping Camera Images
(View Frustum)

Since the cameras are set at an angle with respect to each other, the film planes are not parallel. This causes keystone distortions in the left- and right-eye images. These may present as object height distortions that introduce artificial vertical disparities that can become uncomfortable to view if not corrected. *Also* **verging cameras.**

twin camera stereo photography   Recording both left- and right-eye stereogram images at the same time using two identical cameras.

twin-lens camera   A stereoscopic camera with two separate lenses and an integrated imaging system that allows for the capture of two images at the same time.

U

unfusable images   Left- and right-eye images in a stereoscopic pair that contain conjugate points with excessive parallax, either positive or negative, such that the individual images cannot be fused into a 3D view.

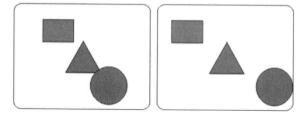

V

vergence;—eye movement   The coordinated inward (convergence) or outward (divergence) turning of the eyes when focusing on an object or when adjusting one's gaze from one point to another point at a different distance. This has the effect of projecting the object of interest onto the fovea at the center of the retina where clear, full-color vision is possible. Vergence is only effective for objects up to about 200 meters away (stereo infinity). When viewing objects beyond this point, the eyes are held parallel. Unlike other types of eye movements, with vergence, the eyes move in opposite directions. *Also* **angulation; stereoangle.**

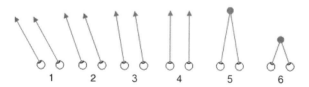

vergence point   The point in space where the lens axes of eyes or toed-in cameras cross. This also defines the zero disparity plane for images recorded with toed-in cameras.

vertical alignment error; vertical misalignment   A vertical deviation between left- and right-eye images in a stereogram where one of the images is higher than it should be so that horizontal points do not align.

vertical disparity; vertical error; vertical offset; vertical parallax   The vertical distance between conjugate points in the left- and right-eye image pair that makes up a stereogram. Only disparity in the same plane as the viewer's eyes (generally assumed to be horizontal) contributes to depth perception, so vertical disparity should be avoided. Small amounts can be ignored, but too much vertical disparity will interfere with three-dimensional image fusion, leading to viewer discomfort and double vision. *Also* **height error.**

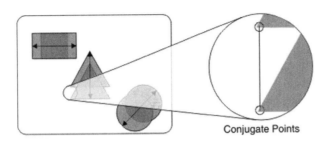

Conjugate Points

vestibulo-ocular reflex; VOR; oculovestibular reflex   Automatic eye movements, based on motion data recorded by the vestibular system, that help stabilize images on the retina and allow for clear vision when the viewer's head moves. VOR is reflexive and operates in complete darkness or when the eyes are closed.

view frustum; viewing frustum   The flat-top pyramid that encompasses the volume of space recorded by a camera, particularly a synthetic camera recording a computer-generated image.

The view frustum through a lens is conical, but photographic images are recorded with a rectangular aspect ratio, so a camera's view frustum is shaped like a pyramid. The front plane of the view frustum is defined by the closest object visible to the camera. In computer graphics, near objects are excluded from view by a clipping plane so the computer does not have to perform unnecessary calculations. Similarly, the back plane of the view frustum is defined by the farthest object visible to the camera or the back clipping plane in a computer-generated image.

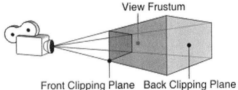

View Frustum

Front Clipping Plane   Back Clipping Plane

viewing angle 1. The figure formed by extending a line from the center of the viewer's gaze to the surface of the screen, measured in relation to both its horizontal and vertical offsets from a line perpendicular to the surface of the screen. **2.** The horizontal angle of view when observing a display screen. An important factor in stereoscopic calculations. Calculated as a function of the screen width and viewing distance and measured in degrees.

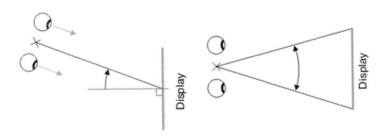

viewing distance The length from the observer to the display surface. An important factor in stereoscopic calculations. Generally measured from the center of the viewer's gaze to the center of the screen.

viewing zone The volume of space within which a viewer's head must be placed in order to perceive the full stereoscopic effect. A particular display technology may have one or more viewing zones, often a central zone and side zones. *Also* **head box; sweet spot.**

viewing zone angle A measure of the extent of the viewing zone measured as an angle from the center of the display, either horizontally or vertically.

visual/brain conflict; visual confusion A contradiction between a visual image and what the brain has come to expect from the natural world. For example, if left- and right-eye stereo images are reversed, then objects will appear inside-out (portions that should be near will seem to be far and vice versa). Alternatively, if an object with negative parallax (seeming to extend out of the screen and into the audience space) is cut off by the edge of the screen, the brain will not know how to interpret this. Far objects cut off by the edge of the screen are natural (this is how a window behaves), but objects closer than the window should not be cut off by the edge of the window, leading to a visual/brain conflict.

visual mismatch When an object appears in only one half of a stereogram or when there are significant differences between the same object in the left- and right-eye views that cannot be explained by visual parallax (the offset between the left and right eyes). Generally caused by compositing errors (as with depth mismatch and partial pseudostereo) or by rendering errors in computer-generated images.

volumetric 3D; volumetric display An autostereoscopic presentation system that physically creates an image in three dimensions, generally one that can be viewed from any angle. These include holographic displays, swept-volume displays (where a display element moves through space at a high speed—often by rotating on a central axis—to present a different view in each position so that persistence of vision blends the individual views into a single, three-dimensional view); static-volume or layered displays (where a block of transparent voxels—often created by stacking 2–20 flat image displays—are selectively activated to create an image in three dimensions); and varifocal lens displays (where lenses position multiple image slices at different optical depths from the viewer).

voxel Volume element; a three-dimensional pixel; the smallest addressable space in a three-dimensional computer model, having height, width, and depth (where a pixel has only height and width). Computer-generated images are generally presented in two dimensions (on a screen or on paper), but are often created and calculated in three dimensions.

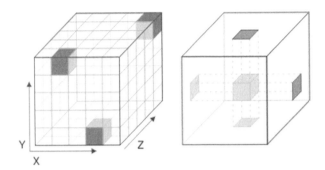

Z

z-depth   The horizontal offset between conjugate points in the left and right images in a stereogram. Larger z-depth values result in an increased 3D effect. Positive values provide depth away from the viewer while negative values provide depth towards the viewer. *Also* **3D depth.**

Z distortion   Unintended deviations in the z-depth of a stereogram causing visible image depth distortions. Most noticeable along horizontal edges.

zero binocular retinal disparity   When the images recorded by the left and right retinas in an animal with binocular vision are perfectly aligned, resulting in zero parallax between the conjugate points.

zero disparity plane; ZDP   The distance in a scene at which objects will appear to be on the screen in the final stereogram. The ZDP divides a scene into objects that will appear in audience space (in front of the display surface) and in screen space (behind the display surface). *Also* **HIT point; plane of convergence; zero parallax depth.**

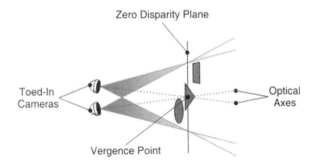

zero interaxial   When the two images recorded by a 3D camera system exactly overlap—there is no interaxial distance separating them. The greater the separation between the images, the more pronounced the 3D effect. At zero interaxial, there is no 3D effect.

zero parallax   When a point in the left-eye image is perfectly aligned with the conjugate point in the right-eye image in a stereogram. Conjugate points with zero parallax have no stereoscopic depth information and appear to be at the same distance from the observer as the screen.

zero parallax setting; ZPS   Adjusting the relative horizontal offset of the left- and right-eye images in a stereogram so that the conjugate points that lie on the intended display plane have zero parallax.

RICHARD W. KROON

Richard W. Kroon is the Director of 3D Services for Technicolor's Media Services Division in Burbank, California. In addition to being an award-winning videographer and published author, Mr. Kroon is a member of the Society of Motion Picture and Television Engineers (SMPTE), National Stereoscopic Association (NSA), International Stereoscopic Union (ISU), and Dictionary Society of North America. He is a Certified Project Management Professional (PMP) and PRINCE2 Registered Practitioner. Mr. Kroon holds a BS from the University of Southern California (USC), an MBA from Auburn University, and post-graduate certificates in Film, Television, Video, and Multimedia from UCLA Extension's Entertainment Studies program.

Richard Kroon

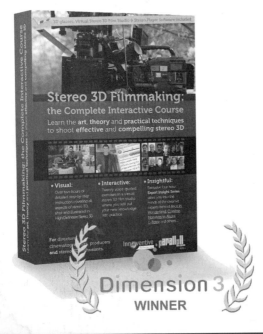